Review the Books

MR. SMITH

Books by Louis Bromfield

A MODERN HERO
TWENTY-FOUR HOURS
AWAKE AND REHEARSE
THE STRANGE CASE OF MISS ANNIE SPRAGG
A GOOD WOMAN
EARLY AUTUMN
POSSESSION
THE GREEN BAY TREE
THE FARM
HERE TODAY AND GONE TOMORROW
THE MAN WHO HAD EVERYTHING
THE RAINS CAME
IT TAKES ALL KINDS
NIGHT IN BOMBAY
WILD IS THE RIVER
UNTIL THE DAY BREAK
MRS. PARKINGTON
WHAT BECAME OF ANNA BOLTON
THE WORLD WE LIVE IN
PLEASANT VALLEY
A FEW BRASS TACKS
KENNY
COLORADO
MALABAR FARM
THE WILD COUNTRY
OUT OF THE EARTH
MR. SMITH

MR. SMITH

By Louis Bromfield

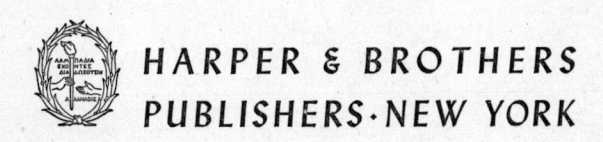

HARPER & BROTHERS
PUBLISHERS · NEW YORK

MR. SMITH

COPYRIGHT, 1951, BY LOUIS BROMFIELD
PRINTED IN THE UNITED STATES OF AMERICA

ALL RIGHTS IN THIS BOOK ARE RESERVED. NO PART OF THE BOOK MAY BE USED OR REPRODUCED IN ANY MANNER WHATSOEVER WITHOUT WRITTEN PERMISSION EXCEPT IN THE CASE OF BRIEF QUOTATIONS EMBODIED IN CRITICAL ARTICLES AND REVIEWS. FOR INFORMATION ADDRESS HARPER & BROTHERS, 49 EAST 33RD STREET, NEW YORK 16, N. Y.

FIRST EDITION

G-A

For ANNIE and DAVID RIMMER
with the Affection and Gratitude of
LOUIS BROMFIELD

MR. SMITH

Prologue

Two years after the end of the war, I received a telephone call from a stranger describing himself as Sergeant Burke. He asked for an appointment saying that he had with him a parcel which came from an old friend of mine. He had, he said, promised to deliver this parcel to me by hand. The old friend, he said, was someone called Wolcott Ferris from the town of Crescent City where I was born. For a moment the name lay dead and unrecognized in the echoing spaces of a rather poor and fairly overburdened memory. It was the words "Crescent City" which gave me the clue.

I told the Sergeant to drop in about five o'clock and hung up the telephone.

Then slowly, as I leaned back in my chair, the name of Wolcott Ferris became a reality and took form physically in my memory. But the form was not that of a man but of a boy of perhaps fifteen or sixteen years of age. I had not seen Wolcott Ferris in at least twenty-five years and I was puzzled as to why the Sergeant had referred to him as an old friend. True, he had been a friend of my boyhood, but I had not seen him since that happy period.

In my memory I saw him again, slowly at first and then clearly, on one of those expeditions which the boys of our neighborhood used to make in the early spring, into the country along flooding streams and through woods where the first anemones were beginning to show their pale blue and mauve blossoms among the fallen leaves.

He was a cheerful fellow, good-looking, and never afflicted

with the pimples that were the plague of most boys during adolescence. He belonged to the same Scout troop as I did and he was good at sports. I remember that even in those days he always seemed to me one of those people who had everything on his side. He came from a family which was prosperous and even rich, a family whose history virtually followed that of the town in which we lived. People liked him, and in high school he was, if anything, plagued by the attentions of the giggling girl students. He had everything that was needed to make for a pleasant, successful, happy life.

And then I remembered that twice during the twenty-five years since I had last seen him he had written me rather friendly letters. I answered them although there wasn't much to say except to recall the pleasant times of our boyhood. The only clue as to why he should have written to me was contained in a single sentence or two which I remember only dimly. They ran something like this, "Since we last met you have not only had a successful life but a wonderfully interesting one. I often envy you the experience of knowing so many kinds of people and of having seen so much of the world. Sometimes I feel that I would like to take up writing, but of course all that is nonsense. It is too late to begin now."

At the time I thought, "He just thinks that through me he might meet a chorus girl or an actress." I had had other letters from men like him who seemed to believe that I lived perpetually in a round of champagne, women, and gaiety. In both letters he had written that the next time he came to New York he would give me a ring. But he never did.

Now I was puzzled as to why he should send me a parcel to be delivered personally by a third person. Why did he not deliver it himself? Or send it by post? Or why was he sending me a parcel at all?

The answer came at five o'clock when the Sergeant appeared. He was one of those square, heavy, muscular men who seemed ageless, with unruly black hair and blue eyes. I guessed that he was about thirty-five, but he probably looked the same at twenty-five and would look exactly the same at forty-five. He came in shyly, impressed, I think, not by prosperity or prestige, but by what such men conceive to be evidence of superior brains and education. My office is a pleasant place filled with books.

We shook hands, and with some difficulty I got his hat and the paper parcel away from him, after which he accepted my offer of a drink and sat down.

"I hope I'm not bothering you," he said. "I would have sent the package or just left it here but I kind of felt that I had to see that nothing happened to it. I kind of owed it to Captain Ferris."

I said that I understood.

Then as if he remembered suddenly, he said, "You know he was killed in the South Pacific?"

"No," I said, not feeling anything in particular. "I'm sorry to hear that."

"You see, I liked Captain Ferris," he said. "He was a square shooter and we got along fine. It was kind of tough going with five guys stuck on a little island and forgotten by the Army for more than two years. You know . . . I guess . . . what that could be like." He grinned. "Sometimes it was hell and we wanted to kill each other."

I gave him another drink, noticing that perhaps out of nervousness he had downed the first one in a couple of gulps. The drink seemed to dissolve a little his shyness.

He said, "When he was killed it was kind of like losing a brother. I'd got to count on him. It was worse too because he wasn't killed in combat."

"How was he killed?"

"Well, nobody really knows. But he was shot one night by a sentry who said he thought the Captain was a Jap trying to infilter the camp. This here particular sentry had a grudge against the Captain, and the rest of us always thought the sonofabitch did it on purpose." He sighed suddenly and went on, "But you couldn't prove anything so the sonofabitch got off free. He was lousy white trash from down South some place . . . you know the kind . . . Ku-Kluxer and nigger hater."

Then he turned to the table where I had put the parcel, picked it up, and gave it to me as if merely leaving it behind in my possession wasn't enough. He had to put it into my hands. The presentation had the quality of a ritual.

"The Captain was always writin'," he said. "Sometimes he wrote all night like he had to get something finished. This is it. After he was killed I found it in his hut addressed to me sayin' that if anything ever happened to him would I see that it was delivered personally to you. I just wrapped it up and brought it along with me. I carted it around with me till I got back to the States and out of the lousy Army . . ."

"You never read it?" I asked.

"No. I'm not much on readin' if there's anything else to do. I kinda got into the habit in the South Pacific because you had to read or go crazy but once I got out of there I didn't have no more time for readin'."

That was all he knew and all he told me, save that he had gone into the Army at twenty-four and had become a top sergeant and that after the war he got out of the Army as soon as possible.

"I used to like the Army," he said, "but it soured on me. The next time they get me into the . . . thing, it'll have to be with ropes."

There wasn't anything more to talk about. The Sergeant seemed to have no remarkable conversational gifts and we had nothing in common save a joint acquaintance with a dead man I had not seen in twenty-five years and even then the man he knew was not the boy I had known. So after an awkward silence or two, the Sergeant stood up and said, "Thanks for the drink and the time. It's a weight off me to get the package safe to you. I almost lost it a couple of times knockin' around. But it was like . . . what do you call it? . . . a mission. The Captain seemed so wrapped up in it." His square solid face seemed to soften a little. "He was a funny guy. He could laugh or drink or tell a dirty story and there wasn't nothin' high hat about him. But he always seemed kind of sad. I guess he thought too much." Then he grinned. "It's something I try to avoid as much as possible."

"Better leave your name and address," I said. "I might want to get in touch with you."

I gave him a pencil and pad of paper, and, clumsily, as if they were not used to spelling or writing, the hamlike hands wrote out a name and address. Then he handed it to me, saying, "I haven't got no address at the moment. I'm just knocking around looking up old girl friends." He laughed. "Makin' up for lost time. I got a lot of scrounging to do to get caught up with what I missed during them lousy two years with no women around but dirty fuzzy-wuzzies. But you can always reach me care of my mother in Roxbury."

Then we shook hands again and he went away and I opened the parcel. It contained two or three hundred pages of manuscript, some written in longhand and some by typewriter. The paper was of all kinds and descriptions and was discolored and stained by the tropical sun and perhaps by salt fog. I started reading it, and when dinnertime came I had my dinner brought into the office and went on reading. I finished about two in the morning, and on the last page, typed as a sort of P.S., I found a note addressed to me.

It read,

"If you think this could be published I'd like it. It might help some other poor bastard with the same disease as mine . . . rotting from the core outward, you might say. W.F."

And then another thought occurred to me. The Sergeant had said that Ferris' death had not been cleared up, that it had never been established either as accident or murder. If the Sergeant had bothered to open and read the manuscript he would have found a third possibility which seemed the true solution. . . . Ferris may well have gone out with the express purpose of being shot by a sentry. Perhaps his end may have been a confusion of all three—of accident, murder, and suicide. It seemed planned that way. . . . Perhaps for the sake of his extraordinary wife and his unfortunate children. . . .

In any case, I did think the manuscript worth getting published and here it is. I have called it "Mr. Smith." Perhaps you will understand why.

L. B.

1 Oakdale

THIS TIME I THINK I CAN DO IT. IT IS THE FOURTH TIME I have tried but always something got in the way, something like a fog or a wall or something in between and perhaps a mixture of the two, but it wasn't any good. I would get to a certain point and could go no further. What I was trying to do would simply get beyond my reach. When I tried to go on putting on paper what I felt, everything became confused, and no matter how long or how late I sat in the rumpus room working, I got nowhere and afterward whatever I had written had to be torn up and burned.

It couldn't be left about the house for anyone to pick up and read. I did not even dare to risk tearing it into bits and putting it into the garbage lest some person, maybe the garbage collector, might out of curiosity begin piecing it together, and I knew that if anyone put together enough of the pieces, he would go on because he might recognize someone in the tale and be compelled to patch and piece and read on and on. You see, it is all about my own life and Enid's and the lives of all the people in Oakdale.

All that I had written was chock-full of dynamite, because, in reality, it was written for myself alone as a kind of purge. I had to put *everything* down and am doing the same thing now, because that is the only way it can be done. Any cheating, any disguise and compromise, I discovered very early, simply destroyed the thing I was compelled to do in order to save myself. And so I wrote about everything truthfully and objectively, perhaps as much as it is possible for one man to do. You see, this is to be my one accomplishment in life, the single achievement in which I can take pride—if I ever get it finished. All else I have done is largely meaningless, routine, average, banal, without savor or satisfaction. Perhaps too late in life I discovered that I must do something in which I could take satisfaction, but more than that I had to find out why I am, what I am, why my life should be such a desert. It would, I hoped, act as a purge which would permit me either to go on living or to regard death with a contented eye and a satisfied spirit.

Try it sometime, if you have the leisure and the inclination. Try writing down *truthfully* (or as near as you can come to truth) everything about yourself—what you have thought, what you have done, how you feel toward your neighbors and your own family. It is very difficult. Perhaps it is impossible—even for myself—sitting here on this godforsaken, rank, and hellishly beautiful island in the midst of the South Pacific, as detached from the world which made me as it is possible for a man to be detached from his past . . . without being dead.

In writing the truth, I find, as I found even at home in the house in Oakdale (which is the rich suburb of Crescent City), that I was cutting myself off from everything and everyone about me. You understand, I *saw* my friends, my acquaintances, even my wife and mother clearly for the first time. And so I stumbled upon things which should scarcely be spoken, let alone put on paper, and I found, very quickly, that what I was writing should never come to the eye of anyone, at least so long as I was alive. There were too many people involved, people who were friends or acquaintances or even enemies (if I ever had any real enemies), and most of them lived and still live in Crescent City. I knew some of them from childhood. Some lived in the same suburb as I, in nice expensive houses built by middle-class people moderately successful in life like Enid and myself—houses which were "decorated" by a professional who came from Chicago.

They were all decorated alike in rather rich-looking muddy colors because the decorator, who was a shrewd man and became very rich by knowing his clientele, was aware that these people (like Enid and me) wanted nothing revolutionary. They wanted something that looked "rich" but not strange. The reds of the curtains and the upholstery were never quite red, nor the yellows yellow. All the colors were dimmed and muddy. "Off-white" was an expression he was fond of using when he gestured with his long white well-kept hands, and "off-white" got somehow fixed in my brain as a symbol of so many things in the lives of all my friends and of Enid and myself.

The decorator—Mr. Banville by name—had a whole jargon which infuriated me the whole time he was in and out, doing Enid's decoration after we built the new house. He spoke of "occasional chairs" and "scatter rugs" and "gorgeous drapes" and "lovely homes." It was a kind of chatter, a kind of second-rate decorator's gobbledegook which was used by all of Enid's friends. It belonged, I suppose, with the vast amount of hogwash, shady thinking, and falsity which has been sold us by the hucksters of the great advertising agencies—things like "pure" salt and "fortified" bread and "toasted" cigarettes.

Who wants to use pure sodium chloride on food when rock salt or natural sea salt is so much better for the health and makes food taste so much better? No Frenchman could be sold "pure" salt. He knows too well what good food is. And who wants "fortified" bread when nature provides all the vitamins and minerals and a better flavor than any great chain baking company could ever provide? And what does "toasted" tobacco mean? They are all slogans and ideas, false and meretricious, which advertising has sold us all. They assault our eyes from hideous signboards desecrating the landscape, they ravage our ears when we are listening to radio, the news or a good piece of music. And presently everybody, like a herd of ducks, begins to believe the nonsense and hear it in his sleep and to repeat over and over again saying, "Quack, quack! quack! Pure salt, fortified bread, occasional chairs, scatter rugs, vitamins, ranch-type houses. Keep your movements natural. Quack! Quack! Quack!"

That is exactly how Enid and her friends sounded when they

talked about Mr. Banville and his decorating. Since he it was who decorated virtually all the houses in our suburb, they all looked alike. Except for the shape of the rooms, you couldn't tell whether you were in your own house or someone else's. But it made the women all happy I suppose. They did not envy each other unless one of them, whose husband had suddenly made a rich strike, bought a near Old Master or a genuine piece of antique furniture. Such an event always caused great excitement and discussion and criticism as if someone had thrown a stick into the circle of ducks in a pond and set them all quacking more loudly than ever. And sometimes, as when Mary Raeburn came back from Europe and furnished part of the big old family house with the beautiful things which she had collected over there, it confused some of the newer and richer inhabitants of our suburb and led to the wonderful remark attributed to Mrs. Hershall, who didn't have much background but a great deal of depression money (owing to Hershall's being very liquid financially and buying up all the things other people had to sell in order to keep their heads above water). She was quoted as saying, "What a pity Mary Raeburn's money gave out before she finished the house and she couldn't afford *new* furniture!" This, of course, was an absurd statement because, as everyone knew, Mary Raeburn was rich enough to buy and sell the Hershalls many times over.

But during those long evenings when, after the kids had gone to bed and Enid had left me alone in the rumpus room to work, all of these things and many more kept getting in the way of putting down on paper what I knew I had to put on paper. Somehow just when I was getting to where I could see things clearly and put it all down in writing, I would become lost in a cloud of "occasional chairs" and "scatter rugs" and golf scores and building plans and servant troubles. It was like drowning in a flood that was filled with flotsam and jetsam made up of all sorts of rubbish which looked like junk but when regarded separately and individually all became terribly important. I knew it was junk and that our lives were cluttered up with it, but the knowledge made no difference except that it simply confused me still further.

It was a struggle to get those few hours of peace late at night when I could sit down and try to think things out. I wanted to get it all on paper because I felt with a terrible urgency that if I could once get it on paper in concrete form, it would stop troubling me, gnawing away at my happiness and the happiness of Enid and the children and their futures, as well as because the whole thing was affecting me and my business. I hadn't any heart in the business any more. I couldn't go on building it up, increasing the amount of my income by more and more commissions on more and more insurance premiums. I was confused and I was tired, and it isn't right for a man to be tired in his late thirties. Then he should be at his best and most vigorous with the vigor of youth blended with the wisdom and experience he should have acquired by that time.

It wasn't anything physical. I was strong as an ox in that way with a good physique and no sign of a slight potbelly or any excess weight. I was tired in the head and in the spirit. Now I think it came partly from never being alone, because in the world in which I lived, nobody ever seemed to want to be alone. Indeed, they seemed to have a terror of it. They all wanted to lunch together, or play golf together, or go to the country club or the women's clubs together, or meet in the hotel bar or in the corner drug store to kill time over the pinball machines. And in the suburbs, with all the houses built close to each other, where a two-hundred-foot lot was an estate, there was never an evening alone. Either we were going to some party or outdoor barbecue, or someone was coming to us or just dropping in "because they didn't have anything to do that evening." And even when I was at home, there were always Enid and the children, Ronnie and Esther.

They all had the idea that no one could enjoy himself unless there were several people in the room with the radio playing. Even reading wasn't possible because the children were always interrupting and Enid, who had no taste for reading, would insist on conversation, not of a sustained and interesting kind on any particular subject, but just rattling along, always breaking in upon your thoughts just when something was becoming clear, or raddling your attention just as you had lost yourself in a novel or a biography or popular book about science.

Of course, it got a little worse as she grew older and fell into the habits of our neighbors and insisted on having a cocktail or two before dinner when we were alone. I didn't mind the cocktail. I liked it because often enough I came home tired and bored. The office had been full of people, and then I had had lunch with the boys at the hotel or the Club and after that the office again and then to the drug store to pick up the big-city papers and more of the boys there around the pinball machine and sometimes it meant going into the hotel bar for a quickie with more greetings, more drinks, and more confusion, and then home. The only time I was ever alone for a moment was in the toilet, and even there I nearly always found some other man who hung around talking over the partition rather than be alone or go back to his work.

When I got home one of two things happened. I found Enid with all the cocktail apparatus laid out and herself full of housekeeping troubles and gossip or with another couple or one or two women who had come in because their husbands happened to be out and they were left alone. Or it would be a party somewhere and we'd go for dinner at seven-thirty and finally, after so much drink that everyone had become boisterous or quarrelsome, sit down to eat about nine or nine-thirty. The interim had been spent in drinking enough to reach that level where they could all enjoy themselves and forget that flooding torrent of little things which made them both tired and unhappy. Sometimes weeks would go by when I was never alone for a second, because even after I had gone to bed Enid was there beside me in the other bed imposing upon me secretly and powerfully, even when she didn't speak, the fact that she was there and that we were (by God!) a happily married, prosperous couple who might serve as a model for the rest of the world. At times there seemed to me that there was a certain malignance in this silent, psychotic pressure.

She was very determined about our being a model happily married couple. She was determined about it even in her sleep. You could almost feel her imposing the illusion upon you. I do not know whether she believed it or not but she certainly believed that she believed it. I have always been a fairly good-natured man and, I think, honestly, kindlier than most, but sometimes I have been known to lose my temper and when that happened I was for a little while quite insane, perhaps with the stored-up repression of not speaking my mind when I should have done so. On such occasions I would never have wanted to face myself for I am aware that I could become viciously cruel and say things which were like stripping the skin from a living body.

In our world that was an easy thing to do, because it was largely a world of illusion and to shatter any illusion was a criminal thing to do. That, I think, is why so many people in our world were afraid to be alone—because, in spite of anything they could do, solitude would permit the creeping in of small thoughts and corroding doubts which were like maggots, little doubts which could, as they grew and multiplied, destroy the whole fabric of existence and create in its place the bare skeleton of despair. Once in our small world and many times elsewhere, when a man or a woman committed suicide, people would say, "I can't imagine why he (or she) did such a thing. He had plenty of money. He had a nice family. Apparently he had no worries."

But I think I know the reason. The maggots had gone to work, and presently the whole structure fell because a man or woman realized with a horrible and devasting sense of futility that everything added up to nothing, that nothing had ever happened to him or ever would, that he was merely killing time until he died, like those men about the pinball machine in the corner drug store, nice fellows, kindly most of them, prosperous enough at middle age to take it easy, who would spend hours each day around a pinball machine killing time until they died. Only *they* kept themselves distracted by talking and drinking and playing golf and watching the little lights light up and never being alone so that the maggots could never go to work on them. And a few years later a heart attack or kidneys weakened by too much drinking in order not to think or to drown the boredom would get them and nobody would miss them very much and certainly not the world itself. They left enough money to take care of their families and that was all right and pretty soon they were forgotten. On their tombstones might have been written with a monotonous uniformity, "He lived without ever being alive. Nothing ever happened to him."

Of course presumably love can happen to you, the kind of overwhelming love which annihilates all else, which partakes of passion and voluptuousness and cleanses the spirit, even presumably a love which goes on and on; but it never happened to me and certainly it never happened to most of the people I have known. Marriage in the world I know is usually a process of finding someone congenial, of "good" family, and possessed of a little money, with whom at the moment you experience a rather vague and somewhat temporary desire to sleep. If it's the first time the experience has happened to you, you think the whole thing is "Tristan and Isolde" but presently it turns out that it isn't and the whole thing breaks up or you get used to it or presently you get bored with it and go out and buy it by the night or take to half-tipsy necking with some middle-aged woman in the back seat of a parked car at the country club or down some suburban lane. Or maybe you're pious and churchgoing and don't step out at all and finally put love on the same level as old-fashioned Saturday-night bath or a dose of Carter's Little Liver Pills. But Tristan and Isolde or Hero and Leander! I never heard of it in my world. I know some nice well-adjusted elderly couples who have made a go of it, and they are perhaps the nicest and wisest people there are because with all passion spent they were still able to remain on affectionate terms, with common interests and a respect for each other's individuality and personality.

Enid, if you had asked her, would have told you that our life together was radiantly happy and that we were the ideal married couple, but anything on the level of Tristan and Isolde she would have considered frightening and dirty. That wasn't love; it was passion. Real love was respectable like the muddy colors Mr. Banville used in his "gorgeous drapes." It wasn't that she was frigid or that she disliked going to bed with me. I think she liked it well enough if I wasn't too demanding and I know she wanted to keep it up long after I was willing to call it a day (which didn't help matters). It was only that love should fit into its proper place in her picture of things and not crowd out anything else.

More than once I have overheard her discussing the whole business with a couple of other women and they all seemed to be in agreement. The only time any of them in our world kicked over the traces was when they got well along into middle age and the maggots got to work and it occurred to some of them that maybe they had missed something and had better make up for lost time before it was too late. That was when they took to the back seats of parked cars with a bottle of Bourbon and a middle-aged neighbor. Sometimes it was pitiful and sometimes comical, but it was always a little frantic and never very romantic.

The trouble is that in our world—and indeed among most Americans—nobody ever experiences passionate love. Nobody ever cares enough to murder or kill themselves over love. They just arrange a divorce and then marry again somebody they think they love, sometimes again and again in a kind of chain-store legalized adultery. Or they take to a bottle of Bourbon and the back seat. It must make it very difficult for those who try to write tragic novels. You can't make authentic tragedy out of trivial superficial characters. Nobody could make tragedy or even drama out of Enid.

The trouble with Enid was that she was always living up to the pattern or rather the illusion she had created for herself. In a way she was always acting a part—that of the devoted wife and mother with an adoring husband who could not live without her. If I went to the end of the garden to lie alone with a book in the hammock she would presently appear with some mending, to sit on the bench and begin one of those thought-shattering running commentaries on life, the neighbors, the cook, etc., etc., etc. She had persuaded herself completely that I was much happier having her there with me and, subconsciously, of course she was not seeing a husband who wanted a little peace to read and think and was in reality quietly hating her, nor was she seeing herself as a very limited woman, emotionally and intellectually, just quacking like a duck because she could not be alone and because she thought she was fascinating and "holding" her husband (a subject under constant consideration in her circles). No, it was not like that at all. She saw it in her own way and convinced herself of the truth of her vision of us as a couple who preferred constantly to be with each other and were restless and lonely if not perpetually in each other's company. It was a hellish illusion but a very common one at which she and her friends actually worked.

Of course when I found that the only peace and solitude was to be had after midnight and took to shutting myself up in the rumpus room to work at this thing which I *had* to do, she became disturbed. I sometimes think she resented this rebellion of mine, which broke her great pattern and illusion, more than if she had actually discovered I had been unfaithful to her. By shutting myself into solitude away from her I had betrayed her and the role for which she had cast herself and me. Sometimes I struggled with what I was trying to do until two or three in the morning, but instead of sensibly going to bed and to sleep, she would remain awake no matter how tired she was, wandering aimlessly about the house with the radio playing, changing from station to station as they closed down one by one for the night.

At other times, just when I would begin to make some progress on what I was trying to do, I would hear her footsteps overhead and everything would be ruined. At first I believed this was accidental but later on I think she came to know that by turning up the radio or banging the door of the refrigerator or walking across the floor above my head she could thwart me and presently force me back into her pattern from which I had rebelled so mildly for a little while. You see, what she could not bear was not only that I had broken the illusion by wanting to be alone and shutting myself up but that I had escaped from her. When I was in the rumpus room working, the thin door put me in another world into which she could not enter and roam around.

The rumpus room was built into the house long after it was finished and we moved into it. I don't really know why we built it because we had above-stairs a perfectly good and big living room, a pleasant screened veranda, a terrace, and I had a small room for my fishing rods, some papers, my guns, and my books, few enough in the beginning but increasing in number as life seemed to lose something of its excitement and I took to books as an escape and for a time as a kind of hobby.

The rumpus room occupied some unused space in the basement and was finished in waxed cypress. At one end there was a bar with four high stools upholstered in bright red leather. The chairs were covered with a kind of red dyed sailcloth, and for some reason I have forgotten, since there was nothing whatever nautical in my life or my family's, it was decorated with pictures of sailing vessels and bits of rope cable. It is likely that Enid saw some such room in the Garden and Home magazines and proceeded to copy it. There was of course a card table and several rather expensive unused games stowed away on the shelves and a radio, an old one replaced by a newer model. It was the only room in the house in which there was any really pure color that was not muddy or "off" some other color. I suppose this was to encourage and even possibly to *denote* gaiety. The curtains were of red and white checked cotton stuff.

Such a room was, I suppose, remotely descended from prohibition times, but by the time we built our own room everyone seemed to have one. They were a part of all the houses constructed in Oakdale, as much a part of every house as a bathroom. At first the room seemed to bring something into our lives, but I am inclined to think that what it brought in was not simply what we thought it was—a new element of gaiety and unaccustomed spontaneity. The real pleasure it brought us was the pleasure of *creating*, a pleasure rare enough in our world. When the house itself was built, everything was left to the architect, partly because, despite the fact that both Enid and myself had spent four years in college and been graduated "complete" with diplomas, we did not know anything about architecture or the history of architecture beyond what was called "colonial" or "early American." We had heard about "Gothic" but not much more than that. It was not that we had skimped our studies in the field of architecture or had not remembered what we had been taught. It was simply that in all the years we had spent in school we had never been taught anything at all about architecture which was a curious commentary on four years of training which was designated as a course in the "liberal arts."

We did not even allow the architect to bully us, for we had no ideas strong enough to provide any opposition. We had just what everyone else had in Oakdale and ours was wrapped up in a package which the architect labeled "Georgian." But in the creation of the rumpus room he had no part. The contractor did the whole thing under our direction, and so in a way the rumpus room was the only part of the house with which we had anything to do or which properly we could call our own. Perhaps that is the reason I liked it best of all the rooms in the house and chose it as a kind of fortified refuge against Enid and indeed all of Oakdale.

At first we used to bring people down there for a drink or two but after a time we came to use it less and less. It was more comfortable to sit upstairs in the living room or in summer it was pleasanter to sit outside on the terrace. And presently we came to abandon it altogether to the children and as a sleeping place for my setter who, I think, never really liked it. Essentially it was an ugly room, with its marine affectations and checked curtains and ugly uncomfortable early-American furniture. Finally it came into some real use when I discovered that it was the one place in the house where for a few minutes at a time I could lock myself in and be alone, not "sharing" everything with Enid.

After a while she developed a new angle—that I must not stay up so late because it was ruining my health and I was not getting enough rest and then on top of that grew still another angle—that because I was staying up so late I was neglecting my insurance business, and with prices going up and the children to educate we wouldn't have enough money to go on living in Oakdale in the kind of house we were living in. I think there was at least a certain sincerity in this because she, like most of her friends, lived in a perpetual terror of having to scale down the way they lived. If anyone in their world encountered such a catastrophe, the others leapt in for the kill with slobbering lips like animals pouncing upon and killing one of their number who has been hurt. It would begin, "Have you heard Mrs. So-and-So has had to give up her cook?" or, "You know, Molly is doing her own cleaning now. Tom must be losing money." And sometimes the very rumors and gossip would bring about the final collapse, hardship, and tragedy. To fail materially in that world, to slip down the scale, was as much a tragedy as having one's sixteen-year-old daughter go on the street. That was why such morbid emphasis was placed upon all material things from bathrooms to interior decorators to automobiles. They were a symbol of wealth like strings of shells worn about the necks of savages. I think Enid did actually worry about our sliding down the scale of material things.

But she kept trying constantly to thwart me, to disturb and disrupt what I was doing, always of course with the inference that she loved me so much she was worried about my health and happiness. I have no doubts that at times she did believe all this sincerely, but for a great part of the time this was not at all the motive of her concern. It is one of the confusing things about life that all is not black or white but very mixed up, and from the moment I began writing and shut myself away from her, our relations steadily became more unsatisfactory. Of the two of us I was the one who suffered least from the whole experience, from the late hours and the lack of sleep—at least to judge from physical appearance and reactions. She it was who became more and more nervy and short-tempered, who lost weight, who developed dark circles beneath her eyes. If anything I was happier and felt better, probably because the hours which I spent alone there in the rumpus room, doing not only what I wanted to do but what I *had* to do, were more restful to me than the hours of disturbed sleep spent in the twin bed next to her when I could feel, awake or asleep, that curious, almost desperate determination to *impose* upon me the pattern of an existence which was what she felt our life *ought* to be.

At first she would not even leave me in peace but would come to the door of the rumpus room from time to time and open it and walk into the room and say, "Darling, don't you think it is time to go to bed? You've been working too long."

And at first I was polite and told her to go on to bed and that I was quite old enough to decide for myself, but when the annoyance continued I had the courage at last simply to lock the door. The first time she made the discovery of the locked door and, on trying it, failed to get any answer, she went around the outside of the house and climbed into the small areaway outside one of the cellar windows opening into the basement room in which I had shut myself up. She could not quite manage to squeeze herself through so small an opening. The knocks on the door had disturbed me in what I was doing, and I had scarcely re-established my train of thought when the scuffling noise in the areaway (at the back of the room where she could not see me) ruined everything all over again and I left the card table on which I worked and went to investigate.

There she was, as you might say, "stuck" in the areaway. The window was too small to admit her into the room and the areaway was too small and deep for her to climb out unaided. She was merely trapped and threshing about.

I tried to keep my temper and said, "Wait, I'll go outside and give you a hand."

When I got outside I reached down and pulled her out. I said, "What on earth were you trying to do?"

But she was hysterical and crying and could not answer at first. Then standing there in the darkness she said, "I thought something had happened to you. I thought you'd had a heart attack or something."

"I only wanted to be left alone," I said.

Then her hysteria began to turn to anger and she answered, "I don't know what you mean. I don't bother you. All you needed to have done was answer my knock. That wouldn't have hurt you."

I started to explain that interruptions upset me in what I was doing and then checked myself. What was the use? She would merely go back to trying to find out what it was that I was doing.

"It's only because I love you so much," she said. "I was frantic when I thought something had happened to you."

So my solitude and all chance of writing was gone again for that night. I had to fetch whisky for her and make a pretense of contrition over causing her such alarm, although for the moment I wished her dead.

All this you might have said was caused by my own weakness and lack of decision. You might have said that I should have told her to mind her own damned business or that I should have gone away to Maine or the Rocky Mountains. But it is not so easy as that, as any decent married man with reasonable kindness and affection in him well knows. I liked my children. Indeed at times I loved them in genuine fashion. I liked to find them there when I returned from the office. I liked occasionally to read the funnies to them. And in a physical sense I liked my own house and the garden which I had made painfully and slowly out of bare, unfertile, filled suburban soil into a small and blooming paradise. I liked peace and remained a peaceful man and even a patient one save for those rare outbreaks of violent temper when physically it became impossible for me to bear any more. "Bear any more what?" you might ask, and I could not really answer you because what I had to endure was at once so confused, so intangible, and yet so concrete and real.

It was not Enid alone. It was the whole of that life, all outwardly so prosperous with two cars in the garage, a country club, a large, beautifully "decorated" home, two children and a moderately good-looking and well-dressed wife—all, in short, which you might say the average American man could possibly want or desire. Enid was perfectly a part of the pattern and acted her role as if superbly cast for it, and like the possessive American wives of so many prosperous and apparently happy American husbands, she wanted not to lose her husband, and I speak not only in the physical sense but of something far more subtle. She wanted to keep the domination of him so that he did what she wanted, provided her with what she desired, shared every thought with her, made her friends *his* friends but all *without* his ever suspecting that these things were happening.

She had too, of course, an extraordinary faculty, perhaps not so singular and uncommon as it appeared to me, of lying in small things and believing actually that she was telling the truth. It was a part, I think, of her acting a role. So long as she kept within the role she had conceived for herself in the domestic drama she had created to include me and the children and the house and the neighbors, she believed herself sincere and honest and justified in almost any tactic. And of course in the back of her mind there was always, without any doubt, the steel-clad conviction that she knew "best" and that everything she did was for my good and the children's good and that in reality she was perfectly selfless in the whole matter. These tactics lie, half recognized, deep in the minds of countless American wives, and as the method succeeds with the passing of time, it becomes a rigid and relentless thing, so calloused over by practice that it is not recognized at all. It becomes merely a daily way of life. At times it seems to me "the American way of life," at least in the prosperous upper-middle-class life I have known. The variations are infinite but the pattern is the same.

This process may drive a husband close to madness and it has undoubtedly caused more than one murder, or he may simply ignore it and spend more and more time at the Elks or playing golf and restrict his misery merely to the hours which, for the sake of his children or out of profound sense of respectability, he spends at home with his wife.

The situation centering about the rumpus room grew worse and not better. It infuriated her, I think, that I had at last devised a way of being alone for a little time. Her own pride was strong enough not to permit a repetition of climbing down the areaway to get at me, and she realized, I think, the absurdity of screaming and pounding on the door in order to force me to open it. But never would she go to the bedroom until I myself went to bed. She even took to washing odd bits of clothing in the washing machine of the adjoining basement room, an action for which there was no necessity since she had a laundress for two days a week as well as a part-time cook and housemaid. When at last we went to bed it was usually in silence, a very *hurt* silence on her part, which she made certain I would recognize not only by the thickness of the atmosphere but by deep sighs and much tossing about, so that she kept my irritation alive long into the night and at times made me hate her for being even in the same room with me.

You see, she managed always, in her own eyes at least, to put me in the wrong, to imply that I neglected her and was cruel to her and caused her great suffering, and in her heart she sincerely believed this, tending and fostering a whole situation which in fact existed only in so far as she created it—all of this simply because there were times when I wanted to be alone from her and from everyone.

Of course what maddened her most—and I cannot quite blame her for this—was not merely the knowledge that I had found a way of locking myself up alone so that she could not reach me but the fact that beyond the faint pounding of the typewriter, which late at night was always spasmodically in her ears, she did not know what I was thinking or what I was putting on paper. When she asked me what I was writing, I answered truthfully enough that I did not know. It might be a novel; it might be a kind of autobiography. It might merely be a pile of rubbish, but it was something I *had* to do if I was to continue living.

To her, of course, this was the merest hogwash. Nobody *had* to behave in such a ridiculous fashion. What did I mean by "continue living?" et cetera, et cetera. No other husband behaved in such an absurd fashion.

She would not even believe that I was telling her the truth as nearly as I was able to tell it. She wanted to read what I had written, but I refused because I was genuinely shy about my ability to write anything and because if I had let her see it she would have understood none of it and some of it, in which I wrote about her and her friends, would have driven her into fury or perhaps into despair. It never for a moment occurred to her that I had a right to privacy or even to my own thoughts. I was merely betraying her.

I had great trouble in concealing the few pages which I preserved from time to time because they seemed to be what I wanted to accomplish. I knew well enough that in the curious pattern of behavior and illusion she created, she would have no scruples whatever in reading the stuff if she could lay hands upon it. She felt, I knew, that this was her right, even as she felt it her just and honorable right to examine at times the contents of the drawers in my desk and the cards and addresses in my wallet. Early in our marriage I found that she felt it perfectly all right to open and read letters addressed to me, and when I protested, although there was at the time nothing for me to hide, she said, "I don't see what's wrong about it. My mother always read all our letters, even my father's. We're married aren't we?" She stopped the practice openly, but she continued to steam open and reseal much of my correspondence.

At this pilfering she was not very skillful. She put things back in what she believed was the proper order and sequence but always the contents of drawer and wallet were just enough disturbed for me to know that she had been at it again. She never mentioned this practice perhaps because she never found anything that might have been incriminating, yet she could not stop doing it over and over again. She did it not, I think, because she suspected me of infidelity but simply because she *had* to know everything about me (which of course she never did know). It was all a part of what she called "sharing" our life. "A happy husband and wife," she would say, "should share everything. There should be no secrets."

This deformity even extended in reverse to her own behavior. If I did not ask her each evening where she had been, whom she had seen, what she was planning for the next day, she would pout in her peculiar way, which was not a pout at all but a kind of acid aggressive sulkiness, and say that I was never interested in what she and the children were doing or in what happened to them. It wasn't only that she wanted to share me, inside and out, but she wanted me to *share* her whether I wanted to or not or felt like it at the moment. Of the two, I think the latter was, if anything, the worse experience.

So you see, I think, why I tried four times to do what I am doing now and each time failed, lost and befogged by the life around me, so that my purpose and any pattern I had devised soon began to crumble into chaos. This time, sitting in the wet hot jungle on the other side of the world, with no companionship but a tough extrovert Army sergeant whose only concern is his appetites and his functions, and three younger soldiers who lead their own separate and somewhat peculiar existences, I may finish up what I must do, which is to straighten out and put on paper in some concrete form the pattern and significance, if any, of my own existence. If I do not succeed I may kill myself. I have been very near to it a dozen times and I have not committed the final act simply because of the strong feeling that I must live until I have done this job. Then I may kill myself or I may feel that, in putting down on paper the pattern, I shall be freed not only of the life and the little world which I came to hate but even perhaps of *myself*—the self who got me into all the mess and then was not courageous enough to smash everything in a determination to escape.

This passionate desire all began one October morning nearly a dozen years ago while I was shaving and suddenly looked into my own eyes and *saw* myself. Perhaps it has happened to other men and perhaps it failed to affect them in the same way as it affected me or perhaps they shrewdly and quickly turned away from the mirror and then back again in order *not* to find *themselves* this time but merely a face, a characterless almost inanimate face, from which they were scraping a few bristly hairs as they had done thousands of times before. Perhaps that is what I should have done ... but I didn't.

I stood there with my razor poised, looking into my own eyes, thinking, "This is you? This is the guy you have to live with for the rest of your life? What is *you*? Are you decent and kindly or a monster? What is it you want? Whither are you bound? Why are you shut off from everyone and everything in spite of every effort to lose yourself? Where did you come from and where will you end? What are you here for? What are you doing with this short space of time permitted you on earth? What becomes of you when this flesh dies and withers away? What are you missing? What precious experience ... what richness, what unknown pleasures and delights and satisfactions have you *not* had while life rushes on day after day with never any time to be alone, to think, or to do anything but the monotonous secure round of a mildly prosperous existence? What is your significance—a mere speck in the universe but immensely important to yourself? In short, what are you? Why the hell do you exist? Why do you go on living?"

These were morbid and even dangerous thoughts for a prosperous insurance broker living in a suburb with a wife and two children.

I do not know how long I stood there looking into my own blue eyes which somebody—it sounds like Ruskin—referred to as "the windows of the soul." The face was perhaps a better-looking than average face, with a straight nose, a rather full mouth, blondish slightly curling hair, a rather stubborn chin, and large close-set ears. The face was agreeable enough and told the passer-by something—the stubbornness in the chin, the sensuality of the mouth pinched a little at the corner as if that sensuality had never been satisfied, the vigor that was in the large ears. But it was the eyes which told everything, rather large blue-gray eyes set fairly well apart. It was the eyes which fascinated me, for they came nearest to telling me what I was, the eyes which betrayed to me on that October morning the doubts and fears and dissatisfactions which I had never recognized or allowed myself to recognize until that morning.

Something extraordinary happened in that moment. All the surroundings, I was aware, were the same—the familiar bathroom with the initialed towels, the birds singing in the garden outside, the occasional yelp of one of the children as they quarreled while getting ready for school, the voice of Enid admonishing them. It was all the same but suddenly everything became different. The sounds I heard, even the familiar initialed towels (selected by Mr. Banville to match the walls and toilet seat), took on a significance. They meant something, all fitting together in a pattern of—what shall we say?—oppression, monotony, futility, imbecility? I cannot say. Suddenly I hated my house, my wife, my daily existence, even for a moment, my own children. Everything has remained different ever since that morning.

Presently I heard a knock on the door and I heard Enid's voice asking, "Are you all right? Is there anything wrong?" and I knew that I must have been staring at myself for a long time, completely lost to such things as time or appointments or offices or whether someone else wanted to use the bathroom.

Startled back into reality I answered, "I'm okay. I was just thinking," and I heard her faint laugh as if something deep in her soul found the process of thinking merely ridiculous.

I finished shaving and dressing and went off to the office and presently forgot all about the experience, but the forgetfulness was merely temporary. In the days that followed the memory of the unnerving experience kept returning to me, and I found that unless I deliberately shaved in a hurry without once looking into my own eyes, I would slip back again into regarding myself as if I were a stranger—a questioning and querulous stranger.

You might say that this whole process was, in the terms of the new psychology, the beginnings of narcissism, but this would not be true since narcissism implies love of self even to the point of the physical, and this was certainly not true of me. It was not *my* self but another self in which I was interested and which I tried to study. It was not even egotism. I think I can describe it only as a fierce desire to explore the thing which in the last analysis was *me*, and in exploring it, of course, I could not exclude the things, the influences, and the people around me and in a way the whole of living as it touched me and I touched it.

Well, that is how it happened, and I advise you never to begin such a process of examination for there is no end to it until you cease to exist and it is very certain that even though the body dies and decays, we still have no assurance that the spirit, the ego, the soul, or what you will dies with it, so there is perhaps really no end to the thing at all. Better live like an animal, directly as my Sergeant does, concerned only with food and women and enough money to provide him with both. He likes doing things with his hands and is very good at it. He can make up radio sets out of tin cans and rig up elaborate laundry machines and trick shower baths. He has no doubts. He is, I think, incapable of worry. He can only be annoyed when he has not enough to eat or there is not a woman at hand when he wants her.

II The Jungle

THE HUT IN WHICH I AM WRITING IS CONSTRUCTED OF corrugated iron, about twelve by fifteen feet in size. At first it had a roof of corrugated iron but the heat became intolerable and the Sergeant and I covered it over with plantain leaves thatched together thickly in an amateur way. It keeps out the rain, until it rots, which everything does very quickly here (even men's minds and bodies), and it is much cooler now. The boys have done the same thing to their own huts. It appears that back in Washington it has never occurred to the Army bureaucrats that iron absorbs heat and that in the tropics it is scarcely a material suitable for roofing. Perhaps one of these days an inspecting officer will visit us, make a great row and insist that we remove the plantain leaves and restore the corrugated iron because plantain leaves are not "regulation." The roof has a life of its own for it was scarcely finished before it became inhabited by every sort of rodent, spider, lizard and centipede. Living their own nocturnal lives, there is a perpetual sound of rustling throughout the damp nights.

In my hut I have an Army cot, a crude wooden table, two homemade chairs, a typewriter, an enameled wash basin and some books. It is simple enough. Many might consider my home lacking in comfort and constricted in size, but to me it is a kind of paradise. In it I live alone. It is all mine. I share it with no one save when the Sergeant or one of the boys comes in to talk, which is seldom enough. And when they do come in, I find for the first time in my life that I know a man and can talk to him. In a place like this there is little to hide and small reason to hide anything. It is extraordinary how frank and honest our conversations can be and even at times how sympathetic and understanding. I think that is because all of us, save Homer, the wool-hat, feel that we are lost and abandoned and that all the conventions, the restrictions, the hypocrisies of ordinary everyday life back home have no place or meaning here in this primitive world. We are all in the same boat.

Meyer doesn't talk much . . . indeed hardly at all, but when he does talk he reveals things which I am certain he has never revealed to anyone, even his wife, back home in Brooklyn. But Al, the Kansas farm boy, talks quite frankly about anything at all and has a collection of the finest hair-raising physiological stories ever heard. And the Sergeant tells you everything, every tremor, every nuance, every technical detail of what might be called only by the wildest stretch of romance his "love life."

Outside our huts there is a row of Quonsets and a white beach between the coral reef and the place where coral sand turns suddenly into thick, black constantly decaying soil and the jungle rises abruptly like a wall in a tangle of wet, lush, dark green growth. It is virtually impenetrable save for a path leading to the nearest village, less than a mile away—a path which is kept open by the villagers themselves, who come to us on visits of curiosity, and by Homer, the wool-hat, who uses it in his rutting animal-like excursions.

The village is built on stilts for protection against flood and wild animals and beneath the houses there lie perpetual heaps of garbage and excrement in which a race of razorback pigs scrounge for a living. When the wind comes from the east you can smell the village and of course you can smell it whenever a villager with oiled kinky hair and greasy body comes to stare at us and make grunting noises.

It rains perpetually, at all hours of the day and night, the rain coming, it seems at times, out of nowhere. But when the sun shines, it is with a dazzling light reflected from the white coral sand so brilliantly that all of us, even Homer, the wool-hat, perpetually wear dark glasses and live in fear of losing or breaking them. Yet when you enter the jungle even for a distance of a yard or two, the brilliance vanishes and is replaced by a thick deep green gloom in which the vegetation feeds upon itself in a constant cycle of birth, growth, death, decay and rebirth. Yet with all this fantastic growth there is little to eat and what there is consists mostly of nitrogen, carbon and starch. In the midst of all this opulent growth, the natives suffer from malnutrition and are the victims of every kind of disease. Homer, the wool-hat, brought the flu with him when we arrived and passed it on to some native woman. Within ten days there were five deaths in the village.

Yet the place has a wild and extravagant beauty, especially at dawn or at sunset when the water between the outer reef and the coral beach turns crimson and gold. But the beauty is too much. It cloys in its extravagance and at times even grows terrifying. Yet I like it. Even when I sit at my typewriter naked with the sweat pouring off me in the wretched damp heat, I like it. I am relaxed. I am myself. I am free. I am, to all intents and purposes, alone, at least in spirit. No one is sharing or possessing me. I have to make few compromises. My responsibilities are simple to the point of being primitive. I even like my fellow prisoners here on this island, with the possible exception of Homer, the wool-hat, and even he does not bore me because I find him a fascinating specimen unlike anything I have ever met before in all my existence. He seems a combination of jackal, wart hog and hyena.

With the Sergeant I have the greatest bond of sympathy, perhaps because he is nearer my own age and because, happily for him, he seems to have been born without all the conventions, the false values, the hypocrisies which I have had to strip away with great effort and pain until I stand at last almost as naked and free as he is.

The other three, the Army privates who are here on this hateful but beautiful island, are a mixture. Al is a farm boy from Kansas who wants only one thing—to return to his father's farm and marry the daughter of the next-door neighbor. Meyer is a swarthy little fellow from Brooklyn. He has a tailor shop and is married and has one child. He suffers from being away from his wife and child and even from Brooklyn which to him is paradise. The third, Homer, is a shambling, long-faced, "wool-hat" Georgian who can barely read or write. He is apparently quite happy because everything in the world astonishes him, from the size of ocean-going ships or the inside of a radio to some of the peculiar facts about sex which he never dreamed existed until he got out of his backwoods cabin into the Army.

In another world and background I should probably be bored by all of them and never get to know them at all. Here I have no choice but to know them and in doing so I have discovered that very likely no human is in essence a bore or a mediocrity. It is only that we do not have the time to explore or that we are blocked by our own limitations of interest. In this lonely jungle they make gardens in which radishes and beans grow up and mature and rot away in a few days. They fish in the muddy swollen river to bring up monstrous-looking tropical fish which they refuse to eat but give to the wild bad-smelling villagers who surround them the moment they begin operations. They listen to Tokyo Rose and sometimes, with great luck, get programs crackling with static from some distant station. They sweat, they smoke endless cigarettes. They curse a good deal and occasionally the Georgia boy goes into the bushes with one of the greasy, smelly native girls. Color does not seem to trouble this Georgian when nature presses but even the Sergeant draws the line; he says it is the smell he cannot stand and the yaws from which most of the natives suffer.

We read and read and read. I think the war must have taught many men to make a sustained effort at reading and concentration who before then had concentrated only long enough to get through a comic or the baseball score. The Sergeant likes detective stories and can read them over and over again even though he has long since learned "who dun it." And the Kansas boy just reads over and over again a book about an American farm. It is, he says, almost as good as being back there himself.

The dark little Jewish fellow likes mystery stories too, possibly because he never read anything before he came into the Army and into a life in which the principal problem is killing time. Homer, the wool-hat, doesn't read anything. It may be that the effort is too great for him. When he is not talking or working he just sleeps at any hour of the day or night, flat on his Army cot or, if the day is nice, leaning against a palm tree with his mouth wide open.

All of it, of course, is escape reading, and most of them regard the printed page as a kind of magic and hold in the greatest awe and veneration the writers who can put all that on paper. "Gee!" the Kansas boy will say. "I don't know how he can do it with only words. You can smell the warm milk and the mint in the pasture."

None of us has ever been in combat. We are what is left of a detachment sent here months ago to guard the stores kept in a row of steel Quonset huts, watching them day and night to see that the tropical rain doesn't come through the roof and that none of the natives get in and pilfer the supplies. We are all just sitting here in time and space, lost for the moment to the rest of the world. The heat is bad and the continuous Turkish-bath rains and the insects and the monotony of the food and the company. We all get on pretty well together and until now there has never really been a serious quarrel, despite our isolation. We are all waiting, for what?

The trouble is that here we *know* we are waiting. There is no future. We seem to be living suspended in time and space. There is no interest or activity to distract us. There are no women but the dirty greasy-haired female savages whom no one but Homer, the wool-hat, would touch even *in extremis*. There is no conversation, as such. There are only the reminiscences of the men about their boyhoods or their home towns or their experiences with women which, except for the dark little Brooklynite and the Kansas farmer, seem to be pretty primitive and indiscriminate. The Brooklynite has, I gather, never known any woman but his wife in a marriage not of choice but arranged between families, and the farm boy has messed around a bit at picnics and homecomings but I doubt that he has ever had any complete experience. "Horsin' around," he calls it. He knows all the facts of life and he has the girl picked out, and when and if he gets back he will go through the ceremony and then the breeding operations.

I haven't much to contribute to such conversations, not because I am wholly without experience like the Brooklyn boy, but because my own experience has been on a different level and I could not discuss it in a fashion which would interest them, even if I had any inclination to do so. Only two or three times have I had what might be called "functional" experience on the level of their rough-and-tumble affairs, and each time the experiences were unsatisfactory and even unpleasant, so that I find no pleasure in recalling them. A man doesn't discuss his own married life, and the whole business with Mary Raeburn was no subject for discussion. I could not talk of it and in any case I doubt that, if I had, any one of them would have understood what I was talking about. The Sergeant would have observed that "She must have been a hell of a good piece" and envied me.

The jungle has a sinister extravagant beauty which, unexpectedly, is singularly monotonous. The trees, the ferns, the strange snakelike lianas and other fantastic tropical growths are all outsize and seem at times, particularly at night, to have a life and animation of their own, as if the rustlings you hear in the darkness were the sound of their growing and reaching out to overwhelm and smother and devour each other. In the daytime the birds and the butterflies, drifting through the half light which is green like deep clear sea water, seem to be flashes of light.

They are like those flashes of light which sometimes come to me here when I find my mind working, really for the first time, when I see people and things clearly—even myself—and I understand that somehow I have missed the boat all along the line and this in spite of my having had what you might call every advantage and every opportunity. These flashes of light are as painful as they are illuminating, and the odd thing is that they are followed by a spirit of the blackest depression when I find myself hoping that the war will go badly for both sides and that there will be enough destruction so that we may go back to the beginning and start to build a wholly new world. All this serves to convince me that a man like myself should never really *think*. He should go round and round his treadmill until at last he fades away, or live as the Sergeant does intensely and directly, rather like an animal who is comfortable and sleeps when his stomach is filled and his senses and desires put to rest.

All of this separates me in a sense from the other men on the island, none of whom have ever been corrupted by thought. We wonder, no doubt (all but Homer, the wool-hat), what goes on in each other's mind, and even though we live so closely, so intimately in such spectacular isolation, none of us will ever really know what goes on in the inner recesses of the other's mind. The less the mind, I suppose, the less it matters.

The terrible thing is that in our modern world there is so little place for thought or for its effects, for the mindless multiply far more rapidly than the intelligent and all the forces which surround us seek to destroy thought, to reduce everything to the level of codes and brevity, radio and movies, condensations and predigested pills of information. At home Meyer sits in his tailor's shop, cross-legged in the old-fashioned way (that's the way he sits on his Army cot), and he does not think, he does not consider himself, nor his surroundings, nor his faith, nor the universe. He is listening to the radio. It does not much matter what the program is. It is merely a noise that fills a void. Probably the whole of his conversation is limited to the baseball score or the latest gag by a radio comic. He has neither conversation, nor picturesqueness nor any quality whatever. He lives, breeds and dies, and that is the whole story.

It is not because Meyer is in himself a mediocrity. He has been made so by the world in which he lives. I think he talks more here on this beautiful wretched island than he talks at home and even here he talks very little, but he *must* think, for one cannot arrest the working of the mind save by sleep or by perpetual noise and distraction. I suspect that all of us have done some thinking we have never done before. Now and then the results of it burst out in the most unexpected way.

Al has been thinking about his farm and he says, "When I get back and can live a decent life again, I'm going to make my farm the finest in all of Kansas. I've been thinking about it. I know what I want to do and I've already got plans laid out. It's not going to be just a good farm. It's goin' to be super. I've got to make up for all the lost time."

Probably a lot of other boys on other beaches and islands, in other deserts, are thinking too, for the first time, because there isn't anything else to do when the detective and mystery stories run out and can't be read again for the fifth time. So maybe there is some good or purpose in this idiotic war.

Al has lovable qualities. He starts at you suddenly when an idea strikes him. It's as if he experienced a kind of wonder at such an occurrence. He will scratch his head and grow intense and think on from that idea to another one. I believe he and his fellow farmers are the only ones who have mastered mechanics and machinery rather than permitting these things to master them. To Al, farm machinery is a slave, to be put to use to do things more quickly and efficiently so that he may get through his work and turn to better things. The rest of us are enslaved by radio, by automobiles and planes and telephones. We tremble and leave whatever we are doing to answer a telephone, as if we were slaves who would be punished by torture if we merely sat and permitted it to ring until it had worn itself out.

There is something supremely idiotic about our position here. I am the only one who does not wish earnestly, even passionately, to return home and get on with his life. We have been here nearly two years and may remain for God knows how long. Why are we here? To guard a depot of food and supplies which is slowly rotting away and will, when and if the war is ever finished, be dumped into the sea or burned, and all around us are these wretched natives starving in the midst of this mad unhealthy vegetation. Yet if some martinet should come on inspection to check on supplies and find that a half-dozen tins of soup were missing, the discovery could have serious consequences for me, if not for the others.

All about us among the islands are other men occupied in the same useless death watch, and here and there are a few hundred wretched Japs who have escaped and hidden away like shy animals. They will not come out of the jungle even if you leave them messages or call to them over loudspeakers to surrender. We have none here on this island and the nearest island is forty miles away, so at least we do not have the worry over being attacked and having our throats cut silently in the middle of the dark tropical night. Perhaps that might be better. It would make things a little more exciting . . . at least for the other fellows.

I have the excitement of writing all of this down, this search, this exploration into what I am and how I came to be what I am. It is like exploring the jungle itself. One goes on and on, deeper and deeper as one new dim and misty vista opens up into another. I was tired when I came here but I have been in a sense reborn by what I am doing. Yet in the back of my consciousness is a perpetual fear and dread of what will happen when I come to the end of the exploration. At the moment I am living over again everything of importance that ever happened to me and it is all new and different because in a way I see it for the first time, as I could never see it *when* it was happening. That I suppose is what disturbed and agonized Faust himself. That is why he wanted to live it all over again, for the enjoyment and the savor which he missed the first time he passed that way. Yet there is an enjoyment merely in the whole of the exploration. I have made a new and interesting acquaintance. I have encountered someone I never knew before. It is myself.

III Oakdale

I WAS BORN IN THE TOWN CALLED CRESCENT CITY OF WHICH the suburb Oakdale is now a part. My birth took place in a large and rather ornate house with towers and cupolas and plate glass windows, a very outsize house considering the fact that the city lot upon which it was placed was only seventy-five feet wide and in depth not more than a hundred feet. The big house occupied most of the lot so that it stood very close to the houses on either side, and in the evening, unless the shades were drawn, it was possible to see from our windows what went on inside the houses on either side. I can remember seeing family quarrels taking place and what in those days was referred to as "spooning." I have seen fathers strike their children, and even in the case of old Hazeltine, who late in life married a young bride, I have witnessed as a child the rather repulsive intimacies of that particular bedroom from my own second-story bedroom window.

The house was a symbol of many things. It belonged to the era which lay between the frontier when Crescent City was a village and the day when, as factories moved in, the village grew to be a town and then to be a city, and finally the people who once would have lived on the main street in such a house as ours took to the suburbs and the main street became a "dead area." In time the old big ornate houses went unpainted and the dooryards unkempt, and at last the big trees which once shaded the street were cut down to widen it. The old houses first became boarding houses and presently went half empty save for one or two which housed a funeral home or the establishment of a chiropractor or disappeared before the enameled front of a shiny filling station. The day of the old house and the way of living which went with it passed and the whole neighborhood became "a dead area," a phrase which might well describe much of American life.

In the very beginning the houses of the village had been close together as a protection against the attack of the Indians, the French, and finally the British. Then as the town grew, the houses remained close to each other because the only transportation was by means of horses, and even the rich built houses on small squares of valuable land within the limits of the city itself. And when the automobile came and changed the element of space into that of time, they moved out a little way into suburbs like Oakdale; but still, even when there was no longer any peril from attack or any limitations of transportation, they still huddled together in the suburbs, building their houses on plots only a little larger than those in the city. Farmers lived on farms and townspeople lived in towns, but a country house was and still is largely unknown—a house where there might be solitude and wildness and beauty of a kind that is connected with space and the breathing of the spirit and cannot be found in towns and cities and suburbs. It was as if the people were always afraid, first of the Indians and the raiders and afterward of being alone or in any way different from their neighbors.

The fear of solitude grew, I think, out of the thinness of their resources and the lack of thought or even the capacity to think. Never as in Europe did they put walls or hedges about their properties so that they themselves might have privacy and be spared the indignity of witnessing, as I did in childhood, unfortunate or unpleasant things going on in the house next door. They did not cherish privacy and, like Enid, actually *wanted* neighbors to know what was going on within the limits of their own small properties, and so, in a sense, they developed a kind of falseness related to play-acting, concerned wholly with the appearance rather than the substance, with the façade rather than what lay behind it. And all of this became a part of the thing which might be called American culture or civilization, or perhaps more accurately the lack of both. At any rate, it added up to a kind of sterility and still does.

In her way Enid is a humble symbol of what I mean. With her it has become so profound that she play-acts even in bed so that there is no satisfaction in any relationship with her, physical or otherwise. In reality she in a way resembles a prostitute who also play-acts as a part of her profession. There is no way ever of reaching her—in the essence, I mean, or the spirit or the reality, if indeed by now she has any longer any essence or spirit or reality. That is why, long ago, I gradually stopped trying to talk to her about anything whatever—the welfare and future of the children, a political issue, or even the behavior of our neighbors which is always a source of relaxed and easy gossip. When I tried I found myself talking, not to a warm and honest human being, but to an attitude, a pose, a character part in a play, in a setting behind which there was nothing.

It is an extraordinary thing how the life of a town like Crescent City and a suburb like Oakdale has ceased to produce "characters." Among the early pioneers, tough men and women who knew the satisfaction of building something with their own hands and minds, their own courage and dignity and self-reliance, "characters" among old people were so common that they were very nearly the rule. And even in my childhood there were plenty of characters in the town—people who lived as they wanted to live with a certain freedom and even luxury of expression and action, indifferent to the opinion of others. They made life much richer for the whole of the community and infinitely more colorful. But as I grew older they gradually died off and no new eccentrics came to take their places, and both the town and life itself became much duller until now the whole community at times seems insufferable since every door in every house admits or releases people who are just alike in what they believe, in how they act, in what they think. The odd one, if he occurs, is likely to be shut up or treated as mad. I think it could be said that eccentricity and "characters" are the measure, as they were in the eighteenth century, of an independent and dynamic society, a civilization, or a culture in any nation.

At least three of my grandparents would certainly be regarded today with pity or alarm as eccentrics. My Grandfather Weber came from the Palatinate in the Forties at a time when liberty and independence of thought were of much concern to certain elements among the German people. He fled into exile in order to avoid capture and prison because he was one of the leaders in a movement of revolt against the tyranny of a government which sought to curtail his freedom and deform his personality, and to him such things were unsufferable.

He was a heavy, strongly built man who by trade in the old country had been an ironmonger and blacksmith in a prosperous way, and until the day he died he spoke with a strong South German accent. In addition to being extremely skillful and even an artist in the fashioning of wrought iron in all its forms, he was also something of a musician, played the trumpet, and sang regularly in the bass section with the fellow German refugees who formed a Liederkranz society immediately upon their arrival in Crescent City. He was the father of seven children, including my mother, and so far as anyone knows he remained happily faithful to his wife from the day he married her until she died, at forty-seven. After that he had some kind of a happy relationship with a middle-aged milliner named Mrs. Schontz. How far it went I do not know, but I would suspect that it went all the way. She was a buxom, blonde woman who made wonderful *strudel* which she always gave us children when we stopped in at the millinery shop. I do not know why they did not marry, but I remember hearing as a child some talk of her feeling that she was not capable of becoming a stepmother to a family of children some of whom already had children of their own. Also there was talk of a ne'er-do-well husband who had disappeared and might possibly return unexpectedly with potential embarrassment to all concerned.

I do not think any of it mattered very much. Whatever happened was carried on in a dignified way. There were no bottles of Bourbon and smooching in the back seat of a car at the country club. They made each other happy, and on occasion she went with him to the Liederkranz society and sang with him in the contralto section of the chorus when the German element did "The Messiah" each year at Christmas time. And she always superintended the annual beer-garden picnic and reunion of the old Germans who came over, during the revolutionary troubles, from Bavaria and the Palatinate.

It was a warm relationship to which nobody, so far as I could discover, ever objected, even the old man's own children who always regarded Mrs. Schontz as a friend. She supported herself through her millinery shop, and the most he ever spent upon her was to buy a little gift or treat her to beer for the evening. I think that my grandmother herself would have approved of the relationship because it made her Caspar happy. Her Caspar was one of those big strong men who could at the same time be helpless when it came to small things. Mrs. Schontz looked after him.

When she died he became a lonely old man who actually cherished his solitude. He refused to come and live with any of his children and stayed on in the old house where he had lived the whole of his life. Sometimes he came to meals with our family and always he carried sweets of some kind in his pocket for the children. He had worked hard and brought up a large family comfortably, and when Mrs. Schontz died he said, in his funny accent, "Sure it would be nice to live with one of you, but I would be in the way with so many children, and I am old enough now to deserve solitude. When I want to think I can think. When I want to remember the happy times I have had and the blessings God gave me I can sit on the front porch and watch people go by and call out, 'Good Evening,' and have a beautiful time all by myself. I have put aside enough savings to live comfortably. I can even keep my own house clean and neat. When I want company I can go to the Liederkranz or the beer garden or come and have supper with one of you."

He did not want to be "kept." He did not want the state to make his decisions. He did not want to conform. He had been a good citizen, contributing his share and much more to the general good of the community. He had no fear of being alone. There was his music and his ironwork, and as he grew older he carved little figures out of wood—elves and trolls in the South German tradition, which he painted in bright colors and gave to the children. Even as a very old man he never "killed time" until he died. On the morning my mother found him dead he had been at work creating something up to the last minute when the Lord called him. He left behind, not quite finished, an ornament of wrought iron designed to hold flower pots for the balcony beneath the turrets and scrollwork of my mother's house.

He was content to die at eighty-one, and it was probably just as well that he did for I remember, even long ago, when I myself was old enough to notice such things, that sometimes the children mimicked his accent as he passed in the street and my cousins complained that they were ashamed of a grandfather who could not speak good English. It made him seem different and so reflected upon themselves who each day sought more and more to be as much like everybody else as possible.

But there was another reason, far more profound. He died before he saw the fiery spirit of the French Revolution, for which he had made himself an exile from the Rhine country he loved so much, begin to be transmuted into something else, something derived from the Marx whom he had always detested and who was a materialist and the bitter enemy of the human spirit which the French Revolution glorified through blood and strife and suffering. He would have resented bitterly the materialism which ordered him to pay taxes so that he might have an old-age pension, the materialism which crippled his own independence and reduced him to the level of men incapable of taking care of themselves and their families, which treated him as part incompetent and part indigent. It was not materialism for which he had conspired and fought and been exiled, nor for a state potentially as tyrannical and much less colorful than the state against which he had rebelled. He had fought for something quite different which concerned the dignity rather than the material security of man. In the New World he had found that freedom which permitted a man to be a man and live with human dignity, aware of his own strength and thought and abilities and trustful of the good will of his neighbors. He did not live long enough to see that right of freedom and independence begin to fade into commonplaceness and conformity and the sacrifice of the spirit for which he had fought, turn into a dull paternalism as vicious and perhaps more deadening than the old tyranny had been.

My paternal grandparents were of another tradition altogether. My father's father was already well past middle age when my father, one of twelve children, was born, so that he seemed immensely old when I knew him as a child. He died when I was very young, at the age of ninety-three, and had lived through most of the nineteenth century when the whole country about Crescent City was transformed from a near wilderness into a huge and modern industrial community. Despite the great distance which separated him and me, my memories of him are vivid. He was a man, I think, who, once seen and known, made an impression as on a photographic plate, which remained forever.

He was a tall, thin, very tough old man who always seemed younger than his years and was vigorous up until the moment he died. By blood he was mostly north of Ireland Scottish with some English blood, and he possessed both the ruggedness of the one people and the adaptability of both. Essentially he was a pioneer, but you couldn't make a career out of being a pioneer, and during the course of his life he had tried his hand at many things. Apparently he would undertake a job and, once it was accomplished, he would lose interest and set himself at once to another, which is I suppose a characteristic of the pioneer. As a young man he had fought in the Indian Wars in the Great Plains and the Southwest and he had traveled a great deal inside the borders of this country.

He was a great storyteller and his tales of the Southwest had a passionate interest for me. They were better than any I have read since, and sometimes, when the memory of those tales returns to me, I feel a great sense of sadness, injury, and loss that the country he talked of no longer exists and that I never had the opportunity of knowing it. Of course, the flood-stream beds, the mountains, the mesas are still there, but the excitement and the struggle and the perils have gone and everywhere there are shacks and filling stations and motels. That country has become a shrunken thing, and to find again a wild country like it one would have to search the wildernesses of the earth.

I think that more and more most of us suffer from an increasing claustrophobia. The next town is too near and the distance between it and our own town is built up with bungalows or their successors—the ranch-type house. Great cities which seemed to me as a child romantic and distant places are only a few hours away by plane or even automobile. Europe is too near and Asia threatens us. More and more we feel a sense of uneasiness at this mechanically projected process of shrinking the world. More and more there is a universal and shadowy psychological sense of alarm and even dread, as if there were no longer enough room in the world. And all the time there are more and more of us—more Chinese, more Americans, more Russians—and the more people there are, the more complex and difficult become the problems of the world and consequently our own personal problems.

My paternal grandfather, who was called Colonel Jared Smith, lived in a free world filled with a sense of space and of boundless opportunity. He could be an Indian fighter, a settler, a merchant, a trapper. He could set up a small business which might grow into a great industry or do any of a hundred adventurous and fascinating things. We hear much in these times of how the span of life has been extended and how fewer and fewer people die of tuberculosis or plague, of how such dread things as syphilis are cured overnight, of how the weak and handicapped who might have died are kept alive to go on breeding. We hear about the great advances in transportation, of plumbing, of radios and television. . . . I don't know. Maybe it *is* a better world. But in return for all of these things we have sacrificed much and have raised for ourselves, and above all for our children, complexities and problems which may never be solved and which in the end may mount up until the heap collapses and thrusts mankind and civilization back again into the Dark Ages. I don't know. What do you think?

We live in a world of short cuts, many of them brutally contradictory of natural law, yet the whole swarming ant-mass of this planet is insignificant in relation to the universe and its immutable laws.

Anyway, Grandpa Smith had always gone his tough way, using brawn and wit to make for himself a fascinating life, to build and create, at least in part, the world into which I was born, a world which even on my entry into life was beginning to become a static rather than a dynamic world, a world resembling more and more closely the tight crowded world of Europe where there were too many people and not enough free land and there has long been a shortage not of men but of land and space and opportunity.

In any case, I was born into a world very different from that of the old gentleman Colonel Jared Smith. The look of his world was in his eye—the kind of look one rarely sees in these times save in the eye of an eccentric hermit, if you can find one. It was at once a look of peace and of arrogance. There was in it the fierce independence that is in the eye of the eagle but beyond that there was the look of peace which is in the eyes of people who have lived full rich lives and, when old, find peace and no regrets either for the things they have done or have not done. It is the kind of look one finds in the eyes of people who have discovered that in old age there is a richness, a quiet satisfaction they never attained earlier in life. They are the people who have lived, you might say, in rhythm, completing the full arc of man's existence from fiery ascending youth through the solid accomplishments of middle age into the quiet, peaceful decline toward death. They are not people who dread death or struggle to evade it, for their lives have been complete, rounded out, and realized like a great work of art. They have never feared life or denied it. They do not welcome death through frustration and despair but because they have fulfilled their cycle with richness and satisfaction. How few of them there are in our times!

He was a great horseman and as an old man he rode an old spotted mare which he had brought from the West twenty years earlier. Actually he died while riding her and was found dead in the fields of his farm lying on the ground with one hand holding the reins. She was not a pretty beast. She was heavily built and had a Roman nose but she was smart and looked after the old man. They were devoted to each other, and she ran loose like a dog about the farmhouse. When he died she was never able to understand that he had gone away and this time was not coming back. In the summer mornings she would come to the back door and neigh as she had done hundreds of times before, but he was no longer there to give her an apple or a lump of sugar. She died during the following winter, perhaps of old age, perhaps out of loneliness. We could never quite explain to her what had happened.

This grandfather had great good luck in his wife. He had found her in California where her father operated as a rancher on one of the last Spanish grants. She had Spanish blood which showed in her dark hair and black eyes, and it is not impossible that there was some remote Indian blood in her. She was very trim and very spry, even as an old lady, and she was a wonderful cook. I think it is by her cooking that I remember her and I know of no better way by which to remember anyone. The children always liked going out to the farm for meals since the food was excellent and of great variety, including even Spanish and Mexican dishes which seemed very hot until we got used to them. She must have been very handsome as a girl with her brilliant black eyes and firm full-breasted figure and trim ankles.

In any case, she seemed always to have been in love with my grandfather, and I suspect that the basis of the love on both sides was founded on complete physical satisfaction in each other. From that stemmed in turn tenderness, devotion, self-sacrifice, understanding, and even common interests. It is on the physical side, which is usually the foundation of any lasting love affair or marriage, that so many marriages in the world I have known have failed, because this part of the marriage has been a bungled and unsatisfactory operation without abandon, or ecstasy, or complete surrender. It is, all too often, a messy affair brought about by physiological pressures with urgent brutality on the one side and a contrived and patient endurance on the other. And so comes divorce or that dreary limited compromise which is varied only by sordid adventures on the side.

My grandmother's name was Pilar, a pretty name, and she always encouraged the impression that my grandfather not only dominated her but bullied her. He was always ordering her about saying, "Pilar, do this," or, "Pilar, do that." She usually did it in her own good time, if it suited her, and all the while it was she who in reality ran everything. She kept charge of the money and took care alike of his children and his investments when he went away on one of his long trips. She ran the house and the farm and the livestock, patiently and with satisfaction, until he returned, when there was a turbulent reunion lasting for days from which there inevitably resulted still another child.

She appeared a little strange in Crescent City and the surrounding countryside, and I think that always most people looked upon her as alien. There was always a Latin elegance about her carriage, in her habit of dressing nearly always in black and white, and even about the way she kept her house. Whether she was aware that she seemed strange I cannot say, but if so it did not appear to trouble her. The odd thing was that, although she had been brought up as a Catholic and a Spanish one at that, her children had contact with no particular faith save that whenever it became necessary to have the services of a clergyman, the Presbyterian preacher was summoned. She did not appear to miss the consolations of religion perhaps because she lived very close to nature and the animals, both wild and domestic, on the farm which next to my grandfather was the most important thing in her life. These two elements, together with her children, made up the whole of her existence.

She died suddenly of a stroke a little over a year after my grandfather was found dead beside his mare. None of the children seemed to have inherited either her taste for country life or my grandfather's wild restlessness, and presently the farm which we all called "Pilar's Farm" was sold. The old buildings have been long since torn down and no memory or even physical vestige of the place remains. The fields have long since been broken up into suburban lots and the farm is a part of the fashionable suburb of Oakdale. My own house is not far from the site of the old farm house.

Biologists tell us that we do not inherit directly from our parents, who are merely the carriers of seed, but from our four grandparents, and this may account for the fact that none of Pilar and the Colonel's own children seemed to inherit their tastes. They were all on the whole respectable and commonplace and conventional. It may also account for the fact of my own restlessness and frequent melancholy. With Pilar and the Colonel the restlessness, the physical passion, the color, and the delight in purely physical things were all realized and satisfied. With me these things have been suppressed and frustrated, partly by circumstance and partly perhaps simply by my own weakness and indecision.

It raises the old question between inheritance and environment about which there seems to be no really definite decision. I only know that at times I can somehow *feel* Pilar and the Colonel in my blood, in wild but suppressed and concealed outbursts of disgust and frustration, and on those occasions when in my mind I considered secretly the easiest and quickest way of getting rid of Enid altogether.

Enid, of course, never knew of these secret plottings, when in a vicarious way, entirely in the imagination, I destroyed in a single wild explosion all of my Oakdale life, killed her, escaped, and lost myself forever. Nor do I think that she ever suspected what I was thinking and even plotting since that kind of violence was something quite beyond her understanding. It was her way to go on patching and compromising and pretending. Well, that is what I did too because I could never bring myself to act and could find no way out until the war came along and dropped me here on a steaming tropical island as far from Oakdale as it is possible to be in this world.

My own father was as little like his parents as it was possible to be, unless it could be said that he inherited something of Pilar's sense of stability and outward orderliness. The only inheritance left by Pilar and the Colonel was the farm and the livestock and machinery which went with it, so their children had very largely to make their own way, and my father got a job early in life in the office of old Mr. Hargreaves who had the first and the biggest insurance agency in Crescent City. As the city had grown and the country developed, his insurance business became immensely lucrative, and when he died he left it jointly to a nephew and to my father to whom he had taken a fancy. So at thirty my father was very well off with a business which he liked and for which he had a talent.

In some ways my father was the perfect small-town Middle-Western businessman of his time. He belonged to half a dozen fraternal organizations. He helped to organize the first Rotary Club of the town. He was a regular attendant of the Presbyterian church. He knew nearly everyone in the town and few had a bad word to speak against him. He was outwardly a good husband and definitely he liked his children although he never came very near to them. Whether he ever loved his wife or not I do not know. He must have married old Caspar's daughter out of love since when the old German's estate was settled she inherited only a few hundred dollars.

How long that love or the desire which accompanied it endured I do not know. I was the third child, and by the time I was old enough to be aware of such things there was very little evidence of love or even affection between my parents. It was not that they quarreled or even showed any evidence of disliking each other. They simply went their own ways, seeing each other at meals morning and evening and sharing until he died a large double bed. They spoke to each other occasionally but they never *conversed*. Exchange of words was commonplace and habitual but I never remember their showing any great interest in each other or any interest in what the other was doing or saying. In all their conversations there was never the slightest evidence of an idea or of any thought.

My mother is still alive, a solid rather square-built woman with the heavy reliable energy which came down to her through my German grandfather. Most people would call her handsome. She should, I think, have been the head of a great business or engineering corporation and perhaps in these days would have held an executive position or even have founded a business of her own. But when she was eighteen there was no place for a woman to go, and so she married my father, which seemed the obvious thing to do. He was good-looking, three years older than herself, and very well off with an insurance business which was about as solid as anything could be. I do not know how much they were in love with each other or indeed do I know what love is because it can be so many different things to so many different people. Certainly neither of them was very hot-blooded or passionate, or at least neither of them seemed ever to have discovered either passion or desire. That, I suppose, is how it is with many people who live lives which are like a pudding without salt or sugar or spices.

They were what are called good citizens. They were prosperous. They had three well-behaved and satisfactory children. I suspect that the family was limited to three not because of any effort at birth control but simply because my parents lost interest in each other. I think that both of them missed much in life and that, partly aware of this, they lost themselves and partially cured their frustrations by becoming frantically "busy."

My father went early to the office and came home late. He was away a great deal on business trips. I think he really loved the immense files and the complicated forms that went with the insurance business. All this did not make him either a very attentive father or a very interesting one. Until he died he always seemed something of a stranger to me, and even now I find myself thinking of him not as "Father" or "Dad" or "Pop" but simply as "Mr. Insurance Man." His business constantly grew and finally he bought out his partner, the nephew of the man who had befriended him and who preferred hunting and fishing to insurance. The partner took a smaller house and presently a small farm and sold some farm insurance on his own, enough to keep his wife, himself, and his five children, and gradually he became half-forgotten by the town in which his uncle had been one of the richest men and one of its most prominent citizens. When people thought or spoke of him it was to say, "Isn't it a pity the way Tom Hargreaves has gone downhill? It would certainly be a disappointment to his uncle."

Sometimes, because one of his boys was about my age and a friend of mine, I went to stay at their small farm for a few days. Everything went wild there, including the children. We camped out, scared at night by the rustling sounds made by the wild animals and the calls of the screech owls, and in summer the swimming hole behind the house was our bathtub. Tom Hargreaves may have gone downhill, but he certainly had more fun than my father ever had and he gave fun and excitement to many other people.

After such a visit I always returned home saddened and filled with wistfulness because I always wished I had a father like him.

My mother was a good housekeeper and we were able to afford a cook, a "day" girl, and a laundress in the big house with the towers and the fretwork. She did little housework herself and actually disliked it. Most of her heavy energy went into her women's club activities and into raising charity funds and attending conventions. The house was always well kept and the food good, but there was a sterile emptiness about it and an almost total lack of warmth and never any excitement at all. It was as if we were all hypnotized, paralyzed, and embalmed in material security, order, and convention, in a big ugly house on a seventy-five-foot lot.

My mother was fair and just and a good disciplinarian when she was with us, and we three children grew up to be a well-mannered lot and extremely conventional, but I think now that all three of us married very early in life simply in the half-conscious hope of having a "home." What we had had all our lives was a comfortable, even luxurious house and good food, but none of us had ever had a home. It was only when we went on a visit, as I used to go to Hargreaves' farm, that we understood what it was that we did not have.

Yet despite her apparent indifference and her preoccupation with other things, my mother exercised over us an iron control. She always "knew better" than anyone else, including ourselves, what was good for us, and she somehow, in her spare time, managed to get us all married to "suitable" mates of what were considered good families and which she described as "well situated." In this she displayed her powers as a manager and an executive, and long afterward I came to realize that she was as much responsible for my marriage to Enid as I myself was.

She managed this in a hundred small ways—by praising Enid, by throwing us together, by rather backhanded hints about our being suited to each other, and by suggesting that it would be a perfect match. I think she would not have objected if I had got Enid into trouble so that a shotgun wedding would have been necessary. Of course such a thing with Enid would have been quite impossible unless Enid had found a man who was absolutely indispensable to her future security and position, and then it would never have been the result of passion or deception but of calm calculation on her part. It was the marriage my mother wanted to bolster up her own sense of success and perfection and help complete the planned pattern of what to her was a satisfactory existence. Now, as a still powerful and firm old lady, revered as past president of the American Federation of Women's clubs and honorary member of the Lord knows how many other women's organizations, she can look back with satisfaction upon a life which she ordered and planned from the very beginning.

She failed only in the cases of two of her children. My sister's husband is a hopeless and partly secret drunkard, and it is scarcely possible for a man's marriage to have been more drearily unhappy than my own eventually became. These failures, however, did not disturb her for she simply refused to recognize them. When once or twice my sister tried to discuss the tragedy of her husband, my mother simply turned her off by saying, "Let's not discuss it, my dear. We all have our problems and you have yours. You must try a little harder to make him happy and he will forget about drinking. I always managed in my own life to iron out these little difficulties and I think I can say that I succeeded." What was a great tragedy she treated as little more than an annoyance.

In this attitude she was not too different from many of the American women of her generation, or indeed men as well, for it is a great trait of Americans to believe what they want to believe or to ignore or distort any truth which may be disagreeable.

They are, I think, as fearful of facing the truth as they are of being alone, and the two fears are inevitably linked and blended, since it is when one is alone that the truth is faced and revealed, and so they hunt in packs and move in crowds and attend conventions and drink themselves into the sleep which is a little like the death they await while marking time in emptiness.

And so my sister had to bear alone the burden of her husband's tragedy of disintegration which began, I think, when his parents forced him to become a lawyer—something he never wanted to be but which was in the family tradition. And so he was a bad lawyer and a failure and ashamed before the wife whom he sincerely loved. He drank because whatever he did was a frustration and against his nature.

My brother, happily, married a girl from Seattle and so went far off to live and seldom returned to the East. So far as I know they are happy, but he showed little desire ever to see his parents again after his marriage.

So far as the trouble between Enid and myself, I have never discussed the matter with my mother, but she knows, I am sure, the misery of the household. But she ignores it and only contributes to the fiction of our perfect suburban life as the "finest type of American family." I have overheard her saying as much on more than one occasion when she knows perfectly well that it is not the truth.

It is very difficult to describe my mother or give her any particular character because in some respects she was and is like a machine with an incredible power of riding over everything and everybody. She accomplishes this without any violent struggle or even intrigue but always quietly and almost sweetly, as if the crushing effect of her passing over you like a steam roller were good for you. Always, of course, she has operated in the tradition of the "accepted thing" so that she has behind her the vast power of convention, of conformity, of a crushing mediocrity.

She is now a venerated, distinguished, respected character in the community and even in a small way in the nation. She has very white hair which, with her rather cold blue eyes and high-colored complexion, makes her very handsome and "aristocratic-looking"—a common phrase and description which belongs with the "lovely homes" and "gorgeous drapes" and "occasional chairs" school of formula and vulgarity. Two things subtract from any look of genuine distinction. One is her taste for fussy dresses and elaborate hats. The other is the pince-nez which she always wears attached to a fine gold chain that snaps in and out on a spring from a gold button attached to her broad bosom. These two things rather give her away. In one sense she could in her prime have posed for a composite portrait of the typical middle-aged middle-class American woman of her era.

She belonged, and as long as she lives will still belong, to a particular era in the development of American sociology, and the key to her story is that very likely she should never have married at all but have gone into business, a thing that was very nearly impossible in her time. Today it is quite different. Such a woman can undertake a career and either never marry at all or marry and relegate her family to the second position of importance in her life and thus be able to avoid many frustrations and small deceptions and hypocrisies. Although my mother has been very active all her life, there was never any sense of adventure in her, nor any real fire. Her life was satisfactory, according to her lights, and dull, and she, so help me God, was the dullest thing in it. Before I was fifteen years old I knew that she was a dreadful bore. Now in her old age, since she has come to consider herself a "character" and to *demand* reverence and attention, she has become insufferable.

It is true too that she lived toward the end of an era in which the frontier was passing and in which women were scarce and simply under the law of supply and demand, if for no other reason, became desirable. It gave all women, unattractive or otherwise, a great advantage. It gave rise to the absurd fashion of placing all women either on a pedestal or in the gutter. There was nothing in between and no allowance made for the mixed-up thing which most women are, part mother, part bitch, part beauty, part ugliness. This mixed-up quality is what makes women charming and interesting, but the women of my mother's generation and situation were not allowed to be mixed up. They were all supposed to be pure and virtuous and motherly whether they were or not, and most of them spent their lives in giving a performance of all of these things. Not only did it make them dull and false; it turned them into hypocrites who practiced their bitcheries never openly but secretly and in a veritable web of intrigue. Sweetness of nature was rarely genuine; it was usually the sugar coating on a bitter pill of frustration and envy and baffled ambition. Of course Enid, in her more subtle way, was a remote product of this same tradition.

Motherhood, a physical fact, arrived at often enough bitterly and unwillingly or by accident, was a sacred word, regardless of whether the mother neglected her home, tortured her husband, or devoured her children after first deforming their lives. Good mothers are purely accidental and they are rare enough. It is a pity that the word "mother" suffered the debasement it experienced during most of American sociological history. Things have begun to change, and it is gradually becoming recognized that many mothers are merely monsters. There is nothing sacred about the fruition of the act of copulation. It depends upon what a woman makes of such a situation.

I have been able to avoid my mother pretty well for the last ten years, but there were the inevitable yearly visits which fortunately could not last for long since it was impossible for two such women as herself and Enid to stay for long under the same roof without a violent explosion. Fortunately my mother never stayed more than a week, but at the end of that time the tension between the two women, aggravated perhaps by my own corroding inward misery and weakness, became unbearable. In a Latin country like France such an atmosphere would have led to physical violence and even perhaps murder. The nearest it ever came to violence was that furious quarrel when they joined forces against me. I know now that the only thing which prevented violence in our house was the composite pattern of illusion and play-acting in which both women lived. Enid wanted always to be able to say, "I don't understand mother-in-law trouble. I get on so well with mine. I think the solution is fundamentally based on our attitude toward each other," . . . then with a smile, as if she were saying something witty and original, "You know, bear and forbear." And my mother wanted always to be able to say, "My daughter-in-law is utterly devoted to me. When I visit her the place is turned over to me. Nothing is too good for Grandmother."

In the presence of strangers or friends who dropped in, the performance between the two women could only be described as "revolting." They fell into their roles and really "hammed" and "mugged" them. Each built up the other's act with "dears" and "darlings" as thick in their conversation as currants in a bun. Then the moment the door closed on the visitors, the overanimated, falsely eager faces drooped again and a kind of bristling like that of two hostile bitches circling each other came into the atmosphere.

Of course I caught it both ways. Enid, throughout the visit, would keep saying to me, "You know, darling, your mother is a wonderful woman but she is a great trial. She's so used to being the center of everything and running everything. I'm always so tired by the time she leaves that I could lie down and die" (the very last thing indestructible Enid would ever dream of doing).

And on my mother's side, I would get, "It's a pity Enid doesn't show more interest in cultural things. I never thought she'd turn out this way when you married her. She seems to think only of neighborhood gossip and the housekeeping. She has plenty of help. Why doesn't she manage them so that she doesn't have to spend all her time house-cleaning? It's very difficult to talk with her about anything serious. I don't see how a woman could have spent four years at college and come out with so little."

Of course during the annual visit I had to give up altogether the luxury of my solitude behind the locked door of the rumpus room. If I attempted to escape I was persecuted by both of them with hints and hurt looks and implications of an almost sinister sort. In short they ganged up on me in a bitter and unholy alliance. And I was weak enough to be concerned about the horror involved in the spectacle of the two of them sitting over my head alone together in the sitting room, hating each other and making nasty remarks. Even if I had tried to escape to the rumpus room, I could not have accomplished anything because the picture of the whole thing would have been in the back of my mind, disturbing me and upsetting any attempt to think or put anything on paper.

So I would sit there with them, usually playing records on the player as loudly as possible in order to make conversation difficult and try meanwhile to get a little reading done. And presently my mother would rise and suggest that it was time to go to bed and perhaps that both Enid and I would be the better for a little more sleep and a few less cocktails. Enid would never give in and go to bed first. By the time the evening broke up I was much too exhausted to think of going back to the rumpus room and find a little solitude. I merely did what was expected of an American husband approaching middle age who has no longer any interest in his wife—go upstairs to a single bed next to hers as if they were going to bed to perform the marital act, as if either of them still wanted to. The mere thought of my occupying a separate room while my mother was in the house was, of course, unthinkable to Enid, who wanted my mother to feel that it was Enid who had possession of me now and that we were still passionately in love with each other—something we never were.

Of course all of this came partly from my own weakness, but essentially I am a man who likes peace and wants people to like each other and get on well together rather than to corrode the whole of their spirits and everybody else's spirits by intrigues and envy and jealousy and hatred and that horrible desire to possess and devour others which is popularly called "sharing everything." The odd thing, which I have never been able to understand, is that the two women actually seemed to find pleasure and satisfaction in hating each other.

It was curious that, despite my mother's immensely "successful" life, her mouth turned down sharply at the corners and there was a line almost like a gash from her nostrils to the corners of her mouth. As Enid grew older, her mouth too began to turn down at the corners and the same line like a gash began to develop. It is very common with American women of middle age upward. Of all the lines which come into the human face with increasing age, this is the ugliest and most frightening, for it comes from an inner and carefully hidden torment and an unhappiness and frustration which is terrifying to contemplate.

I have gone at some length into my ancestry, for ancestry and inheritance are of course an immense part of all of us. We do not perhaps inherit acquired characteristics but we certainly do inherit glands and physiological factors which tend to reproduce the same traits which have been observed in an ancestor. We can, for example, inherit a bad liver and develop the traits of most other people with bad livers or a thyroid weakness which makes us more or less like all other people with thyroid weaknesses. To be sure, the variety of the combinations of inherited genes and factors are enormous, but some still follow through from one's sources of inheritance.

Like most Americans, my own blood came from many races and subdivisions of races. In that respect I could scarcely be more typical in a biological sense of what is today called an American. My background of ancestors and of the culture and civilization of their times could scarcely be more conventional. All of these things produced me and some other millions of American men very like me. I am forced to examine all these things to find some answer to who and what I am and why I come to find myself now on a remote tropical island with a sense of failure and the desire each night, when I turn in on a damp hot Army cot, never to waken again.

IV The Jungle

TONIGHT THE SERGEANT CAME IN AND WANTED TO PLAY GIN rummy. I knew it was coming on because he has been restless and nervy all day, almost as if he were afraid of himself. Gin rummy and poker and pinochle are the only games he knows. None of the others knows anything about cards but Meyer, the little dark fellow from Brooklyn, and I fancy he finds little pleasure in playing away from his family and his own special friends in Brooklyn. The muggy solitude and boredom of the island simply drive him deeper and deeper into himself and he spends hours lying on his cot under the mosquito netting in what I am certain are veritable orgies of brooding and self-pity.

Homer, the wool-hat Georgia boy, simply sleeps, eats, and goes off into the bushes with one of the black greasy native women with sores on their legs. He has to be kept dosed up with penicillin against yaws most of the time. When he talks it is mostly about how the Yankees don't understand the "nigger problem" or of the times he took part in "nigger hunts."

Al, the Kansas farm boy, tries to fight off boredom by reading books and farming on the small patch of ground cleared out of the frightening, ever-crowding jungle. At this he does a very good job, keeping us in fresh vegetables which are large and flamboyant and quick-growing but rather tasteless. He and Meyer take turns with the cooking and sometimes I put my hand in, a thing normally regarded as reprehensible on the part of an officer, but I like to eat well and I learned to be a pretty good cook at the backyard barbecues in Oakdale. I do not think it hurts my prestige as an officer. I never have any trouble with the boys, and of course I always have the Sergeant to back me up with strong-arm methods if necessary. I have to restrain him sometimes in dealing with wool-hat Homer for whom he feels a contempt which he shows by occasionally giving Homer what he calls a good "going-over." Probably it does no harm since that is the only kind of thing Homer understands, but it sometimes seems to me unfair since the Sergeant is a bruiser and Homer a poor weedy specimen of Southern white trash, undernourished all of his life on a diet of fat pork and cornbread, grown on miserably poor land, worn out under three hundred years of wretched agriculture. Homer is the only one who ever mentions little Meyer's being a Jew.

Commonly the Sergeant refers to Homer as the Rat, and he is right, but in a way you can't help feeling sorry for Homer because the others dislike him so much. Yet there isn't much to be done about it. If you try to talk to him about the virtues of cleanliness or of responsibility or of one's duty toward others, you get nowhere at all. He simply doesn't understand what you are talking about and, what is worse, he wouldn't care even if he understood. He never reads but looks at the paper comic books by the hour, apparently finding pleasure in them no matter how many times he has seen them. He said once that he did not get the full pleasure out of them until he had gone over them three times.

I have tried to imagine what it was like in his own community back in the hills of Georgia and what sort of position he occupied there, but I never get much out of him. I suspect that back there he was a loud-mouthed bully, but the Army has long since taught him that the same tactics do not work outside his own small community and he has come to adopt the one other alternative of the bully—a hangdog, whining manner. Now and then there comes into his eyes a curious cornered, desperate, vicious look which gives me a terrifying indication of what he might be like on a "nigger hunt."

I don't know what there is to be done about such specimens as Homer or the people in the background out of which he came. Certainly they cannot be cured overnight no matter how many "do-gooders" undertake the job or how much money is spent on them. Behind him the trail of poverty and prejudice, ignorance and bad nutrition and possibly even incest, is too long and too intricate. If there are forgotten men in America they are Homer and his relatives, who are worse off than the pitiful Negroes from the same kind of poverty-stricken sordid background, for in Homer's kind there is no merriment and little emotion other than hatred and bitterness. I had never known his sort until I came into the Army, for they do not exist anywhere near Crescent City or even anywhere at all in my own prosperous northern state. I had read about them, but that was a pale experience compared to the reality. They are a contradiction of the pure Mendelians. The original genes, as many sentimentalists suppose, may have been of the finest Anglo-Saxon stock (a theory which I believe can be heavily discounted, especially in Georgia), but something certainly has deformed them—a mixture of poverty and sordidness and poor diet continuing through generations.

But enough of Homer, although he is for me a perpetually fascinating if loathsome study. Even the fact that he is heartily disliked by all of us does not seem to disturb him.

The five of us, so dissimilar, manage to get on pretty well despite steaming rains and bugs and boredom, and I have been able to maintain my prestige and discipline. Perhaps this is because I have been completely and utterly objective, removed from all of them and very nearly as impartial as God himself should be. Of course, the backing of the Sergeant is important, just as a police force is important in a world in which mankind is still not sufficiently civilized to do without one, as the Anarchists propose. The Sergeant holds me a little in awe because I can read and can write and speak passable English. Sometimes he scratches his head and declares openly his regret that he quit in the eighth grade of the Roxbury, Massachusetts, schools.

My four companions in this morose green hell are as dissimilar in appearance as in character. Meyer is small and dark with great liquid eyes which seem perpetually filled with unshed tears. His beard is very heavy and blue-black whether freshly shaven or not.

He is very orthodox and will eat no food cooked on Saturday, observes Friday prayers, and I think would like a *masusah* attached to the door to kiss as he goes in or out of the Quonset hut.

Homer, the wool-hat, is lean and sallow with very small cold blue eyes and sandy hair and a skin that never tans but merely turns red and is covered with freckles. He has a rather squashed nose, which may have come from some fight, and a large loose mouth with uneven teeth usually stained with tobacco juice.

Only Al, the Kansas farm boy, has any pretensions at good looks, and these pretensions are certainly wholly unconscious. He is a well-built boy, with a very clean look always, as if he had just come out of the shower. He is rather like the photographs of "the healthiest Four-H boy in the state." There is nothing of the "hick" in him, but there is a kind of profound simplicity in his approach to life and a good deal of genuine innocence. He is a "nice" boy, as the ladies would say. He performs his tasks efficiently and has a genuine talent and love for the earth. He does not seem to be homesick, but the farm in Kansas is his idea of paradise and he wants the war to be over quickly so that he can go back there.

As for the Sergeant whose name is Dennis Burke, I thought as I sat playing gin rummy with him tonight that he might well be called, "The Male Principle." If it is true, as many psychiatrists claim, that there is no such thing as the absolute male or the absolute female but that we are all only in varying degree combinations of male and female, then the Sergeant would come pretty close to the extreme male end of the yardstick.

He is not very tall and is immensely muscular. It is difficult to discover where his chest ends and his stomach begins, but there is no fat on him. He is just thick-bodied and heavy with big feet and hands with fingers like clusters of sausages which are nevertheless extremely and surprisingly deft in performing delicate operations and putting things together. He is in charge of the medicine department, and when Homer, the wool-hat, got his head bashed open somehow on one of his night prowls, the Sergeant washed and sewed up the scalp wound with as delicate a touch as that of any expert nurse or surgeon. He is very hairy with a kind of beard sprouting from the top of his undershirt, and the dark hair on his head is rough and almost bristly. It is difficult for him to say "Yes" grammatically. In my presence he makes a desperate attempt to speak correctly and falls into the vulgar overelegance of the people who say, "he asked he and I" to do something or other. Also, like the classic sergeant, he has a fine vocabulary of elaborate profanity. We get on very well together and I think he likes me, although I clearly puzzle him. In his brutal directness he cannot understand all the inhibitions, the conventions, the restraints, the hypocrisies of the life which has complicated the whole of my character and existence. With him there are no reticences about what he thinks or what he does even to the most intimate details of his experiences with sex in almost all its forms. I puzzle him because he cannot make out whether I am without experience or whether I simply prefer not to discuss such things. He is further puzzled by the fact that I do not seem to disapprove of his behavior. He has been used to lectures with slides, warnings, and moral exhortations from chaplains, Y.M.C.A. workers, and "P.I." officers, none of which has, of course, made any impression whatever upon his behavior.

When he plays rummy he plays with all his might. If he loses he is depressed and if he wins everything is fine for the next twenty-four hours. He seems to forget even about women. So whenever possible I let him win. I think he feels that victory over me is a real triumph, much better than defeating Al, because I have been to college.

Tonight he seemed to be in a particularly good mood perhaps because we shared between us part of a bottle which I managed to have sent on to me along with some other things.

He said, "I don't know what the hell we're doing out here. I only hope that they don't forget us when the war is over and leave us here forever. Sometimes I think I'm just dreaming all this and it ain't happening at all. It shouldn't happen to a dog."

As long as he has something for his hands to do he is fairly happy, but when he finishes a tinkering job and is at a loss for one to follow it he gets into a bad temper and is likely to give Homer a "working-over" or make derisive remarks to poor little Meyer who just wants to be left alone to feel sorry for himself. I am probably the happiest of all because I have time and am resting, and out of all this thinking and writing I am doing the same kind of tinkering job which Dennis does when he is putting together some new Rube Goldberg contraption. Only my tinkering is steady and consistent and continual and doesn't, like his, come to an end so that I have to think up something else.

When I think of Dennis it occurs to me that it would be a good thing if half our colleges were turned into trade schools where boys could learn to use their hands (and their brains) in creating new mechanical marvels so worshiped in our civilization. But there is still a lag from the nineteenth century and the frontier which induces most people to think that what is called a "college education" is not only important but indispensable. The country is filled with engineers and lawyers who are unwanted and can't make a living and are unhappy when they might be infinitely more prosperous and happy with a machine shop or honestly working a good farm. And there is the whole residue of the "liberal arts college" graduates, most of whom add up to nothing in so far as learning and culture are concerned. After Dennis, well oiled, finally went to bed, I lay under the mosquito netting for a long time thinking about myself and how I had never found out what it was I really wanted to do.

Every now and again the rain would come down, in torrents, as if someone had opened a gigantic water tap, and in the moments between the deluges the night was unnaturally still so that you could seem to hear the jungle breathing, and above the soft breathing there would be the sound of faint rustlings and the occasional raucous cry of a bird or some tree animal. It is these sounds, this mystery, this hostile terrifying feeling of the awful jungle fertility, which binds us all together far more than any other factor in our existence. In the end, of course, it will have a disastrous effect upon some one of us, if for no other reason than because each day we seem a little more lost and remote from all the rest of the world, as if all restraint, all convention, no longer applied here, as if we had to start all over at the beginning of things to create a society and manners and civilization and devise ways and means of living with each other without violence or murder. I do not know how long it can last without trouble of some kind. I am better off perhaps than the others because I have gone backward into the past.

The odd thing is that even after months of this monotony I am happy here and most of the time I am alone and I have time to exist and to *be*. Most of us have no conception of what time is. The man back home whizzing along the road by motor or in the air by plane from one town to another thinks he is saving time, but when he gets to his destination he merely starts out whizzing off to the next objective. The man riding a horse or driving in a buggy along the same road in the past had much more time, for he could think and reflect and doze and *grow* in his mind, in his spirit, and in his soul. This is the first time in many years I have had *time*, and there is no one preying upon me to do this or that, to play golf or to drink, to go to conventions or any number of meaningless things. There is no one who wants to "share" me. The boys here don't prey upon me. They are friendly enough but I think they consider me a bore.

The tired feeling has been dissipated a little. Now and then I feel a faint desire to return to Oakdale and see my friends and live again in the house with the dull rich "drapes" and Enid constantly emptying the ashtrays and flicking up invisible bits of dust or cigarette ash from her precious carpets and chairs. But it is never Enid I want to see. I know now that everything concerned with Enid is finished. I would like to see the children and my bit of garden at the back of that suburban plot. By now the hedge must have grown high enough to shut out the eyes of the Burdens who live on one side and the Prescotts who live on the other, so that I could go there and lie in the hammock and read in the certainty that someone was not watching me out of a neighboring window every time I scratched myself. Of course there would always be Enid coming out at once to join me with her mending and sit near me so that she could "share" everything, even the beauty and solitude of this little corner which I think she actually dislikes.

When I planted the hedge, she didn't like it. She said she thought it was unfriendly, like a spite fence. It is not impossible that when I return home I shall not find it has grown but that she has in my absence dug it up because it prevented her from calling across to the Prescotts or the Burdens whenever she felt like it and because it prevented her from seeing what they were doing and sharing that too.

But perhaps I shall never return home. I don't know. If it were not for the children, there would be no question. I would not return. Children anchor you down because they are a part of you and because you have a responsibility toward them. But with me there is a third reason—that I am afraid of what Enid will do to them, of how she may limit them and warp the fabric of the rest of their lives by forcing them into the pattern of her own shallow, superficial world in which the greatest terror is of thought or of solitude.

In these times it is little use to work hard in order to save money to leave to one's children. With taxes you can't save very much, and even if you put it into insurance the government takes most of it from them when you die in order to use it for other people who need bureaucrat's jobs or are shiftless or lazy or improvident. So you kill yourself to make money only to have it taken from you and given to those who have never worked or saved or contributed anything to society or even to their own welfare. And, anyway, every year money becomes worth less and less. For fifteen years I have been paying in hundred-cent dollars for annuities and life insurance, and already if I chose to cash in my annuity I would be getting back only sixty cents for the hundred cents I paid in, and if and when I die my children may get back only five cents for every dollar I worked hard to accumulate for them, and the government will take the better part of even the five cents. And even if the company went on paying the commissions to my family on the insurance I have sold, their incomes would shrink and shrink as the cost of everything went up. And all this is done, so they say, for the benefit of the American citizen, to make life richer for him and more secure, not in his will and spirit but in plumbing and electric blankets for everybody.

So working to make and save money for your wife and children is scarcely worth while. Like as not you will leave them not security but liability. The best thing you can leave them is an education, preferably for a trade, in the world that lies ahead of us—the means of making a living with their hands since less and less do brains and education receive their reward save in terms of vicious and corrupting power. Or in rewards for having designed some evil new missile which can tear living men, women and children apart or burn them alive. You can leave your children, perhaps, a sense of values, a taste for music or the out-of-doors or something which can make life more interesting and more possible of endurance.

Here in the wet jungle I have had time to think. It is perhaps the greatest pleasure I have ever known, but at times I become the victim of some grotesque and terrible thoughts. At moments it seems to me that mankind has devised all the means of his own destruction always in the deceptive guise of scientific advance. But there are other factors—the careful preservation of all idiots and physical weaklings and the lowest elements of the human stock which breed and increase their numbers far out of all proportion to those elements which might improve the race and make the world a better and more civilized place. And there is the great American illusion that plumbing and water closets and automobiles are civilization, when a hermit living in a cave may be a million times more civilized than the country-club member with three cars in his garage. And there is the great materialist illusion which has corrupted, like the yaws which afflict the dirty jungle natives, both Russians and Americans, where all value is placed upon machines and radios and plumbing and material security. One hears a great deal about material living standards and how many hours of labor it takes in one country or another to produce a pair of shoes or a loaf of bread, but never anything about freedom of the spirit or the intellect or the simple delights of leading a civilized existence or even the pleasure and satisfaction of eating good food or making something with one's hands. And there is the plague of statisticians, the falsest of all men, who measure everything in numbers, or in dollars, or in inhuman abstractions, lacking the intelligence or sensitivity or perception to understand that man is neither a mechanical invention nor an adding machine nor yet an angel. Most of the "do-gooders" concern their anxious thoughts not with any plans for the spiritual or the intellectual sides of life or the things men really live by, such as work and love and creation. They are concerned only with doing away with the outside privy, the amount of income, with providing "security," with keeping alive the unfit. Their philosophy is a baffled, perverse, unnatural one, but it makes them feel warm inside and good regardless of its long-range evil results.

Sometimes it seems to me that Enid is the perfect product of the age in which we live. She leads an existence which is almost wholly material and even mechanical, without depth or perception, without questioning anything save those who rebel against her kind of living. She lives in a world of conformity in which she herself has no freedom (although the thought never occurs to her). She has no right to be an individual or a character or an eccentric because this is the unforgivable crime. The character, the eccentric has gone out of American life and it is the poorer for it. If one questions the routine materialist world, one is a Red or a Fascist, a crackpot or fit only to be committed. It is in a way dangerous even to speak a fundamental truth. And through it all the professional politicians worm their way like maggots in a cheese, always offering the "peepul" more and more money which comes not out of the politicians' pockets but out of the "peepul's" own. The whole of our political economy is like a monster devouring itself bit by bit, chewing its own tail until at last both digestion and evacuation become impossible and it dies of internal putrescence.

I couldn't think these things out at home in Oakdale. There was never time. And my neighbors never had time. Their mechanical world, full of washing machines and automobiles and bathrooms and airplanes, never left them time from saving time. They never had time to ponder the iniquities of their own government and rise with indignation against it as a monster which swindled and engulfed them. The most they could do was to shrug their shoulders and say, "What can you expect of politicians?" or, again shrugging, "Why bother to vote? My vote won't count for anything. It's just one vote against a million." To vote took time away from their squirrel-cage activities, without sense or meaning. But they never stopped whining over each rise in taxes.

And all the noble plans to *impose* democracy and good government and liberty and freedom upon people like these in this teeming, maggoty East who cannot read or write and actually have no words in their language for these abstractions whose meaning has been painfully evolved through centuries of trial and error, of persecution and martyrdom, of education and enlightenment. They have no words for "freedom" or "democracy" or even "dignity." Small wonder that when they are given freedom they become the immediate victims of the first ruthless and criminal exploiter and dictator . . . the victims of their own animalism. The element of quality seems to have gone out of a soggy world, except among the advertising hucksters who apply the word only to what machinery has created.

I do not think I am crazy. Sitting here in this hot moist solitude it seems to me that all the rest of the world is crazy—a thought which, if I uttered it at home in Oakdale, would certainly bring about my prompt incarceration in a booby hatch. It is the old saying, the supposed test of insanity—that everyone is crazy but you and me and you are a little crazy. It seems to me that if I were shut up as mad, I should only be occupying a madhouse within a madhouse and that in such a concentrated center of madness I might find again at least here and there an element of sense, because through the double madness one might fulfill the circle and achieve at last a return to at least some fragments of sense.

My Sergeant too thinks that he lives in a crazy world, but he has not arrived at that conclusion by any intellectual process but through his senses, since that is how he lives. He merely says, "Me for myself . . . a good meal, some good draft beer, a passable woman, and to hell with the rest of them. I can always make a living because I am smart with my hands and all the rest of them can't live without their washing machines and automobiles and radios. Turn off the electric current and they would be a bunch of helpless sonsofbitches." Sometimes when I think that I may be nuts he reassures me. Quite obviously, by the most basic and fundamental standards, he is not, yet we react and think in a remarkably similar fashion. His scorn of the world in which we live is much greater and certainly more violent than mine.

Sometimes lying awake in the night it seems to me that man has lost his dignity, that he has been robbed of it by the machines to which he has become a slave, by the machines which draw him and his kind together to live in huddled concentrations of huts removed from all contact with the natural universe of which, from the day he is torn painfully from his mother's womb until the day he is laid in the ground with a handful of earth in his face, he is hopelessly and inevitably a part. He has been degraded both in body and in spirit for there is denied him more and more each day the dignity, which belongs even to the animals, of making their own life, or finding food and shelter, of living as free creatures to whom death is but an incident.

During centuries man has built, with suffering and martyrdom and some wisdom, a structure which has begun to disintegrate, to rot from within so that to diagnose the ills and check them has become impossible since man himself is so confused by his mechanical and political achievements that at length all judgment and all standards are lost. He expects machines to do the honest and beautiful work his hands once did and the state (which inevitably is himself and fellows) to make his decisions, to pension him and provide the security which he himself once provided with dignity and with that satisfaction which is the blessing of all creators downward from God and which the kept, the shiftless, the indolent cannot and never will know or understand. He comes to believe that the state is an entity wholly separate from himself which will arrange his life and feed and shelter him. But the state is never a thing apart save in the worst sense, never is it either wise or benevolent, but essentially destructive in its impersonality, in its materialism, in its ruthlessness, in its corruption, in its stupidity. Calling it democracy does not alter its power of destroying the spirit, the intelligence, the creative forces which essentially separate man from the lower animals.

I am but a single man, a fragile spark of life subject to all manner of ills, an infinitesimal speck in the universe, of no intrinsic or basic importance whatever to the operations of that universe, as little in respect to all of this universe as the ant trodden under foot. I am only fighting now to bring myself understanding and consequently dignity without which man himself is of less importance than the squid or the primitive lamprey.

On reading this over it seems to me presumptuous to have such thoughts. I am a mediocrity, limited and bound, who should be content with all the wonders and benefits of modern and mechanical democracy and a "modern" existence. Well, I am not.

V Oakdale

A LITTLE TIME BEFORE I WENT TO WAR I RECEIVED A questionnaire from the University at which I received my degree. Among the questions was one which read, "What benefits do you consider you received during the four years you attended the University?" In a moment of bitterness I wrote, "None," and returned the questionnaire.

In this I was wrong and unfair for I did receive perhaps some benefits. I made some friends who remained friends. I did learn something about getting on with people and came to have some understanding regarding good books and I learned a few facts which remained in my mind. I think, quite honestly, that this was about all I got out of the four years spent there. The tormenting thing is the speculation which returns to me again and again that I might have learned much more during those four years by striking out into the world on my own, and that in doing so I might have lost or destroyed the middle-class complacency and paralysis which reduced my whole life to the monotonous level of uninspired work, material rewards, and conformity, out of which it became slowly apparent that the only escape was neither physical nor intellectual but through drinking. The whole experience at college only tended to fertilize and cultivate the snobberies, the conformity, the shibboleths of the life which had already begun to limit and stifle me. In a sense the four years were spent in a vacuum—four years in which I was protected from almost all reality, four years in which I had neither to go to work nor to face the business of living. I emerged a pitifully immature specimen, in reality no older, no wiser, no more experienced than when I entered. In a way the University only served to arrest my development and preserve my adolescence.

In those four years I might have simply knocked about the world. I might have gone to India or Sumatra or China. I might have met all sorts of people fascinating or strange or even evil but at least real. I might have starved or have fallen ill in a strange country. I might have learned a language or two. But I did none of these things. Instead I spent four years at a university without much work, in the illusion that I was enjoying myself and during that time did not have to be every morning at nine o'clock in my father's office. I joined one of the good fraternities and won my letter in basketball and was on the wrestling team, and I emerged from college no more mature or experienced than I entered it.

The next step of course was marriage and then a family, and by that time it was too late and I was too weak to change a pattern of which most of my friends were the victims. Today those wasted four years when I was young and completely free seem a terrible loss, not only as wasted years but for what I might have done during them—things perhaps which would have changed my whole life and set me free.

I have tried many times to think why I went to the University. My future was assured in my father's business. I did not need the technical education necessary to become an engineer, a lawyer, or a doctor. I was certainly not a genius or even brilliant. I always had good marks which I got without too much work. After thinking and thinking I can only discover one or two reasons—pressure from my parents who, never having been to college themselves, placed an exaggerated value, common to their generation, on what was called a "college education" or "a college-bred man" (another expression which belongs with the vulgarity of "gorgeous drapes" and "occasional chairs"). I also went to college because that was the thing everybody in my world did, whether they learned anything or not.

I found that I was not alone in this situation. Plenty of the boys I knew were in college for those reasons and for some others, equally beside the point. Some of them had been sent to college because "they might make connections there to whom they could sell stocks or bonds or insurance" and some because their fathers wanted them to belong to the same club or fraternity. The idea that a university was a place dedicated to that precious thing called learning scarcely occurred to most of my friends. They managed to stay in college and get decent marks either because they were not too stupid and the standards were not too high or because in order to play on the team it was necessary to get passing grades. Among the others were the men who wanted an education badly enough to work their way through school or the "grinds" or those who happened to be among the elect, possessing brains and charm and good looks and athletic prowess all combined through some special blessing. These last, of course, were in the vast minority. Most of us were simply the sons of middle-class well-to-do parents who were at once in awe of education and in terror of intelligence or intellect or genius.

It did seem odd that there were so few who really wanted to learn or who really emerged at last with any evidence whatever of having been to a great university. Most of them, on receiving their degrees, considered their education finished and from that point believed it unnecessary to learn anything more or to take any special interest in anything. Most of them have remained culturally and intellectually at the level marked by their graduation, as life grew duller and duller and they came more and more to kill time until they died.

I "made" one of the better fraternities for a variety of reasons. I was not bad-looking. I had clean expensive clothes. I was presentable. I showed some prowess in athletics and I had money to spend. These factors, on the whole, seemed to be the qualifications for being invited to join any of the "better" fraternities. I drank beer. I "necked" appropriately on the occasion of college dances. In the last year I had a car of my own. Now and then, rather in a spirit of bravado, some of us went to the nearest city and visited a brothel, but most of us were a little scared and some of us did nothing at all but drink beer after we got there.

The only one who went regularly and for enjoyment and perhaps relief was a dark, tense, brilliant fellow named Frank Saunders. Everybody knows his name now for he is the head of a great corporation and did much to organize industry and carry on the war. At the time he was not too popular and was regarded with mingled envy and distaste for his experienced ways. He was older than the rest of us in his class by three or four years because his father had sent him off on a leisurely trip round the world so that, as the father expressed it, "He would have some sense by the time he went to college." He knew what he wanted in life and went after it. For this he was regarded as being eccentric. There were, of course, a few boys known as "literary" who instinctively drew together through mutual intellectual interests. They represented the one in a hundred and I scarcely knew any of them. During the first two or three years

I would have been ashamed of being friends with any of them.

When I try to remember what happened during those four years I find it very difficult. The years seem to remain blurred in a lazy, agreeable haze in which nothing happened of any importance. That phrase "nothing happened" is a terrifying one when one considers how brief is life and how great and varied are its delights and how immense are the fascinations of a still almost unexplored and unknown universe. It seems to me that I was *driven* by nothing, neither by ambition nor sexual appetites nor curiosity nor indeed anything at all, and in this I was like most of my fellow classmen. There were no torments, no bitter disappointments, no ecstasies, no tragedy, no great honors or great defeats, in fact "no nothing." I suppose this is what some men consider happiness when they talk of the happy years spent in college. It is this, I suppose, which leads them back on class day to make fools of themselves in a foggy, sometimes drunken effort to recapture that happy dullness. Few things are sadder than the class-day reunion with its hordes of middle-aged, rather baffled and puzzled men attempting to recapture not only something which has gone forever but should have been gone and been forgotten as they grew into maturity and achievement, something which, often enough, never existed at all. This immature institution of the reunion, it seems to me, is a bitter commentary on the failure both of education and indeed of a civilization. It is very special to this country.

I went back twice to reunions before I came out to this island, but the pleasures I found there were very mixed. In the beginning I was glad to see some of my old friends, and then after a little time I became bored and saddened because the tie between us was so artificial and so faded and because it quickly became even more frayed and worn. And so I too began to drink and in drinking I found the illusion which I had returned to find. With alcohol in my veins I began to think that the others, like myself, were very amusing and I fell back into the flow of conversation confined entirely to the category of "Do you remember the time that good old so-and-so climbed the bell tower?" The ones with whom I might have enjoyed a conversation, the ones who had gone out into the world and made a civilized life for themselves, were not there, perhaps because they had grown into maturity and because their immediate lives were so satisfactory that there was no need and no time to return and attempt to recapture the past.

After the second time I never went again to a class reunion, and it is highly unlikely that I shall ever go to another if and when this bloody war ever comes to an end.

Education is, I suppose, largely a matter of the individual, both on the side of the teacher and of the scholar, and both teacher and scholar are perhaps born and not made. I would say that if a man does not want an education nothing on earth can force it down him and, conversely, that if he desires it nothing can prevent him from achieving it. In between, of course, are all the people who do not know whether they want to learn or understand anything or not, and that is where the inspired teacher comes in, the man or woman who can lend excitement to any subject and surround himself with young people whose whole lives may be changed by contact with the flame he represents. These of course are all too rare, for the great majority of those who teach are not thus blessed but are merely making a living at a task which gradually becomes more and more distasteful or maintaining toward their work an attitude of dullness and detail which turns any subject into a misery. And of course there is in the teaching profession itself an element which inevitably leads toward eventual desiccation and academic God-almightiness—the fact that a teacher sits on a throne and dictates to those with less academic knowledge and less authority.

In all my experience in college I encountered only one teacher who possessed the flame and was capable of transmitting the spark to those to whom he addressed his efforts. The others certainly failed to kindle any fire in me and I find great difficulty in remembering most of them or anything they taught me. They have simply faded out without leaving an impression. This single teacher did bring to me something which has remained precious to me and will so long as I live and has been a refuge and a consolation and a bulwark against the buffetings of existence. He taught me to read. I mean, *really*, to read. In Oakdale I doubt that any of our friends read a book a year. The women sometimes talked about books but had rarely read them. They got their information from professional female book reviewers who dressed elaborately and badly and used extravagant hats for "bait."

It seems to me that most people never arrive at much achievement or even satisfaction in life because they do not know what they want or because, if they do from time to time have an inkling, the objective constantly changes. And of course there are those who are always looking to get something for nothing and those who will work harder to keep from working than if they simply buckled down and did a job. I do not know what it was I wanted and I do not know today except that I would like the life which I have missed, a life full of excitement and fun and recklessness and satisfaction and achievement. (I write all of this with a kind of agonizing truth and bitterness. It is my own story, my own failure but, God knows, I am not alone.)

I could leave my family today, throw all responsibility to the winds, set out as a tramp around the world, run off with another woman than my wife. Oh! there are a lot of things I could do, but after forty they seem a little silly and the whole effort would be a phony. There is nothing at once sillier or more tragic than the middle-aged man who discovers he has missed the train and tries to make up for it when it is too late.

Twice . . . only twice did I have a real glimpse of that life which under other circumstances I might have had—if I had been brought up in a different background, with different parents, and if I had been a different character with just a spark of something. It happened the first time on the only visit I made to Frank Saunders' family.

They lived in summer in a big house in the East. Frank's father was an architect and a very distinguished one and the house was a Georgian house, although even as a junior at the University where I was supposed to be receiving a cultural education I had not yet learned that there were such things as Georgian houses, or Renaissance or Jacobean houses, or any other kind of houses. All I knew was that there was a type called Colonial and one called "English Rustic" and of course "Early American" which is scarcely architecture at all. The Saunders' house was, I recognized even by my uninformed standards, a very beautiful house. I knew it because when I stood near the entrance to the grounds the sight of the house with its great windows and pink brick, partly covered with ivy, and the horseshoe-shaped stairs leading to the main entrance all made me feel good, much as some music makes me feel.

The hall inside made you feel the same way, with its high ceiling and the great door at the far end and the curving stairway which mounted to the rooms above. At one side there was a big table which always carried a tray on which stood drinks of all kinds so that anyone coming in from tennis or a long walk or a ride could have a drink at any hour of the day or night. Near it there was a wooden chest in which, standing upright, was a collection of walking sticks and umbrellas to be used by the family or guests for walks in every kind of weather.

At the right was the dining room which I remember as one of the most beautiful rooms I have ever seen, dark with paneled woodwork but gay and bright with the light which came in through the big square-paned windows. It glowed with silver and porcelain and crystal and there were always flowers, not just tight little bouquets but huge exuberant bunches of flowers of many kinds and colors. They were not simply stuck into vases. They were not arid garden-club "arrangements" compounded self-consciously out of aspidistras and old beer cans. Always they were what might be called "creations" in which a variety of colors and forms were woven together in a kind of exuberant architectural pattern. They gave me the same satisfaction that I found in looking at the façade of the house. They were "right" for the house and for that particular room and I had not seen many things that were "right" ever before in my life. Frank's mother always did the flowers herself every two days. It was the first time I ever realized that flowers could be more than a mere bunch of carnations and roses or that they could become architecture or painting or music.

On the opposite side of the hall there was a big room called sometimes the living room and sometimes the drawing room. It had big doors which stood open day and night during the summer overlooking the garden where the flowers were not in "beds" but existed in a kind of ordered riot of design and color. There was a big table covered with books and magazines, many of them French or English or German. There were ashtrays everywhere for smoking and, mixed with the English furniture, a great many comfortable sofas and chairs upholstered in bright chintz. There were none of the mud colors so favored in Oakdale. The colors were clear and gay and positive without timidity or conformity.

The floor was covered by a huge Chinese rug spotted here and there where drinks had been spilled or puppies had let themselves go. One evening Frank's mother indelicately remarked that she favored rugs with intricate designs on them since the puppy spots showed less and eventually seemed to become part of the design. I never saw the room in what might have been called a "state of order" let alone the inhuman meticulous order of my mother's house or Enid's. The drawing room too was always filled with flowers. The odd thing was that the English furniture and the great rug had a value many times that of the constantly polished, perpetually dusted stuff in my mother's house or the things which Enid later bought for our "lovely home" with "gorgeous drapes" in Oakdale.

I remember at first a feeling of shock at the disorder and a suspicion that Frank's mother was not a very good housekeeper, for my mother never allowed dogs in the house and she kept in the living room a set of minute ashtrays arranged in a rack just in case any not too welcome sprawling smoking guest entered the place. The ashtrays at Frank's house were huge affairs of heavy glass, and usually by the end of the evening they were pretty well filled unless someone emptied them into the fireplace behind a paper screen made in the shape of a fan simply to hide the rubbish until it was burned the following morning.

Frank's mother was a warm handsome woman who must have been very beautiful as a girl. She was big and rather plump and appeared nearly always during the day in a rough tweed skirt and plain blouse with a small ruffle down the front. In the evening she dressed almost as simply as in the daytime and wore as adornment rather heavy gold jewelry. There was nothing fussy or "dainty" about her. You got the impression that she was so busy living that she did not have time for fussiness. Yet somehow the handsome simple costumes were a symbol of her character, her serenity, her taste. They defined and indicated a person of quality.

She was at the door waiting for us when we arrived, and after an introduction and a warm greeting she enveloped Frank in a great hug and kissed him on both cheeks. It was the first time I had ever seen such an embrace. My mother always kissed me full on the mouth almost with the violence of a mistress, and I have never been able to persuade Enid that I hate the taste of lipstick and the smell of cold cream, probably because both have become associated with Enid and because I have never had the courage to say to her that I could not bear going through the farce of kissing her on the mouth when there was no longer any passion involved. But this mouth-kissing business with its simulation of passion is all part of Enid's show and play-acting. If in public she were ever seen kissing me in any other fashion, the other women in her world would begin at once to say that things were not going well between us. I suspect that she likes the smell of tobacco and shaving lotion no better than I like the taste of lipstick and cold cream. But she has to put on a show.

Frank's mother took me up to the room I was to share with him because she said the house was full of people. The younger children had even been moved out to sleep on cots in the play house by the tennis court. She was delighted to have me if I didn't mind not having a room of my own. It was a big house, although it probably had no more rooms than the ornate house in Crescent City in which I was still living, and it struck me that if the house was filled there must be a lot of people there. And there were....

At home we rarely had an overnight visitor, and my mother frowned upon my having a friend to stay overnight when I was small. The only visitors I can remember were relatives who stayed with us over the funeral of my grandfather and an occasional big-busted, aggressive female who was a fellow member of one of my mother's many organizations and whose visit seemed more like that of a general or an institution than a visitation from a human being.

Even now, years later, as I sit here in the jungle the memory of that visit is a glowing thing. In the beginning I was perplexed by it, by the people I met there, by their vitality and grace and by something I only came to understand much later—their capacity for living. None of the people in that house ever seemed to have enough time, not because they were rushing about in planes and automobiles or from bar to country club to convention, simply killing time until they died, but because there was so much to do, so much to see and hear, so much to learn and understand. In that house I heard conversation for the first time, and by that I mean conversation for the sake of conversation, for the delight in the exchange of ideas, for the give and take of good argument which sometimes waxed furious and angry because the individuals believed passionately in the idea or the theory they were expounding or defending. I had my first insight into the thing called principle as opposed to the thing called prejudice. Most of the arguments I had heard until that time might have been encompassed by the words "bickering" or they were flat statements of inflexible uncompromising intolerance.

Thinking of it now, it seems to me that in the world I had known until then the violent opinions and principles of the early pioneer had simply degenerated into statements of prejudice and intolerance based upon nothing much but ignorance and petulance and conformity, and in that same world opinions and ideas rarely rose to the level of intellectual discussion. So conversation as such became a revelation to me as something stimulating and even exciting, which left me, when I was again in bed with the lights out, excited and sleepless and confused, and although I was perplexed I was aware that I was having a glowing experience in which I myself was an outsider, and this knowledge created within me two things, a gentle melancholy and a sense of envy for Frank who had been so lucky as to have grown up in such a world.

And I began to understand why Frank, at college and in the fraternity house, was not popular and was taciturn and sometimes sullen, why he worked hard and made a brilliant record and seemed to find, without ever saying so, the activities of the rest of us a little juvenile and boring. He did not talk much because there was no talk about anything except beer drinking and football and jokes that were pretty bad. The fraternity had made a mistake about him. They had been fooled by his good looks, his air of worldliness, the certain dark intensity which he had, and the attractive violence of his personality. I think most of our fellow members would gladly have been rid of him. For his mere presence in the same room with them induced an almost universal and annoying sense of clumsiness and inferiority. He had quality, a characteristic rare in these times and steadily becoming more so. It was something intangible but inexpressibly irritating. The only thing he brought to the fraternity was the brilliant scholastic record and a real mind, which to the other boys was of little importance as compared with the record of any quarterback who barely managed to stay in school on "scholarship" through the unmoral connivance of the University authorities.

I did not know why he asked me to visit his family and I do not know until this day. We were not especially good friends, and my only guess is that he found me more tolerable and perhaps possessed of a little more potential intelligence than the others and that he perhaps detected in me a spark which has never grown into a flame but only weakened and threatened, at last, to destroy me—a spark that was a kind of yearning for something better than I had known up till then, something which I could not define, much less understand. I only knew that it must exist and even then that in my life it was missing.

As I have grown older and more experienced it has occurred to me that there existed between Frank and myself a kind of physical attraction which perhaps, with his greater experience, he recognized more clearly than I was able to do. It was, of course, something which neither of us could or would recognize and something which most people never quite understand or realize—the attraction of two pleasant, good-looking people of the same sex for each other and the pleasure they find merely being in each other's company. It explains certainly the attraction possessed by certain individuals for others who share few of their qualities or tastes but find pleasure merely in their physical presence. The physical attraction comes first accompanied by the desire that on the spiritual and intellectual side, in the matter of common tastes, there may be a sympathy as great as the original attraction. There is nothing in the least wicked or perverse about such an attraction, although it sometimes leads to the bewilderment and confusion which colored the whole of my brief, fairly intense friendship with Frank. I think he found in me during our college days the illusion of common interests and a sympathy which scarcely existed in reality and that it probably was some faint physical attraction which led him into that illusion. I know now that on my side I was actually dazzled by the combination of his dark good looks, his vitality, his precocious wisdom, and his brilliance. And, of course, my vanity was flattered by the fact that, although he scarcely had any real communication with the other members of the fraternity, he had chosen to invite me to his own home. Even today I am flattered by the thought that in me he at least found possibilities that were not at all apparent in the others.

My mother was anxious to have me make the visit. She knew the celebrated name of Frank's father and I fancy that she believed I might achieve some material gain through contact with the world he represented. I might even make "contacts" among the Eastern millionaires to whom I could sell whopping life-insurance policies.

It was not only that I was confused by the fast-moving and

exciting conversation but I was confused by other things. I remember that on the first night I was dressed for dinner before Frank, and he said, "Go along downstairs to the living room and get yourself a drink. I'll be down in a couple of minutes."

So I went down the big stairway to the sound of wonderful music which came from the living room and which I recognized at once as beautiful just as, instinctively, I had recognized that the house and flowers were beautiful and organized and were possessed of a design, a balance, and a purpose—something which had received neither respect nor understanding in the world from which I came.

Someone was playing the piano, wildly and exuberantly, improvising a flamboyant waltz in the Viennese manner. It was a kind of apotheosis of the waltz which seemed to lift you out of reality and into a world which never existed on land or sea, in which everything was all right and gay and beautiful and there was no dullness nor any misery. I have not heard much music beyond the recordings I have collected through the years and for which Enid has no taste, but I think I never heard any music so brilliant, so effortless, so *good feeling*. My own feet grew lighter. As I descended the stairs it was as if I had no weight at all. Quite literally my heart sang, and I divined, in a sudden flash of emotion and excitement, something which was good and even wonderful that I had never experienced and which lay somehow just beyond my reach. I felt for a second or two as if I "belonged," as if I had escaped. I did not know what it was to which I belonged nor very clearly what it was from which I had escaped, at least momentarily. I wanted suddenly and shamelessly to weep out of sheer happiness.

I did not go into the living room at once but stopped by the table in the hall where the drinks were kept and poured myself a cocktail from a silver pitcher which sat in a pail of cracked ice. It tasted clean and cold and lovely. I wanted to stay there forever just as I was—in the beautiful hallway, listening to the incredible music which seemed to me like very beautiful fireworks against a brilliant blue night sky.

And I thought, "What a wonderful house! In it there seems to be no troubles, but only fun. Everything is pleasant. Everything is beautiful. Everything seems to fit. Nobody is pretending to be anything. Nobody is gossiping or quarreling or getting drunk."

Above the music I heard the sound of laughter and voices and I experienced a faint sense of shock because there was not a complete silence in the presence of such music. I thought, "Surely this must be a great musician and they should be listening with respect."

Then Frank appeared running down the stairs with the peculiar grace and muscular control which was a large part of his attraction. He stopped at sight of me and laughed, saying, "What's the matter? Scared?" and I said, "No, I was just listening."

"It's Scherbatov," he said. "He's showing off for free. There's nobody like him when he gets going."

He poured himself a cocktail and said, "Come on," and put his arm through mine and led me into the living room. I think he understood how much I felt an outsider, like a beggar at the door.

In the big room there were a lot of people, some of whom I never got quite straight during the whole visit and do not even remember very well. They all seemed alike in one thing—that they were gay and that somehow they all seemed to be extremely friendly. Two of them, a dark man and a blonde woman, sat a little apart, listening to the fireworks from the piano. A third turned out to be Frank's father, a big man with a rather florid face and a rich pleasant voice who welcomed me by putting his great arms about my shoulders in a warming gesture, as if by instinct he were trying to gather me into the curious gay atmosphere of the room. And there was a very odd scrawny-looking woman dressed in rather a grim fashion called Lady Fitzsimmons whom you could not possibly forget even after years because of her sharp and entertaining tongue. She looked very ill but it did not seem to affect her spirits. There was, too, a very beautiful dark woman of about thirty with an Italian name which I do not remember any longer except that they called her Paula. She need never have spoken at all, for simply to look at her was enough satisfaction for anyone. I found her beauty almost terrifying and I could find nothing whatever to say to her on the single occasion when I discovered myself for a moment in a corner with her.

And there were other people whom I remember less vividly after so long a time, but they all seemed to be possessed of the same brilliance and good nature. It struck me that these people really enjoyed living. They did not pick at it or turn their backs upon it. Doubtless they had personal tragedies and disappointments and they could not have been consistently as gay and as carefree as they seemed to be in this peculiar new world.

The man at the piano went on playing. He appeared simply to be enjoying himself, pausing now and then for a second to take a swift drink from the glass that stood beside him on the piano. He was by all standards an extraordinarily ugly man with a great prominent nose and a bald head with a fringe of curly hair and rather popping eyes, but he seemed enveloped in a flame of vitality and good humor so that even with all the other remarkable people in the room you kept turning to watch him. Twice the beautiful dark woman called Paula went over to the piano and said something to him at which he nodded his head, and even to an inexperienced novice like myself it was very clear that she was passionately in love with him.

Among them all moved Frank's mother and a whole troop of dogs, a big boxer, a poodle, and two Aberdeens. It seems to me now that there were more dogs, but those four I remember very well. They were all trained beggars, and no one in the room seemed to have any scruples about feeding them bits of the thin excellent sandwiches which were served with the cocktails, a procedure which seemed to me unbelievable. My own mother only allowed me to have a dog after years of begging and then never permitted it in the house except to sleep in the cellar on cold nights since it might ruin some of her expensive, ugly furniture or the hideous fake "Oriental" rugs.

Just before we went in to dinner two of Frank's younger sisters, about fifteen or sixteen years old, came in and said, "How d'you do?" to all the people in the room, explaining that they were going off to a neighbor's for dinner. The ugly pianist stopped playing and swung about and kissed them both warmly on the cheek as they left. They were pretty girls, and I remember thinking that if I married one of them I might by that very act find my way into this magic circle. The odd thing was that the two girls, despite the fact that they were at the awkward age, did not seem shy or resentful or strange as you might have expected. I understood this only later when I came to notice that in this house there was no such thing as age. The young were not separated from the old, and one discovered a great interest and animation and friendliness and mutual respect among them all. At the dinner party there were people of every possible age. To me, accustomed to a society in which people were stratified according to age and the young regarded the old as fossils and the old regarded the young as "squirts," all this was startling.

The food at dinner was wonderful. It was not simply food. Everything had its own taste instead of all tasting alike from soup to pudding. I drew a place between the dark beauty and a Mrs. Somebody or other who was a neighbor. It turned out that she was divorced and had a thriving business of her own in New York which had to do with furniture and glassware. I was a failure, I am afraid, merely answering the questions of the beauty about the part of America in which I was living and which she was about to visit for the first time. The smart, businesslike divorcee had a cousin who had once lived in Crescent City, and the contact helped a little with the conversation. The cousin's name was Mary Raeburn, whom I knew but slightly although much later she was to make a great upheaval in my life. I envied Frank who seemed to be having no trouble at all between Lady Fitzsimmons and a pretty blonde woman of perhaps thirty. I could see now, more than ever, why at school he had been taciturn. Certainly he talked enough now to make up for months of silence. At school he had found nothing to talk about and no one with whom it was possible to hold a conversation.

After dinner some of them played bridge in a small room off

the drawing room and the others talked, and presently Scherbatov went to the piano and played some serious music, and then he and Frank's mother and another of the older men did a wonderfully funny burlesque of an opera which I discovered was *Tristan und Isolde*. Scherbatov improvised fake music with a Wagnerian sound and an occasional Wagnerian theme. Frank's mother, enveloped in a mass of draperies, played Isolde, and the older man, with an aluminum saucepan on his head, a long cape, and an old saber did Tristan, returning from far into the kitchen and singing as he came closer and closer until he joined Isolde on a settee where they sat at arm's length, embracing each other as they sang a boisterous version of the second-act love duet. And after that Frank's mother, leaning against the piano, gave an imitation of an arty and bad concert singer. I remember that one of the florid pieces she sang was called, "D'un Prison," and the other, "L'Esclave." In the midst of it the big poodle suddenly sat upright under the piano, opened his mouth, and joined in the concert with a series of wonderful and mournful howls.

Long after midnight we all had more good sandwiches. Some had milk and some had drinks and at last the party broke up. Half the people were staying in the house and the others went off into the night to other houses near by.

Upstairs, after I had got into my pajamas, I sat on the edge of the bed still dazzled, still thinking, still bewildered, and when Frank came out of the bathroom he looked at me, grinned, and said, "What's the matter? Depressed?"

"No, I had a wonderful time. I never saw people like that before."

"I guess there aren't many of them around. Did you get them straightened out?"

"Some of them, I guess. The Italian woman is the most beautiful woman I ever saw."

"Yes. She's famous for that. Quite a girl. She's Scherbatov's mistress." He noticed the bewilderment in my face. "Yes. That's right. Don't discount Scherbatov because he's ugly. He's a famous lady-killer. Women run after him every place he goes."

Then I stepped into the trap which I suspect he had been setting for me in his sardonic way. I asked, "Does your mother know about it?"

He laughed. "Of course. She's put them in adjoining bedrooms so they won't have to wander about trying to find each other."

I felt the color coming into my face, and Frank seemed suddenly sorry for having exploited my provinciality. "You see," he said, "she thinks things like that are none of her business . . . that is, as long as it doesn't hurt somebody else. If people are nasty or mean it is quite a different matter. You should see her then. Nobody can trample and squelch people like Ma if she wants to, when she finds somebody has been cruel or cheap. She thinks what people do in their private lives is none of her business. Everybody knows about Scherbatov and Paula. Her husband is a Roman Catholic and won't divorce her."

In the darkness I found it all very puzzling, and what puzzled me most was the figure of Frank's mother who seemed so warm and healthy and pleasant and quite obviously a happy and faithful wife and a very good mother. In my world where everything was black or white she would have been considered wicked for having such a couple as Scherbatov and Paula in the house. If sin were such a terrifying and evil thing how could these people be so happy and, above all, so gay? How could she permit her young daughters to speak to a woman like Paula who was living in sin, nay, even in open adultery.

There is no use in going further into the rest of the week. People came and went. It seemed that the big beautiful house was always filled with dogs and people and children, all of whom seemed to get on admirably together regardless of age. A good part of the time they talked about things of which I had little or no knowledge so that, even if I had been less shy and awkward in such a society, I still could not have taken part in any conversation worth listening to.

On Sunday evening when the servants were out Frank's mother turned in and cooked the dinner, and an excellent dinner it was, and the angular, sharp old Lady Fitzsimmons turned herself into a kitchen maid and a good one, preparing the vegetables and washing up the saucepans. Scherbatov and Paula on Thursday night made a wonderful dish of Spaghetti Bolognese, and Frank's father took over the salad. After both meals Frank and I and his two sisters washed up the dishes and cleaned the kitchen, Mary, the prettier of the girls, mopping up the floor with the expertness of a charwoman. Even the dogs took part in the affair, lying around underfoot and being fed morsels from time to time. It was all over and we were back in the living room an hour from the time we left the table. . . . I was useful then, and I think I enjoyed those two evenings the most of the whole visit. I could listen and participate without seeming an oaf.

But the thing which impressed me most was that these people enjoyed what they were doing—that old Lady Fitzsimmons took pride in her job as kitchen maid and probably did a better job than any of the servants. Scherbatov and Paula put their whole souls into the spaghetti along with the meat and tomato sauce, and Mary, Frank's sister, scrubbed the floor probably more thoroughly and efficiently than it had been scrubbed in years.

When the conversation turned upon servants, Frank's mother said, "I've never had any servant trouble. We all get along well and I have had the same couple for eighteen years. My father gave me wise advice when I was a girl. He said, 'Learn to do everything. You can never know too much in this life,' and so I did learn, and if a laundress walked out on me or a cook became insolent, I could always say, 'Leave if you want to, but if you stay try to be good-tempered. There's one thing I won't have around the house even in my own family and that's a sullen sulky person.' I could always say, 'If you leave I am not helpless. I can do your job probably better than you can do it.' I've never been sorry in following my father's advice."

It is something I have never forgotten, particularly the part about "learn to do everything. You can never know too much in life." I have not always followed that admonition. I wish I had.

During the week I developed an intimacy with Frank himself

which had not existed before. This was so perhaps because we were sharing a room and perhaps because for a little time Frank almost felt sorry for me and tried in his abrupt direct way to help me, even at the end when he must have seen that I was bewildered and hopelessly out of my depth.

Once I said to him, "Your father must be very rich," and he laughed. "You'd be surprised how broke he always is. He spends his money on pictures and furniture and on his big family and on his friends. He likes to eat and drink well and he's the kind that always grabs the check. I hate to think how much the old man is in debt. He makes big fees, sometimes enormous ones, but it all goes out of the window. None of us kids will inherit a cent. He keeps telling us that. He says, 'I'm spending it all on you so that you'll know how to make your own living and, what's more important, how to get the most out of life. If you have capital in a bank, the bank can go bust or your stocks and bonds can go up the flue. If you have it in your head it's indestructible.'" Frank laughed again. "I know I'll have to make my own living. The old man keeps telling me so over and over again, and I'm not interested in just making a living. I really want to do something and be somebody."

That night he seemed to have been released somehow and talked more than I had ever heard him talk. Some of the talk was directed at me and more of it I think was directed at himself, as if he were trying to straighten things out.

He said, "I know some of the Christers in the club disapprove of me, especially my going over to Jessie's place now and then, but I know what I'm doing. I know what I want to do. My father sent me out to the Middle West to college because he didn't want me to be provincial and know nothing but fellows from the East or fellows who had nothing but money. He sent me around the world first, telling me to take my time and find out what things are about and then maybe when I went to college I'd have some sense and know the answers and know what I wanted to do. Well, that's exactly what happened. I do know what I want to do. I want to be an engineer and, by God,

I'm going to be a good one. I'm a sexy guy, and when I go over to Jessie's it's to get it out of the way so I can do my work. It's a lot better than seducing the daughter of some campus boarding-house keeper or smooching around in the bushes with some 'nice girl' and getting nothing for it but a lot more agitation. I haven't yet got enough sense to get married and stay married, and I'm not fool enough to get myself handicapped at my age with a lot of kids and diapers. Maybe some day I'll fall in love and that'll be fine, but I hope by that time I'll have enough sense to make it last and enough money so that I'm not going to settle down for good in a six-room house in the suburbs with no prospect of escape. Jeez, if we don't have enough sense to manage our own lives then we shouldn't whine afterward."

And then remembering all the scare stories and the colored slides concerning social diseases we had all been treated to again and again, I asked naïvely, "Aren't you afraid of catching something?"

At that he laughed. "I can take care of myself. . . . If they'd teach kids more about that and less about the horror side, everybody would be better off."

And then he told me that he didn't see the regular girls at Jessie's place. He told me what I had never known before. He said, "Jessie has a list of girls on call. They wouldn't stay in her house and most of them won't even come there. They'll meet you at Jessie's home on the edge of town. Some of them are pretty nice women—young widows or wives whose husbands are impotent. I've had one girl for the last two years. Her husband has an electrical repair shop and she's fond of him and doesn't want to leave him. We meet mostly on Thursday nights when he goes to the lodge. She's a good girl and not stupid at all. She doesn't want to leave her husband and I don't want to get married, so everything is jake. I'm very fond of her."

I left at the end of the week and I saw Frank again the following year at college, but the old brief intimacy seemed to have vanished and he appeared no longer to have any interest in me. He was polite and even friendly, but he never mentioned the visit and he was so set upon what he wanted and what he was doing that he had very little time for me. I still do not know why he asked me in the first place to visit his family. I can only speculate. If he saw anything in me, any possibilities over the other men in the fraternity, he must have become disillusioned when he discovered how awkward and ignorant I was in such a world. He knew as I knew that I did not belong, and he probably felt that I never could belong or that, if I could, it would take too much of his time and energy to accomplish the trick. You must remember that he was nearly four years older than I and in maturity and background and sense of values hundreds of years older. Out of the background of that wonderful house, he had, as a boy, simply absorbed more than I would ever learn or assimilate in a lifetime, or could ever learn in any college or university, and after him the young sisters were repeating the process. How lucky they were!

The visit might have been a cruel thing for me at the time, and later on, after I married Enid and had two children and realized that there was no way out, it did turn into a cruel thing because by the time I was trapped, by myself as well as by Enid, I began to realize what had happened. If I had never had that sudden brilliant glimpse of another, richer, more exciting world, I might never have known, like most of my friends in Oakdale, that I had missed anything at all, and been moderately content. But I had seen beneath the curtain, and when I began to be bored and started to drink like all the others in order to find even the shabbiest kind of satisfaction in life, it was too late.

It is strange that I remember so vividly the whole of the visit. As I grow older it seems to become clearer to me and I remember things and even speeches and remarks which I had forgotten during the intervening time. Clearest of all in the memories is Frank's mother with her warmth and good looks and health and infectious gaiety. How wonderful it would be to have a wife like that! Or a mother! I doubt that I could ever have found a woman like her in my world, and, after all, one has to deserve such a woman, to offer something even to attract her.

What I saw during that visit to Frank's family was a civilized world in which there was a set of sound values and things fell into place according to those values. It is something that does not happen overnight. Many things go into its accomplishment —background and spirit and taste and brains and, above all, values themselves. It was a world in which two cars in the garage was of no interest whatever except as a convenience. A car, whether a jalopy or a Rolls, was simply something to get you from one place to another. It never became a chromium-plated symbol.

I know now that the people in that world looked upon cars and plumbing and telephones and all the materialist, mechanical paraphernalia of our age simply as the means of providing them with more time to devote to those things which *are* civilization and bring deep satisfaction and richness to living. Without all the mechanical, material things, I know now that these people would have been much the same. They would have lived well and richly in a shack or a cave, and out of all the world they would have found each other so that when the time came for them to die they would do so pleasantly and without reluctance or bitterness or fear or regret, because they had very largely fulfilled the destiny set for intelligent and civilized mankind. The cars, the telephones, the radio, the plumbing were not the goal nor the measure by which one's material position was determined as richer and more successful than that of other men; they were merely the means of achieving something far beyond that. The odd thing was that these people were not only much happier than most people that I have known; they were also richer in worldly goods and success and fame. It was as if a sorry world sought them out and forced these rewards upon them as a just compensation for the light they shed, whether it was the music of Scherbatov or the architecture of Frank's father or the beauty of Paula or the gaiety and wit of Frank's mother or the bitter brilliance of old Lady Fitzsimmons. The world, it seems, is hungry for such things and will pay well without ever being billed for the account. It is people like these who provide the real escape. They are the fortunate and the blessed because they are not afraid. Perhaps, being the blessed, there is no need for them to know either fear or despairing boredom.

VI The Jungle

Sergeant Burke came in late tonight while I was reading, not to play rummy this time, but to consult me about something serious which has occurred. It appears that when he inspected the contents of one of the Quonset huts he found that a considerable quantity of canned goods was missing—several tins of corned beef and a lot of canned vegetables and fruit.

He was deeply upset and took the whole business as a personal insult. I think he felt the same indignation which is experienced by the owner of a burglarized house who is furious less over the loss of material belongings than over the indignation of having his privacy invaded by a stranger. The situation also reflected upon his dignity as a sergeant, something which he regarded with as much seriousness as a devout monk regards his vows. This should not have happened to *him*, and he meant to ferret out the mystery and bring the culprit to justice if it was his last act on earth.

He sat down opposite me with little drops of warm crystal rain still clinging to the big, indignant red face.

"I can't figger it out," he said. "I talked to all the boys and they are as much in the dark as myself. At first I thought it might be Homer stealing the stuff to give to his fuzzy-wuzzy girl friends. He must have to pay something for the tail he's getting and money doesn't mean anything to those greasy babes. Homer denied it up and down. I know that he can't tell the truth if it killed him but this time I kind of believed him. Even when I threatened to give him a super going-over he still stuck to his story. When I asked what he did pay for what he was getting, he just grinned like an ape and said, 'I don't pay nothin'. They pay me!' Maybe that's true too. You can't tell about these skinny pink-haired bastards."

He always took a long time going into a story, bringing in all sorts of side issues. I'd been interrupted in the middle of writing and I tried to hurry him along in order to go back to what I was doing. Here in the jungle there are few interruptions but when one does occur, especially when I want to be alone to think and write, it seems monstrous and interminable. I said, "Did you inspect everything?"

He wiped the perspiration from his face. It had been dripping down into the black mass of hair that sprouted above the line of his T shirt. He was a stickler for being neat and clean and such things disturbed him.

He said, "I was just comin' to that. After I questioned the boys I made an inspection for myself and discovered that some of the corrugated sheets at the end of the hut were loose and came off in your hand. They were held in place by a couple of short nails which came out easy. It *looked* all right until you touched it and then it came right off. It must be somebody from outside because if it was Homer or one of the other boys they could steal all they wanted while they were on guard without ever having to break in."

I looked at him. "Who d'you think it is?"

As I told you the Sergeant is a great reader of mystery stories, having discovered them since he has been shut away here in the wet, crawling exile and boredom of the jungle. Like many uncomplex and simple creatures he is likely to take on the color of what he reads or sees in the movies and at times becomes a ham actor. He was in such a mood now, and despite the uncomfortable conditions and his own undoubted bewilderment and anxiety over the theft of the canned goods, he had begun to give a performance with only myself for his audience. He mopped his forehead again and leaned forward toward me. He glanced right and left as if to make certain that we should not be overheard and, in almost a whisper, said, "I think some of them yellow bastards must be hidin' out around here."

Although I was tempted to laugh at the pomposity of his behavior, I knew that I dared not for fear of hurting his dignity, and with the Sergeant dignity was the very foundation, the wellspring of all that he was and hoped to be—the dignity of the Army and of the rank of sergeant.

So I said, seriously, "But there are no Japs around here. There never have been. The nearest they've ever been is on the next island. To get here they'd have to swim a forty-mile channel and then make their way another hundred miles through the jungle."

"I wouldn't put anything past the bastards," he said.

"Did you nail tight the sheeting again?" I asked.

"Yes. They'll have a hell of a time getting it loose without making such a racket you could hear it."

"Well, watch it and tell the boys to watch it. Probably it's one of the local apes that's been stealing." Then I added, "And you might check on the boys and make sure they're not sleeping on duty."

"Okay."

"How about a drink?" I asked. Here on this lonely island with only five of us there wasn't any of the nonsense about officers and enlisted men drinking together.

"Sure."

I poured a slug of whisky for each of us. He took his straight with a chaser of warm beer and I drank mine with some of the lukewarm water we had always boiled carefully in advance. Then the Sergeant returned to his favorite anxiety. For a simple man he had many of them but this was the one that troubled him most.

He said, "Captain, you don't think they've just forgotten us here on this goddamn island? You don't think they're going to leave us here forever?"

I smiled. "No, they know we're here. They send our pay. They ask for reports."

"I don't trust 'em." He crossed one heavy thigh over the other. "I'm in the Army, see?" he said. "And I've got respect for the Army. I've made it my career, as you might say. But I don't

[96]

trust 'em." I poured him another whisky and his tongue grew a little looser. "Christ!" he said. "I'd hate to see any business run the way they run the Army. I'm only a sergeant but I've been at it a long time and I've seen things. I've seen 'em smash up expensive machinery or leave it just to rust away. I've seen 'em dump good stuff like underwear and uniforms just because it was in the way or it took a little trouble to repack the trucks. I've seen them dump tons of food into the sea with people all around them starvin'. I guess the trouble is that in peacetime no really *smart* guy would go into the Army. I guess there must be something a little wrong about any guy who wanted a career in the Army . . . even some of them guys who went to West Point. I went into it because I didn't have to worry. I got fed and clothed and taken care of and because I kinda liked fighting . . . and now look what they done to me . . . shoved me off here in this sonofabitch place." He shook his big bullet head. "I've done a lotta thinkin' since I got stuck off here . . . more'n I ever did in my life . . . and I've about decided there must be something wrong with a guy who wants to get into the Army. You know, he wouldn't be like other guys. He'd have to be just a little screwy. I guess that's why in peacetime an Army private is about the lowest thing you can find so far as most people are concerned. It's even that way with officers too. I've noticed it outside the posts. When they're on the post each one of 'em is a little king. But outside it's different. Why, even a general ain't as good as an admiral socially speaking. I guess the Navy's got something we ain't got. I guess that's why most of 'em like war. It makes them important and nobody cares how much they spend and they don't have to account to nobody. It's all for the good of the emergency and can't be helped." He paused for a moment thoughtfully and added, "I suppose what you call 'the armed forces' could ruin any country if they go on the way they're goin'. Some of 'em are goddamn ignorant too . . . as ignorant as I am." He chuckled. "Maybe more so. They've just had a kind of narrow education but I've been around plenty. Some of 'em don't even know what people are like."

I'm putting all this down because I was astonished at so much wisdom coming out of somebody like the Sergeant. Sometimes the most simple people are the greatest fountains of wisdom because their view of life is perfectly direct and uncomplicated by such things as "issues" and "the good of the country" and "the good of the service" and "humanitarianism" and "the Common Man" and all the crap which muddies up the water of clear thinking and honesty and covers up deceits and hypocrisies and inefficiency and a thousand things—all those expressions and words and abstractions which rarely have anything to do with the case but only confuse the issue and prevent progress while they make the people who use them feel warm all over as if somehow they were superior and more Christlike than other people. Sometimes I think that must be the real definition of a "liberal." Simple people don't get muddled up. They don't always see things, but when they do see them they see them plain and in terms of the truth and the fundamentals. Maybe that's why Jefferson and Lincoln liked the plain, simple people —liked and admired them.

I said, "I certainly think it would be tough on the country back home and on all the whole world if things got into the hands of the generals and admirals once the war is over."

He grinned. "Sometimes," he said, "I think what they'd like best is a kind of mix-up of war and peace where they could get away with all the things they're gettin' away with now and still not have to give up all the luxuries by havin' to fight or live in a jungle." He looked at me anxiously. "I couldn't be had up for what I'm sayin', could I?" he asked.

I laughed. "I don't know. It would depend on who heard it. You needn't worry about me, but when you're away from here I wouldn't take any chances. The regular Army is filled with pompous little jerks."

He was leaning back now as if he were relaxed over relieving his soul and saying what he'd wanted to say for a long time. Then he sat up suddenly and said, "There's still one thing that's worryin' me, Captain. When am I gonna get a chance to get off this island and get on a bender and see some women?"

"I can't answer that," I said. "I've written twice to headquarters to get leave for all of you. It can't be all at once but in turn. I've put you at the head of this list. The only reply is that you are all urgently needed here in line of duty. The second letter they didn't even bother to answer."

"Line of duty! Christ! Why don't they just give all this crap in the Quonset huts to these fuzzy-wuzzies and call it a day. It would be a lot cheaper. God knows why they ever unloaded the stuff here in the first place. Here we are guardin' the hell out of it as if it was gold and diamonds, and after we spend the best years of our life here they'll finally remember us and let us get back to civilization and then dump the stuff into the sea. They won't even give it to these bloody starvin' natives."

"If I'm here, I'll see to that," I said.

"Yes, but you'll be disobeyin' orders. Orders! Christ!" He actually spat on my clean floor in disgust. "Who knows where they come from? Half the time it's from some jerk in Washington or even maybe just a woman clerk. They never know nothing. It's just according to whether they wake up that morning constipated."

"Another drink?" I suggested, aware that for the first time I was really seeing *inside* the Sergeant. But he was cautious.

"No thanks, Captain. Better not. Christ knows what I might say."

He stood up. "You know what I think? I think our whole bloody country is goin' to the dogs and fast. It's gettin' just like any of the second-rate countries anywhere. And I gotta get outa here, Major. I gotta get out. I'm getting crazy ideas . . . ideas like I never had before in my life. I gotta get outa here and go on a bust and lay some women. Jesus! I'm gonna blow up!"

As if to emphasize the passion of his outburst there was a sudden crash of thunder and the rain began to come down again as if someone had pulled the chain on a gigantic shower bath of lukewarm water.

"That goddamn rain!" said the Sergeant.

"What do you mean by getting crazy ideas? What ideas?"

He was quiet again. "Never mind," he said. "I ain't gonna tell you. It's about all I can do to face 'em myself." He picked up his oilskin poncho. "I'm goin' back to the hut and try to sleep. You'd better get some shut-eye yourself. I ain't slept so well myself lately, and every night I keep wakin' up and every time I look across I can see a light over here." He looked at me sharply. "What's the matter? You getting ideas too?"

I grinned. "Maybe. Maybe you'd call it that. I'm thinking . . . and sometimes writing."

"What the hell can you find to write about out here? Nothing ever happens. Jesus, I write to a couple of girls back home just in case I get outa this hell hole sometime and might need 'em again. . . . But I can't find a damned thing to write about except you know what and if I put what I was thinking on paper the censor would send for me all the way from Pearl Harbor and put me in the jug. Jesus! I even find myself makin' pictures of it. Is that what you're writin'?"

"No, not altogether, but that has something to do with it."

He flung the poncho around him and said, "I wish I could write if only to get some of what's drivin' me nuts outta my system. Thanks, Captain, for the drink and the chance to talk. You see, them other guys is so young and inexperienced they don't understand what you're talkin' about."

"Sure, Sergeant. Whenever you want to let off steam, come in and talk."

He went out of the door and the rain came down so thickly that he disappeared before he had gone more than ten feet. The sound on the corrugated roof was deafening. When he had come I had been annoyed because he had interrupted my work, and now that he was gone I felt suddenly at loose ends, wishing he had stayed on to talk. I wondered what the crazy thoughts could be which disturbed him so much. They might be serious or they might be nothing at all. People's ideas of what is crazy or dangerous or what is sin vary so greatly according, largely, to whether they are brought up Catholic or Methodist or Jewish or some other damned thing that you can't even guess very accurately about anybody.

His suggestion that there were Japs hiding somewhere about us in the jungle was disturbing. Although I had pooh-poohed the suggestion I could not altogether dismiss it. They were such hardy, tough little bastards, so determined to go on living, except when they were hysterical in the face of guns or a flamethrower, that nothing was altogether impossible for them. They might have swum the forty-mile channel or made themselves a raft and paddled across under cover of darkness. They *might* even have done what was even more impossible—fought their way through a hundred miles of horrible, tangled jungle. If they were around, if they were able to break into the hut without ever being heard or detected, then all of us might well be in danger of our lives. They could slip in while we were asleep and cut our throats or, if they got hold of any of the grenade supply, blow us all up with no trouble at all. There certainly wasn't anything pleasant about it.

After the Sergeant had gone I went back to my writing, in which I had just finished setting down the visit to Frank's family and the glimpse of the world I found among them, but when I tried to go back I couldn't get anywhere. Nothing would come out of my brain onto the sheets of paper and I gave it up. I wasn't ready yet for the next part. I hadn't digested it yet. It hadn't gone through the process of gestation, coming out clear and formed and understood and developed.

Idly I picked up the letter from Enid which a plane had dropped down on me with the other mail late this afternoon. We get mail about once every three weeks when a plane goes about over the islands dropping mail upon all the godforsaken, forgotten souls isolated like ourselves. For the moment there was something almost pleasant about seeing the handwriting because it involved a life so remote from the one I had been leading for months, a life which some day I might know again.

The letter began, "Darling," which at once set my teeth on edge again. It was an expression Enid perpetually used which always seemed false to me because it is a term which should be used in only two sets of circumstances. Either it is the meaningless expression used by a silly gushing woman indiscriminately and to everyone including the butcher or it is a term of passion shared only by two people to the exclusion of all else in the world. In the case of Enid neither use was justified. She was not the silly gushing type, Heaven knows, and certainly no such passion existed between us even in the beginning. If she had written, "Dear Hank," I would not have been annoyed. I would even have been pleased because it seemed friendly and normal, but "Darling" was superheated and false and a part of that interminable "acting." Thinking about this I suddenly wished that she had been the type who could have addressed me as "Honey" or "Sugar," for there is in the words something at once comical and friendly and warm, like the playfulness of certain uninhibited happy people in the midst of making love. But that did not suit her either. It would have been as false and as revolting as "Darling." I would have settled for "Dear Hank," which she used to call me when we went about together as kids, but of course that didn't suit the picture of our relations as she wanted them to appear to the world. Funny how even a single little word can make you happy or unhappy or filled with distaste when it is all wrong and used out of character.

> Darling [she wrote], I haven't heard from you for three weeks and hope there's nothing wrong. I was a little surprised to hear that you didn't mind the life you're leading. One of the Hazeltine boys who's just back, looking like a skeleton from fever, says the life on those islands is hell, especially if there isn't a club or a bar or anything. But you always were peculiar about some things and I guess you've gotten more peculiar as time goes on. They say geniuses are peculiar. Maybe you're a genius. Ha! Ha!
>
> There isn't much news to write. The children are well and miss you. Ronnie isn't doing too well at school and I had him examined thoroughly—eyes, ears, nose, everything—but the doctors could find nothing the matter with him. He just says he doesn't like school, so I suppose I'll have to work on him to

make him like it. I've been reading books on the subject and one of them says that sometimes children who don't like school have secret frustrations and irritations at home but I know that can't be. Everything runs so smoothly here. It's not because he isn't bright. He's always asking questions sometimes about things he shouldn't be asking. That's where a boy his age needs a father. I've tried to explain to him but I'll be glad when you're back and can take him over. It'll please you to hear that he says home isn't the same with you away. When I asked him what he meant, he just said, "I don't know. It's like the house had got cold and foggy." So there's a tradelast. How about one from you?

Esther is all right. She's a good child and never has made any trouble. She seems always to *understand*, and when I'm in the dumps over your being away, she'll come and put her arms about me and say, "Darling, don't feel bad. Daddy'll be home soon, and when he comes back he'll love you more than ever." Isn't that wonderful? She isn't a bit like Ronnie who sometimes seems to me cold and actually hostile.

The Ferguson boy was killed at Okinawa. I suppose it is a blow to them but he always seemed to me unattractive and fresh and, after all, he did make them a great deal of trouble with the girl from the wrong side of the tracks and being sued in that automobile accident. And the Villars boy is reported missing. I feel sorry for them losing an only child like that. Sometimes war does seem senseless but what are we to do but fight when it is forced on us?

I've sent you a package and I hope somebody else doesn't get it. I won't tell you what's in it. I want you to be surprised. I had the heating system gone over and it was frightfully expensive. Oh, yes, I forgot to say that I had to have the hedge taken out. Something got into it, bugs or something, or it wasn't trimmed properly, and it got to looking mangier and mangier so that I was ashamed of it. It really made the whole property look shabby and dirty. And it always made me feel that I was being shut in and smothered. I hope you don't mind too much. I did do my best to take care of it but I seem to have the opposite of a green thumb. I have only to touch something to have it wither and die. The roses aren't too bad. I've followed your directions but they still have spots and the prettiest blooms were eaten up by some kind of awful beetle. I've had to buy flowers for the house when I have people to dinner. I always *pretend* they come out of the garden so you needn't feel ashamed.

Your mother stopped off here last week for a day and night. She's been on some kind of a tour got up by one of her organizations to sell war bonds. She looked very old and tired and I had quite a long talk with her, pointing out that she wasn't young any longer and couldn't stand what she used to, but it was like talking to a stone wall. I tried to make her rest as much as possible while she was here. You must try, darling, to write her more often. She seemed very hurt and jealous that I got more letters from you than she did. You know how she is.

I'd write more often but it seems almost futile as there's never any certainty when you'll get the letter or whether you'll get it at all. I'm going up to New York for the annual meeting of the class alumni. Wish you were going to be along. The country club seems very funny with hardly any men around. They get fewer and fewer—only boys or old men. It seems so useless for you to be out there in the middle of the Pacific doing nothing when you could be so happy here in the life you've built up for your wife and children.

Now take care of yourself and when you come home we'll make up for all the lost months and years. You can't imagine how lonely I feel every time I look at your empty bed. And write me . . . you don't know what your letters mean to me.

Enid.

Well, that was it. A *nice* letter. Exactly the kind of letter which would be written by a loving wife to a loving husband, from a wife who felt real concern about her husband's mother and left not a stone unturned for the physical welfare of his children . . . a wife you could leave behind and know that she would remain faithful and that everything would be well managed, except perhaps for things like the hedge. Yes, a nice letter . . . impeccable . . . a model . . . But, . . . But what? . . . It was the kind of letter an actor reads aloud in a play on the stage. It was also the letter of a bitch whose bitchery you would never be able to pin down and dissect.

I went to bed and turned off the light so the Sergeant wouldn't be disturbed about me when he awakened with his own worries and torments. At least I didn't feel the need to go on a bender and see some women. But I *was* worried about the children, for I knew suddenly that Ronnie, at twelve, was already beginning to get the pitch and that Esther was going the other way. She was beginning already to act her part so that the production wouldn't be spoiled.

VII Oakdale

WHAT IS LOVE? I DON'T KNOW. DO YOU? I DON'T KNOW BEcause it is so many things and because in reality I have had so little experience. Is it sentiment? Is it mere lechery? Does it involve tenderness? Yes, but it also involves cruelty and jealousy and treachery. Is it the calculated sensuality of the voluptuary or the frustrated sublimations of a gelded Abélard and an intellectual Héloïse? Is it something to be set on one side, formed, made rigid by convention or fear? It is certainly the most carelessly used word in the English language. It is used for God, for women, for heterosexual and homosexual relationships, for children, for mothers, for wives, for mistresses, for pets. The French are much better in their definition of love. When you say *amour* in French you know what is meant with no nonsense, but "love" is a meaningless word in English. Odd too, because English is the richest of all languages but curiously also the least definite and the most vague. Perhaps that is why it has produced the richest and finest poetry in the world. Fine poetry is always like a beautiful structure partially enveloped in mist.

Love is so changeable and so shifting. There are times out here in the islands when I feel greater affection or even love for the dog I left behind than I do for my wife and children. Sometimes I speculate on what member of my household I should like most to have with me here in order to keep me company.

Nearly always the answer comes out, "Why, Sandy, my dog. Of course!" I think what I miss most is having him come to me and put his head between my legs, looking up at me with eyes which speak and yet cannot speak. Perhaps it is vanity, the satisfaction of being worshiped. But it is not altogether that. The extraordinary thing is that I feel *closer* to him than to my own wife and children. He is a wonderful companion. I think we understand each other completely. I think he understands each of us in the family better than we understand each other. He regards Ronnie as an equal with whom he romps and rassels, never hesitating to take a good bite if Ronnie is unfair or too rough. Esther he simply ignores, I suspect because he thinks her rather prissy and no fun. If, as sometimes happens, we forget to put him out and he lifts his leg somewhere below stairs, Esther screams and behaves as if the house were burning down, rushing to her mother and screaming, "Mummy! Mummy! Sandy's done it again!"

He will go to Enid when she calls him and will *submit* to being stroked and petted. He is very polite about it, but he understands, I think, that the petting is not spontaneous. It is an act, a performance in which she finds far more pleasure than he finds. She is thinking without thinking, "What a pretty picture this makes!" The odd thing is that at times she is jealous of the dog, that at times she hates him because he reaches me, something which she has not been able to do for a long time, if indeed she was ever able to do it. He is a not very good Irish setter and a terrible tramp at heart, but I am more worried about him than I am about Ronnie's doing badly at school. I am always troubled lest Enid turn him out at night. I know that the moment I left the house she shut him up each night in the cellar. He had always been permitted to sleep on a special chair in the rumpus room while I was at home, and I always wanted secretly to have him in the bedroom but I never quite dared, any more than for years I dared demand a separate room for myself. Enid is one of those women who puts the neatness of her house above the happiness and welfare of her husband, her children, or any pet. She would have made an unholy row at having a dog in the bedroom. Fortunately, as an experienced tramp he probably knows how to take care of himself.

I haven't had much experience with love, but I have read a great deal about it, mostly in the two or three years before I came out here. I learned to read a whole book in college because I had a good professor in literature—it was the only thing I did learn—but after I left I slipped back again. I read nothing but mystery stories until a few years ago. It was about the time I found out that the endless running about in crowds, usually well loaded with liquor, had become unendurable. Save for the rose garden I had no hobby, and I had to find something to do with my time, especially during the long winter months. Also I found that reading, after a time, became a defense against Enid's endless talking and gossip. If I concentrated so that I could not hear what she was saying, she would eventually give up the struggle and sulk. I did not mind the sulking so long as she kept quiet.

She did not like reading herself. There are so many women and men too like her back in the States. They have been through school and college without ever having learned to read or to enjoy the peculiar pleasure of ideas; people who can really talk about nothing whatever but their immediate occupations and activities. The most they ever read is the more sensational items in the newspapers, the comics, the sports, and easily predigested things out of the *Reader's Digest* and similar publications. It is a fault perhaps of our mechanical, materialist, complex, rushed civilization, but it is a fault too of our colleges and universities.

So many men and women I know seem to have learned or at least retained nothing whatever from the experience of having gone to college. Some of them even leave college without being able to spell or to write or speak grammatically. At times it seems to me almost impossible that they have been to college and have learned so little. They must have gotten good enough marks to have remained in school, yet the residue of learning appears to be nothing. They seem to believe that education ended on the day they left the university, that there is something magical about a college degree, and that there could not possibly be anything more to be learned. The job is over and they can relax.

Enid is like that. She graduated from a great and famous women's college but she seems to know nothing and to be interested in little beyond the daily activities of her life. She is always fussing about. Most of her friends are like her. They have, most of them, had all the advantages of prosperity and education, but the result has been nil. It has always been impossible to discuss anything with Enid which required any concentration or any thinking. She seems to have no background of history or economics or politics. Her reactions are almost entirely emotional. In the beginning she was all for Roosevelt as a second Jesus Christ and now she hates him because taxes are high and she can't get butter when she wants it. The idea that he might be something in between or a charlatan or a demagogue is much too complex for her consideration. She belongs to the League of Women Voters and is active in the Association of University Women, and periodically she comes home from one or the other, all steamed up about some new idea—World Federation or the W.P.A. or something else—about which some woman has given a speech, but she never understands what it is all about and after a few days the enthusiasm dies away.

After the honeymoon a husband and wife begin to have need of something besides bed to hold them together. Was it St. Simon who said that great mistresses, wielding great power and maintaining their positions, were rarely beautiful women in the accepted sense? They were always clever and entertaining and more often than not plain. A man cannot stay in bed twenty-four hours a day.

So after our own honeymoon I found our mutual intellectual life a pretty sterile affair. It was impossible to discuss anything with Enid—ideas or anything important or politics and economics. The discussion promptly became so muddled and eventually so emotional that it ended in a quarrel or with some bitter and savage remark on my own part, not that I am an intellectual genius or in any sense brilliant, but because I suppose most men are more logical and more thorough and more objective than women. Not many women find pleasure in the workings of logic or the mere fact of *knowing*. I suppose that is one of the reasons why even the greatest dressmakers and cooks are usually men, because they employ these elements even in fields which are popularly regarded as belonging to the female sex. More maddening than any other quality was her capacity for inevitably turning every discussion into a personal affair. Eventually everything, even the weather, became related to her own ego. If during the period of hero worship of Roosevelt I uttered even the faintest criticism, it became a personal insult to her.

In any case I took to reading as a defense and a refuge from the sterility and superficiality of my home life and indeed of all the life which surrounded me. And as I read I began to rediscover the immense pleasure of reading, the pleasure of losing myself in a *good* novel in which from the first page I entered a world as real to me or perhaps more real than the life all about me, or the pleasure of following an idea, skillfully and meticulously worked out to the very end. I even began to read books on philosophy. And all this tended to isolate me and make more unendurable those excursions into suburban society which began to be actual incursions upon my solitude and my own inner life. I could not enjoy myself, even after I had drunk a half-dozen strong martinis which at one time in my life had helped enormously. I only grew sullen and resentful, thinking always, above the clatter, that I wanted to be at home exploring the new worlds which I was discovering. It was all a part of the same trouble . . . which began that morning long ago with my actually *seeing* myself for the first time in the bathroom mirror.

We are coming back now to love, for it was out of these books that I began to discover how complex and varied a thing love could be. I should properly use the word *amour* because that is the kind of love I am writing about, not love of God or children or the Parent-Teacher Association or love in any of its careless Anglo-Saxon, Protestant connotations . . . just good old Greek and Latin *amour*.

I began to discover that there were things far beyond my own experience which had properly to do with love or *amour*. I began to make the amazing discovery that love could be a thing in itself, justifying itself as an art or even a career, that love and the vigor and vitality which it engendered could in itself become a creative force of great fertility. And I began to discover the variety of love and to understand many things about myself which I had not understood before, why I experienced certain emotions, why I did certain things, why I had felt warm and eager rushes of affection toward certain girls and even certain boys during my adolescence, why some pretty women attracted me and others, equally pretty, did not, why I had never loved my own mother and resented the fierce proprietary interest and even desire to possess and control me which went on in the very face of her obvious neglect of me in the role of mother. I began to understand why an act which I had once enjoyed with Enid had become in fact an act that was distasteful and could only be carried through because of my own vitality, mechanically, and somewhat as I would take liver pills when I felt bilious. This indeed was a long way from love or *amour,* and I began to see that actually the whole act in relation to Enid was degrading and worse perhaps than any act of perversity. At last, of course, it became intolerable and came to an end but not before I had come close to a real nervous breakdown and lost a great deal of weight.

And I began to understand what it was that drove some of the men of my acquaintance to what could only be described as sordid debauchery and lust on the occasions when they went to places like New Orleans or Chicago on conventions. In short, I began to understand too many things for my own good and perhaps for the good of those about me. I began to see in the men and women with whom I associated things which they believed hidden and perhaps *were* hidden to most people and to see things in them which they did not even know or recognize and admit about themselves. And that only widened the gulf between me and them. If there had been someone with whom I could have talked about these things, frankly and with interest and in confidence, it would perhaps have been all right. But there was no one, least of all Enid.

When I first took to reading she thought the whole thing was just a phase and would pass quickly enough, as a great many former enthusiasms of mine had passed because they were only a part of the restlessness I did not understand and the search for something on which I could take a strong hold, something to which I might attach myself and find both interest and stability.

But when the passion for reading grew and there was no sign of its passing and I refused now and then to go to the eternal barbecues and cocktail parties that were always exactly the same, she decided she would try to share my passion and so bring us more closely together. But despite the fierceness of the original purpose to possess me and to have us *share* everything as if we were one person, she could not follow me into that world which I had discovered without her. Reading bored her, indeed so much that she could not even get through a fairly readable good novel in order to be able to discuss it afterward. If she did attempt a discussion I discovered that she had missed the whole point of the book, partly because she had read it in a hasty, bored, and superficial way, but mostly because she was always identifying herself with one of the characters, usually the one the author had satirized. She did not see the satire. She was as calloused to an understanding of satire as a hundred-year-old turtle. She simply looked upon the satirized character as maligned and abused, and sometimes she observed that the author must be a horrible, degenerate person without any standards or morals.

But it was above all the boredom and the necessity and effort of a moderate degree of concentration which defeated and prevented her invasion of the world I had discovered. Of all things, she took a shot at reading Proust, and of all books, *Sodom and Gomorrah*, called in translation *The Cities of the Plain*. This was at the height of her effort and she stuck to it stubbornly, but she managed to read most of the book without the least understanding of what was going on or the faintest perception of the true character of the Baron Charlus. I did not enlighten her because I knew she would only say, "I don't like to discuss such dirty things," and that would have been the end of it.

I must confess that I did not find Proust easy reading, but I will say that he is the only author I have ever read who is able to keep boredom and fascination both in the air at the same time. And despite all the complications and complexities of his style and content I was fascinated for a wholly unliterary reason. I was fascinated by a world so different from anything I had ever known that I might have been reading a book about people living on Mars or the moon—a life which, however decadent, seemed as rich and exciting as my own daily life was mechanical and sterile and empty from the day I looked at myself in the mirror.

I got most of the books from the Crescent City Carnegie Public Library with the advice of Miss Pritchard, a middle-aged and rather attractive spinster who must have led an intense inner life unrevealed to the patrons of the library. She seemed to have read everything or at least to be able to tell you what kind of book it was and whether it was difficult or easy reading. Outwardly her life revolved entirely around books and the library, with occasional excursions to library conventions or to the Rocky Mountains on holidays, and I think she was a little astonished when I first appeared and asked for some good reading. She advised me, and after a little while she began to discern what it was I liked and steered me in the proper direction. She led me into getting the New York book reviews and out of them I found books which I wanted especially to read. Twice when I asked her about specific books she laughed and said, "We couldn't carry those here. If some of our more respectable readers took them out, there would be an awful row with the library board. It isn't always what you or I might think was the dirtiest book. It's the kind of book that rubs their noses in what they don't want to see. That's what always stirs up trouble. A lot of them rather like what you or I might think were really dirty books. It's the ones that stir them up that they hate and consider dirty."

I think it was that remark which revealed to both of us that we understood a good many things in the same way. The books which she dared not suggest to the library board I ordered by mail from New York. These became, therefore, virtually the only books I owned and the nucleus of a library decidedly of an erotic nature, which infuriated Enid and I must confess did give a wholly false picture of reading tastes which otherwise were fairly catholic. If I died suddenly by my own hand and someone took to investigating he would probably come to the conclusion, on finding that pitifully small library, that I had been obviously deranged through an obsession over sex, which would not have been true at all since such books were only a small proportion of the sum total of my reading.

However, I did develop a lively interest in the substance and the technique of love, partly, I think, because I had been until then comparatively innocent and each discovery came to me with surprise and even with astonishment. What I had known or even suspected dimly had before then come into my consciousness as facts which were suppressed, dirty, dimmed, and generally regarded as shocking and as exceptional in practice as murder. Generally speaking there was a rabbit-like act and that was all. Anything else was dirty. It was tragic but true, and I think that the same attitude was shared by most of the men I knew. It was only when they became older, brutally unfaithful, and went exploring at convention time that they ever extended the borders of love-making, and by that time there was not much beauty and no tenderness in it but only an animal-like quality of lust and rutting. That too is tragic but true.

As for the women I cannot speak with so much authority, but many of them at middle age or after developed the same air of urgency and desperation and promiscuousness and lust as if at last, too late, they had discovered desire but not love or tenderness or beauty. By instinct and sometimes through the greater knowledge of some more experienced partner they discovered the technique of love so late that it could only be practiced with a kind of harsh and indiscriminate animality. Too many times there was in our world in Crescent City the spectacle of a man and woman who had lost interest in each other and drifted apart, practicing separately and promiscuously, with virtual strangers, a love-making which in the beginning when they had first come together would have been beautiful and full of satisfaction but once they had drifted apart became merely a sensual exercise which left them afterward perpetually cold and exhausted and sometimes filled with shame and remorse like the men coming home on a cold gray train from a convention.

How then could this come about? The root of it must lie deep in the puritanical Protestant past of all that is our culture, wherein for generations the idea of sex has been looked upon as shameful and even by some as distasteful. What a preposterous and pretentious business is such an attitude!—that man (or woman) should think himself stronger than the forces of the universe or to believe that he (or she) was so vastly different from his fellow animals. The belief has in itself corrupted the very word "love" and diffused its meaning, making it at once silly and trivial, gross and sordid. Silliest of all perhaps are those who profess to believe that a man and woman should cohabit only with the purpose of having children. I think that Enid perhaps had that idea dimly in mind when we were first married, and then presently she found out that few practiced so rigorous and absurd a doctrine and that she must "give in" in order to hold me. She was always reading articles in women's magazines and "sob sister" columns on how to "hold" a husband.

I know that I got enlightenment neither from my mother nor my father save in a roundabout way. My father was always so remote from me that to have discussed such a thing as the facts of life would have seemed to him like corrupting a strange small boy. My mother did it by books, leaving a "modern" pamphlet recommended by one of her women's organizations on the table in my room where I would be certain to find it. By then it was too late, for I already knew more than the pamphlet contained and knew it with a detail and sureness which certainly the pamphlet did not contain. It was hazy about everything and very dull reading. By that time (I think I was thirteen) I already knew from haymow experience how little girls were made and had even had with Eva Smart (one of those local bad girls three years older than myself) a fumbling experience in which I found little excitement or pleasure. And of course at Hargreaves' farm I had long since learned the facts of breeding and birth and learned other things from the naked little boys at the swimming hole.

If I had been let alone I should have approached the whole question with a fair degree of simplicity and naturalness, but I was not permitted either simplicity or naturalness. The very attitude of my parents, the silence of my father, and the placing of the pamphlets by my mother where I might find them implied that the whole thing was shameful and must not be mentioned. At the same time that the whole campaign sought to suppress the whole idea of sex, it actually served only to give it an exaggerated and distorted importance.

But it did not end there. At the Y.M.C.A., where we went to swim and had as payment to listen at times to the lectures by the physical director on sex hygiene, the subject was dragged up and made not only shameful but hideous through dreadful warnings about venereal disease and even revolting colored slides depicting the horrible price paid by those who "sinned." The whole process was one of creating horror and of making everything connected with sex or even love as revolting as possible.

I wonder how many suicides, how much wretchedness, how much homosexuality was created out of the sessions on sex hygiene. And sitting out here in the jungle, I wonder what they are offering to boys today, now that antibiotics have reduced the wages of sin to the level of a cold in the head, only more quickly and easily cured.

I never have been able to discover how much Enid knew when I married her. It was one of those things which you could never possibly discuss with her because she was incapable of detachment or objectivity in anything you discussed and because there was in her none of the merriness which in some women makes of the marital relationship a laughing and satisfactory affair. Her mother was a prim woman whom it was impossible to imagine in any such situation as an *accouplement*. Yet she and her husband occupied a double bed throughout their existence. Very likely she pretended to herself that it was not happening.

Concerning Enid I only knew that she was awkward and submissive in the beginning and I was not much help since the only experience I had had might have been classified as mechanical. I was of course, by many standards, experienced, for many an American husband goes into marriage a virgin with a textbook in one hand, but I was certainly not a lover calculated to make a woman happy or to create out of the contact anything more than a conventional act brought about quickly and awkwardly through the pressure of vitality and good health.

I think I understood the whole of our life together in one flash when, after I had taken to reading a great deal and years after we were married, I attempted to put into practice a caress of which I had read. I felt Enid's body stiffen and heard her say, "Don't! Where did you learn such a filthy trick?"

That was the end and we were never together again. Yet in that single episode there lay the seeds of long and deep tragedy and the bitter sterility of that life together in which there was never any real satisfaction or pleasure for either of us. After that something died completely in me, and I knew that even when she kissed me in public for show there was no feeling behind it and that the gesture was the falsest of all the performances she gave.

Why was it all like that? I don't know. It is one of the things I am trying to discover in writing this all down. I am trying to discover why two people who, until they were married, had been treated kindly by life should have made such a dull and empty mess of things. It would have been better, I think, if we had quarreled violently, if I had beaten her, even if we had separated and divorced. In that way each of us might have had another chance before it was too late. In that way, through quarrels and violence and passion, we might even have broken down the things which paralyzed us and kept us apart. In that way I might have roused something in her which in the end would have brought us together so that we really shared each other. That was the one thing she most desired and the one thing at which she always acted, yet which she prevented by every thought and action. It never occurred even for a second in all our lives together.

In the beginning it started off all right. We married each other because it was the thing to do—what might be called a "natural." On my own side I was a young and vigorous man who needed either marriage or some relationship which might act as a release both physically and emotionally. It is bad for a young man of average vigor to hold himself in for too long (see St. Paul). And this urgency became translated in mind and even in my body into the delusion that I was in love with Enid. She was at hand. She was fresh and young and pretty. The idea pleased both sets of parents. We would marry and start our life together in a small but luxurious house. I would inherit an excellent business and she would come into some money if everything went well. I had been already two years out of college when she was graduated.

I was one of the few young men who had an automobile of my own, and in that first summer the courtship was largely carried on in the automobile and on picnics and sometimes on the golf course of the country club. All this is considered ideal, yet I see now that we had no special fun out of it. Some uninhibited pair of Slovenes or Italians from the Flats along the river would have had infinitely more fun and pleasure and they would have been a great deal closer both to God and nature, from which our middle-class Protestant upbringing had shut us out. Once or twice when I was aroused I had put my hand on her thigh while driving, but each time she pushed it away and afterward she had sulked. Once she said, "Let's not put it on that vulgar basis." On what other basis ought a young couple about to marry put such a relationship? What but that basis was the fundamental purpose of marriage?

If I had had any experience I would have known then that what came afterward was inevitable, or if I had had enough experience I might have changed her afterward. But young men of my age did not have experience or often enough, if they had it, it was of the wrong kind. Of course if we had been like Paul and Virginia, simply two children of nature coming together spontaneously as we reached the age of ripeness, everything would have been natural and simple and playful, but it was not like that. We had both been wrapped in cocoons, different yet alike, of inhibitions, of shames, of hearsay, of convention, of actual horror, and she, of course, had had hammered in her since birth the idea that a girl must not only be a virgin if she ever expected to make a proper marriage but that she must behave even as if the touch of a man's hand on her thigh might make her pregnant. It would be funny if it did not lie at the root of so much suffering, so many divorces, and even on occasion of murder.

You see, what I am trying to get at is this—where did all this come from and why did such superstitions and nightmares and shames exist? Perhaps it will be different with many of the young people in the future and I have been told that it is different with the boys and girls now growing up. Certainly they are all far more mature for their ages than we were when we married. Young people and indeed all people are to some extent the products of the forces of the generations and times in which they live. These young people coming up in a distraught and trying world are perhaps like the young people of the eighteenth century when Pitt at twenty-one was Prime Minister of the British Empire and men and women assumed responsibilities before they were properly of age. Most men of my acquaintance and age, whatever the number of their years, have in reality never reached the age of twenty-one.

I wonder whether there was less morality and less suffering in a bawdy time like that of the Restoration than in a dull respectable hypocritical age such as the Victorians knew. I doubt it.

You see, I keep fumbling and fumbling, trying to unravel the tangled skeins that lie behind my own personal emptiness and the futility of my life as a family man and a member of a community and, indeed, that lie behind so much of the hysterical futility of all middle-class American life. And how little of our life is not middle class, in one way or another?

Our wedding was conventional and fine with bridesmaids and ushers and banks of white flowers and long articles in the society columns of the newspapers as was befitting the marriage between the "scions" of two of the first families of the town. There was even champagne to drink which was considered rather daring, and rice and confetti were showered on the young pair as they drove off in the new automobile that was the gift of the bridegroom's father.

I asked Frank Saunders to be one of my ushers, but he wrote a polite letter saying that unfortunately he expected to be in Europe at the time of the wedding. He sent us a handsome silver card tray. I blushed when I got his answer because I knew all the time that he would never accept the invitation. I had blushed even when I wrote inviting him to be an usher. I knew somehow that he was through with me, bored with me, and would never see me again save by accident, but I wanted him to come. In my heart there was, I suppose, still a kind of hero worship for him because there was in him something dark and wicked and free, and I would never be any of these things. And there was no doubt that he would bring a certain "class" to the wedding which none of the others could possibly contribute. The girls would all fall in love with him, as girls usually did. And I still wanted to be friends with him. He would have made a difference to the whole of the occasion. There was a radiance and a dash about him which would, I knew, lift the whole tone of the thing. But I knew all along that he would not come. He had better things to do.

We drove away from the wedding in the late afternoon to spend the night in Kentucky, and most of the way Enid talked about how well the wedding had gone off and how well the bridesmaids looked in the dresses she had herself designed and how Mary Everly had had too much champagne and so on, as if nothing had happened that was to change both of us, to bring us happiness or suffering, as if the greatest thing that can happen to two young people had not occurred at all. It was as if, instead of being married, we had just left the Saturday-night country club dance and were driving home and I would presently stop the car in front of her house and come in and sit for a little while and then leave her and go back to my own home.

But I was scared. While I listened to her talk there were even moments when I doubted that I had done the right thing in getting married. It meant that I would have to settle down and now perhaps would never have a chance to do all those things—travel and visit far exotic places—which I had dreamed of in more romantic moments. At any rate I now had the right to place my hand on her thigh and I did so, as if to claim possession of her. This time she did not withdraw or stiffen. She simply went on talking about the wedding as if the hand were not there at all. And I found myself thinking, rather bitterly at so early a stage, "Yes. She has got her man. Everything is settled and she doesn't need to worry any more." Because this was for good. That was the way we were brought up. It was for good.

There is something frightening about that thought, and it must have come to hundreds of young bridegrooms just as it came to me at just that moment. Oh, I was impatient. I was anticipating what was to happen that night when we reached the inn but I realize now that the impatience, and even whatever desire I experienced, was a kind of abstract desire not especially for Enid but for women or any woman and as such was somehow detached from the workings of my mind. If suddenly we had been drawn together spontaneously and kissed with no holding back, with no shyness or fear, everything would have been different. But it did not happen that way, and I am afraid that in our world it seldom does save with the Blessed who have a whole and frank delight in each other with no hypocrisies and no deceits and cocoons of convention.

Ronnie was born three years after we were married and Esther arrived two years later. There was no effort to arrange this. It merely happened that way, and it happened that we never had any more children because at Esther's birth something went wrong. It could possibly have been repaired, but neither of us did anything about it or even discussed the matter. I don't know whether Enid would have liked more children and I don't know even about myself. I think that very probably in Enid's planned scheme of things two children was just about right. It made what she considered the perfect family.

As the children grew older they went to the Oakdale kindergarten and the right school and were taken to the country club to run about or splash in the swimming pool. They played with the other children in Oakdale and became accustomed at times to the spectacle of parents—their own and other children's parents, respectable model parents—who had had too many cocktails and grew rather noisy and bawdy even before it was bedtime for the children. They grew accustomed to the idea of their parents moving about only in crowds and they listened to the hogwash on the radio at certain fixed hours. Once or twice I tried reading to them at bedtime, but they were only bored and restless and, without perhaps enough perseverance, I gave up the whole thing.

By the time Ronnie was fourteen and Esther twelve (just before I went into the Army) they were perfect *average* children belonging in such a suburb as Oakdale with parents who were well-off with two cars in the garage and beginning to think about a third for the children. In the same year my mother arranged, with a good deal of political conniving, I suspect, that we were chosen as the State "Family of the Year" by the Federation of Women's Clubs. It happened at exactly the period in which for the first time I was planning the Perfect Crime.

The "award," I must say, rather startled me, first because, as I well knew, it had been maneuvered by my mother despite her dislike for Enid and her jealousy of her. I could only guess that she wangled it because it gave her ego a reflected glory. It startled me too because it seemed incredible that it had never occurred to anyone that our home life was something far from perfect and that the people around us had never suspected from an exchange of glances between Enid and me or a bitter word or phrase passing between us how false was the conception of our "perfect life" together. Could it be that people saw or understood so little? Could it be that there was among the women a kind of mutual conspiracy in which they were joined with Enid to make *all* their lives seem perfect? Could it be that there was a conspiracy of silence never broken by any of them? Or could it be that none of them expected more than we had and that marriage with most of them had become merely an endurance test involving the "quiet desperation" of which Thoreau writes? Or perhaps the fault was in myself—that I was too idealistic, that I expected more than most men had any right to expect, not only in my own personal and family life but from life in my own small world and indeed from life in general. Could it be that our lives, merely by comparison with those of the others, appeared happy and complete?

If we were the model family and our life perfect, how wretched a world must it be of which we were a part. But perhaps it was merely a matter of discernment—that the others never stopped long enough or were alone long enough to know how wretched they really were, how empty, how time-killing, how dead. What we do not know does not hurt us. Perhaps I, myself, would never have known but for the hateful glance in the mirror. Perhaps I would never have known if, each time life seemed without savor or a dull and dreary thing, I had merely taken another drink— one magic drink or two which would make things seem bright again and make me seem brilliant and entertaining to myself. Perhaps that was why there was so much drinking in Oakdale— that they could not face a single evening without the alcohol which at once blurred and made brighter their existence.

Everyone seemed pleased about the honor, and if there were any catty or vicious comments I did not hear them. Everyone congratulated us and Enid's friends kept saying, "Darling, it's wonderful! They couldn't have made a better choice!" I suspect that some of them said, "I don't see how she can put up with such a dull fellow as Wolcott Ferris" and "Now that he's cut down on his cocktails he's worse than ever." But I never heard them.

The whole thing was a good deal of a bore. There were photographers and newspaper people and pictures in the papers and with all the material Enid started a scrap book in which, she said, she meant to put "everything interesting that happened to us." After this first burst of publicity there was nothing much to put in the book but eventually the fact that I had won a commission in the Army or the society-column accounts of the meeting of the garden club at our house or the listing of our names as among those present at the New Year's dance at the country club.

These garden clubs themselves were a curious manifestation of the life in Oakdale. There were several of them in Crescent City, all carefully graded in their membership according to income and what was known as "social status." At the top on both scores stood the Green Thumb Club of Oakdale, although what the green thumb had to do with it I do not know, for not one woman in ten had any knowledge or even any contact with gardening. Most of them had no garden at all or their gardens were entirely planted and cared for by working gardeners. It appeared that they simply used the name "Garden Club" as an excuse for one more huddling and an opportunity for gossip, and some of them regarded the whole thing with a point of view colored by snobbery. I even discovered that there was nationally a "right" garden club organization and a "wrong" one. The "right" one dominated the East and New England and the "wrong" one flourished in the South and the Middle West. There were undoubtedly a few women who really loved gardening and worked at it and had an abundant knowledge about soils and plants, and these were the ones who arranged the programs and got the speakers, but when the moment came for the speaker the ladies had great difficulty in suppressing the general chitchat which the others found far more interesting than the speaker or anything she had to say. Once I was asked to talk to them regarding the growing of roses because I had done a good job at it and had the best roses in Oakdale. Enid was a leading member of the Green Thumb Club although she had no interest whatever in gardening.

My mother came to visit us during all the hubbub about the honor of being chosen the "Family of the Year" and was of course included in all the photographs as the perfect mother-in-law and grandmother, something which exasperated Enid to the point of fury so that for two days life at home was very nearly intolerable, not because of any open quarrel, but because of what was much worse—the vicious backhanded digs which they made at each other.

And all the time I was planning the Perfect Crime.

I don't know exactly how it began, but I think it came out of the daydreaming which seemed to increase the more I read. In the daydreaming I found myself thinking what life would be like if Enid were suddenly killed in an accident or died of some chronic complaint. Reading had fertilized my imagination, and in periods of daydreaming I even lived through the whole thing.

Someone would call the office asking me to come at once to the hospital, giving me the news that my wife had suffered a bad accident. And I would experience a sudden mixture of emotions involving annoyance and some slight concern plus a secret repressed hope that it might be fatal. And then I would go to the hospital and find that she had been struck by a speeding car and had died in the ambulance and they had not told me the whole truth in order to soften the blow. I would pretend to be overcome and to be taking it very well and people would say how splendid I was, never breaking down. They would say, "It would be better if he gave way. It will be all the harder for him later on," and all the time the heart inside me would be like a stone except for the small flicker of a flame, a flame which, if it could speak, would say, "Now we are free! ... Ronnie and Esther and I. Now when the funeral is over we can go away and take the dog with us. We'll stay away a long time and then sell the house and get out of Oakdale for good. We'll go off to Florida or buy a ranch. We'll start out again some place where nobody will be watching you from the window of the next house, where there is air and space and there won't be a dance every Saturday night at the country club where everybody goes and gets drunk because there isn't anything else to do."

I thought that somewhere, away from Oakdale, the children might have a chance to be something more, to be perhaps like

Frank Saunders' family and the people I had seen there on the one occasion I had ever strayed away from the reservation.

In all that daydreaming, I know now, it was not only Enid from whom we escaped; it was also Oakdale, because the two were inextricably associated and mixed together. Once or twice when I had mentioned the possibility of moving away from Oakdale and indeed Crescent City itself, Enid had looked at me in astonishment.

"What's the matter with Oakdale and Crescent City?" she had said. "They're about as nice communities as it would be possible to find anywhere in the world. Where else could you find so many nice people all leading nice happy lives? Why should we want to go somewhere and have to make friends all over again? The children have roots here. So have both of us. The children couldn't have a better future than in a place like this. Sometimes I think you must be crazy. Certainly you get the craziest ideas of any person I've ever known. What is it you want? What's the matter with Oakdale? Most of the human race would be only too delighted to be as well off as we are and live in as fine a place as this."

"But the children," I had started to say once or twice. "There's so much more for them in life than . . ."

But I seldom got farther than that. She simply dismissed the subject with a snort, adding, "I don't know what you're talking about," which was true, God knows, and in all honesty I cannot say that I knew myself what it was I wanted except that it would be better and at least different.

In the daydreaming my mother would come on for the funeral and we would both go through the mockery of grief and she would take care of all the funeral arrangements, something which she liked to do and at which she excelled, and there would be a big funeral, and maybe when I returned from the cemetery and was seated opposite her with the children at supper, our eyes would meet and there would be a single glance in which everything would be said, but even then she would be saying one thing and I would be saying another.

And beyond the funeral there were the days and weeks that followed when, in the daydream, the children and I packed up and went away looking for the place I had in mind. It was a vague place, but there was sunlight and there was the sea and the children ran around dressed in rough clothing and sometimes we went fishing and at night we came back to a house that was little more than a shack where inside things were comfortable and untidy with a big fire burning that was not lighted by a jet of gas which sometimes burned on and on while the bought, neatly cut logs refused to take fire. And the ashes would be allowed to sift out onto the floor instead of always being swept up neatly every half hour or so. And the logs would be driftwood and you could put your cigarette ashes anywhere at all. And Sandy, the setter, would sleep comfortably on the best chair. And we'd cook our own supper and wash up the dishes afterward and cook on a real fire instead of the electric rings of a shining enameled white stove. And presently the kids would go to bed because the day had tired them out and they *wanted* to go to sleep and not because they had to be sent away at a fixed hour whining for the last trashy radio serial.

But most of all Enid would not be there at all and the telephone wouldn't ring and a neighbor's voice say, "What are you doing? Come on over and play some bridge," or "Let's go out to the club for a few drinks." And in the daydreaming there were always a lot of vague people about, as faceless as the dream was vague and confused. They were salty characters and knew about fishing and trapping and hunting and woke every morning with excitement in their blood because it was a new day. And we'd raise our own food and have some animals like cows and pigs around and faceless people would come to stay with us out of another world, people who could really *talk* and had ideas and even the children would listen to them fascinated.

And always in the daydreaming there would come that day when somewhere, perhaps on the beach among the dunes, I would come across a woman and we would speak to each other and then I'd discover that she lived somewhere near by and I'd go to help her repair something or other and presently we'd become friends and then more than friends so that I couldn't sleep for thinking of her, not only because she was desirable, but because we understood each other in a thousand small ways, so that we conversed without the need of talk, and when at last I took her in my arms a kind of flame would envelop us so that there were no longer two beings, separated and querulous, but only one. And afterward we would run into the sea together laughing and . . . and . . . we would be . . . I would search for the word, but the only word I could find was "happy" and that was not adequate. No word, I think, is adequate for the thing of which I dreamed. Those who have attained it, those few, know that there is no word.

All this, of course, began as daydreaming with the supposed accident in the street, and then week after week and month after month the daydream presently passed into something else. In moments of reality I knew that I was approaching forty, that I was old enough by this time to have sense (which I still do not have) but that I was still young enough to make a warm and satisfactory husband or lover. The dream was all very well, but I couldn't delay forever waiting for Enid to be hit by an automobile while I grew older and more cynical and despairing. And one morning the idea came to me that I might hurry things up by actually bringing about the "accident" myself before it was too late.

At first I thought of the whole thing in terms of an accident and worked out ways in which we might have an "accident" in which Enid was killed and I survived. There were mountains not far from Crescent City with roads cut into the steeper sides of the hills. The car might go over or I might be standing outside the car when mysteriously it started moving and plunged over the side with Enid in it. Or I might shove her off the peak at Lookout Point. Oh, I thought of a hundred "accidents," but always there was something wrong with them. She might not be killed and would live and "know," or I might be killed with her or be maimed so that the daydream could never be realized.

So in the end I thought of poison and I went further into all sorts of complicated plans, but always there seemed to be something wrong with them. This or that might go wrong and I would be found out. One after another I rejected the plans until I came to the one that concerned the sleeping pills. This seemed to me to be the perfect crime.

Enid sometimes took capsules of stuff to make her sleep. I do not know what they were, but the mere fact of her taking them indicated that she too was unhappy, perhaps in her heart as wretched as I was, although she would never admit it, least of all to herself. She would push the thought away from her and blame other things for her sleeplessness and her "nerves." She was the kind of woman who was "determined to make a go of it" and by now the whole performance had become so dominant that she herself had *become* the character she was forever acting. She had imprisoned herself in a net from which she could not escape. She was caught in a web of illusion and self-deception and dishonesty from which she could not free herself.

You might ask, "Why did you not get a divorce? Why didn't you just run away and never come back?" But if you have ever been in such a situation you would know that it is not as simple as that. Many people have been in such a situation and they will understand. For everyone who has run away there are a hundred who stayed behind and stuck it out until at last, through drinking or mere calloused dullness or simply age and weariness, it did not matter any longer. It was not merely that I was tired of Enid and that whatever pleasure there had been in our marriage was done with. . . . That often happens to married people and they find ways of going their own ways while still remaining together and manage to lead fairly civilized and decent lives as individuals. That kind of thing could never happen with Enid or many female monsters like her.

Enid would never give me a divorce and there could be no possible grounds on which I could divorce her since, if the matter ever came into court, she would merely appear there as the perfect wife and mother who lived *only* for husband and children.

There was no possibility whatever of her falling in love with another man and wanting her freedom to marry him. All that was *outside* the picture of Oakdale and the picture she had created. I might have beat and kicked her save that the means was not in my nature and to attempt it halfheartedly would only have ended in deeper and more dismal confusion and failure. I might have said more cruel things than I did say many times and have killed her "love," but the catch there was that she had and has no love to kill. It is something else that held her to me . . . and if I ever return it will still hold her to me to the very end when it will become a bitter contest between us to see who dies first.

And there were the children. Sometimes they seemed very remote to me, as if they were strangers, and sometimes they were very close and I was sorry for them and afraid. I suppose it will be all right if they never "know," if they just go on being like the others in Oakdale. They will never be happy or unhappy. They will never know any depths or any heights. And presently as they grow up and marry . . . There is always a chance that something may happen to awaken them and there is always a chance that as they grow old enough to understand what I am talking about I might be able to get through to them and make things different and teach them the difference between automobiles and civilization, between plumbing and life, between perverse prudery and morality—so that they can live.

Here in the jungle I realize that up to now I have failed them completely, for I have never tried to save them from the *numbness* that will engulf them and has already begun to do so. I have given them as yet nothing to live by, no dreams, no values, no reality. They are moving about in a world of unreality, like tropical fish in an aquarium from which they cannot escape, with the water a proper temperature, fed every morning the right amount and kind of fish food, with the proper amount of air bubbling through the tepid water to keep it well aerated. And there is a little porcelain castle in the tank which might be labeled the Country Club in which the fish congregate, their mouths opening and closing without end and without meaning. I would like to free them from the aquarium but I don't know how, and even if I found the way Enid would thrust them quickly back again if it were possible.

I could have run away and made a clean getaway but I wasn't that kind of man. I was not strong enough or reckless enough or selfish enough or whatever you might call it, and in that I am like a million other husbands and fathers. I am no Gauguin, nor are most of the men I know, and the women are not female Gauguins. If I had been, everything would have been changed from the very beginning. I am, as you might say, "Mr. Smith" or "Mr. Jones." The only difference is that I happened to look in a mirror one morning while shaving and saw myself.

But to get back to the Perfect Crime. I worked it out in every possible detail. I would go to New York and buy poison, perhaps arsenic or strychnine, in a drug store in the heart of the city on the pretext that I needed it to kill rats, and I would never go into that neighborhood again as long as I lived so that no one could possibly remember me. And when I came home I would fill some of the capsules with the poison and make small scratches on the ones I had filled so that I could identify them later. Then I would burn the paper in which the poison came and then one night she would wake up in pain and by morning she would be dead. Probably the doctors would diagnose the illness as some sudden chronic organic failure, or if they had an autopsy and discovered the poison, the discovery would lead nowhere. There would be no trace. I would be shaken and bewildered and overcome with grief. If there was an investigation the little capsules with the scratches on them would not be found because they had been removed and destroyed. Only the genuine capsules would be left in the little box. The death would be a complete and fathomless mystery. After all, were we not a model husband and wife? Was not our family the perfect example of a happy middle-class home? Were we not the "Family of the Year"? There could be no motive. Even if the children were questioned, they could not say that they had even seen a real quarrel between their parents. They had never seen me strike her. Enid did not believe in quarrels. As she put it, "My mother always told me never to let the sun go down on a quarrel with your husband."

If we ever had a disagreement or I spoke to her sarcastically, she would come up behind my chair in the evening, put her arms about my neck, and say, "It's all right, darling. I forgive you." It was in such moments that I came nearest to translating my plot into reality. It was in such moments that I did not even consider the agonies of poisoning by strychnine.

But I never did and I never would act. Despite the fact that in all the daydreaming I never felt the least remorse over having killed her a hundred times, the act in reality was something else again. Plenty of other husbands and plenty of wives have undoubtedly plotted as I plotted, but the number of those who have ever acted is one in a hundred thousand. But there are the few who *have* acted. Some have been discovered but some have not been. There is a line between the daydreaming and the act, the business of quietly putting out of existence another human being. There is a line which, no matter how many have considered it, few have crossed. Those who have killed and been discovered have usually done so carelessly and recklessly, in passion or when they reached that point where things became beyond endurance and temporarily the killer became mad.

The puzzling thing is why people find themselves caught in such a web and why they do not tear it apart and escape. I cannot tell you why I did not smash everything and run off except that it was not only Enid who was unendurable. It was the whole of my life from the moment I rose in the morning and went to the office until at last, almost painfully, I fell asleep. In a sense I, with my weakness, was actually a *part* of the very web which imprisoned me. And so are many of us who are merely killing time until we die.

The odd thing was that I had only worked out the complete details of the Perfect Crime at the very moment that we were chosen as the "Family of the Year" and my mother descended upon us along with the photographers and the newspaperwomen. It seemed to knock the idea out of my head for the moment, and after that came the business of Mary Raeburn and in the end the chance of escape for a time at least into the Army. That was an easy way out and a conventional one in which I would betray nothing but merely seem to have volunteered for the good of my country. And so at last I have ended up in the desolate extravagant empty beauty of this island, alone but for four men in whom I have little interest and almost nothing in common, save that all of us are men.

VIII The Jungle

Tonight it was the wool-hat who interrupted my thoughts and writing. It was the first time he had ever come to my hut and until now our relations had been what you might call formal—a casual greeting in passing and nothing else. Even then the greeting on his side was sullen, as if somehow in the past I had injured him in some way and the act had filled him with resentment. I never questioned him about the sullenness but put it down merely to his hatred of anything that was a little above him or a little different from the world with which he was familiar.

Tonight he came in, saluted, took off his hat, and stood in the doorway.

Looking up I said, "Yes, Homer." (It seemed silly to address the men as "Private." Only the Sergeant did I ever address by his title, and his bearing and professionalism demanded it.)

"Can I speak to you, mister?"

"Certainly. Sit down."

He sat down on the edge of my Army cot and for a moment, remembering the yaws and the native women he frequented in spite of all controls, I felt a sudden tinge of squeamishness.

He did not speak and I said, "What is it?"

He twisted his hat for a moment. "It's about the Sergeant," he said. "He's always pickin' on me."

"How?" I asked.

He twisted his hat some more as if all conversation except when he was talking about "nigger hunts" and life back home was difficult or impossible.

He said, "Well, I get the blame for everything. Now he comes and tells me I musta been stealin' stuff out of the hut."

"I talked to him last night and he says he doesn't believe you took the stuff." I started to tell him the Sergeant's theory about the Japs and thought better of it. Probably the Sergeant hadn't told him, and if I even hinted there might be Japs in the bushes, he wouldn't be any good at all as a guard. He'd just hide away.

"Well, I know he does," said Homer stubbornly. "Even if a storm blows down the radio antenny, he says it's my fault." A look almost of anguish but with a touch too of murderous vengeance came into his face. "And he's always hittin' me."

"Does he ever really beat you up?"

Homer considered for a moment. "Well . . . I guess no . . . but he's always punching me in the muscles and afterward it's sore." He put one hand up to the muscles of his shoulders and rubbed the spot tentatively. "Sometimes it ain't good for a man's dignity."

I wondered where he had come across the word "dignity" and passed over it.

"I'll speak to the Sergeant about it," I said. And then unaccountably I felt a wave of sympathy for him. I said, "How'd you like a drink of real liquor?"

His face brightened. "I'd like it, mister. I ain't used to all this beer. I can drink it and drink it and I only bloat up and feel worse. All I get out of it is a lot of wind. Sometimes I feel like I'd cut off my right leg for one swig of good corn likker."

I got up and poured him a drink out of the bottle of Scotch. He tossed it off in a single gulp without a grimace or a cough. I suppose that after his long experience with the corn likker, mere Scotch seemed like soothing syrup.

"How are things getting on otherwise?" I asked.

[133]

"I want to get out of here and get home. I ain't got anybody to talk to here. I ain't used to bein' in places where niggers and kikes and Catholics is treated better than other folks. Seems like I cain't find anybody to talk to." He looked down at his hat again. "And that goddamn Sergeant. *Him* pickin' on *me*. If it was back home he'd get run right outa town like we do down there with all them papists and union organizers."

"Do you go to church?" I asked.

He looked at me. "You mean when I'm home?"

"Yes."

He nodded.

"What church?"

"The only church they is—primitive Baptists."

There was a look of oppressive bewilderment on the lean face with its freckles and big splay mouth.

"I wanta go home," he repeated, "where a fella can be somebody. I git tired of always bein' treated no better'n a houn' dog."

It occurred to me that any attempts at conversation weren't going to get anywhere. I thought, "Maybe if he gets a little drunk he'll go to sleep and dream he's back home again and it'll make him happy for a little time." I said, "What about another drink?" and then cautiously added, "This is kind of a special occasion—the first time you've ever paid me a visit."

"Sure," he said. "It makes me feel good."

So I gave him another shot of Scotch. He downed it and shook his head. "That Al," he said. "He's teacher's pet. They ain't nothin' too good for him. You know what he says the other night. He says, 'Niggers is just as good as anybody else.' He ain't had to live around niggers. Never saw one till he was twelve years old. Seems they don't have 'em up in his part of the country." The whisky appeared to have reached home and he became almost talkative. "And now you know what, mister? The Sergeant has asked that kid Al to move his sleepin' cot right into his own office."

"It doesn't make much difference, does it? Sergeant's quarters aren't any different from the rest of you fellows. They aren't much different from this." I gestured to include my own room which certainly wasn't much of a place. "I suppose the Sergeant wanted company."

"It's just favoritism, that's what it is."

"What did Meyer think about it?"

Homer spat on the floor. Maybe it was the whisky that set him back to primitive habits. "How do I know what that sonofabitch kike thinks about anything? He don't talk. It's like I ain't good enough to speak to."

"He doesn't talk much to anybody."

"Well, he ain't said anything . . . but it don't look right."

He picked up his glass as if to hint for another drink but I didn't respond. I'd never seen Homer drunk. As he said, beer didn't seem to have any effect on him. Like all the boys he could drink can after can of beer and just sweat it out, but whisky was different. Drunk, you probably couldn't tell what he'd do. Then something occurred to me and I asked, "Who's on night guard duty?"

"Me," he said.

"What time do you go on?"

"Oh, any time now."

I stood up and said, "Well, any time you have a complaint, Homer, feel free to come in and talk to me. I don't think it's very serious about the Sergeant taking Al in with him. Maybe it's a good idea."

He took the hint and stood up and at the same time he gave me a curious look. I can only describe it by saying that the pale blue eyes looked suddenly like the eyes of a turtle. It was a cold dead look but venomous. I think it was the first time he had ever really looked me in the eyes. He said, "Mebbe . . . only if that sonofabitch don't keep his hands off me I might use a gun on him."

At that I stiffened a little. "I don't want any of that kind of talk, Homer, out of you or any of the boys. If you get fresh with a gun you might end up in jail for the rest of your life."

He looked away sullenly. "It wouldn't be a hell of a lot different from bein' here. I might find somebody I could talk to in jail."

I held open the door for him. "Get such ideas out of your head. You'd better go now and get ready to go on duty before you get into trouble again. I'll speak to the Sergeant tomorrow but I guess it's not all one-sided. You can do your part too. Keep your quarters in order and be on time and don't answer back. Good night. Feel free to complain."

I gave him a pat on the back but in return I did not even get so much as a "Good night." He merely walked off toward the huts that stood in a dark row against the thick wall of the jungle.

As soon as he had gone I knew I had done the wrong thing. I shouldn't have offered him the drinks even out here in this damned choked dripping wilderness where the five of us had to get on together or at least to be as friendly as possible. I hadn't made things any better. I hadn't softened him. I hadn't roused any feeling of co-operation or any sense of friendliness. He had taken the drinks and merely decided that I was a damned fool. He hated me because I didn't feel as he did about Negroes and Catholics and Jews. He probably thought that because I wasn't a primitive Baptist I was just as bad as the others. What did you do about somebody like that? What could you do to help him?

I believed now what the Sergeant said—that Homer's only idea was to get out of a task, to put something over on you. If he succeeded he felt good all over, and if you caught him out at it he hated you with a resentment that grew more and more cancerous. If you tried to treat him decently and give him a break he merely thought you were a damned fool.

For a long time I sat thinking about him, unable to get back to my writing. He was, I suppose, the "underprivileged," and nature had made no provision for his redemption. Possibly far back, a dozen or fifteen generations ago, an ancestor or two had been convicts shipped out to Georgia as exiles, and presently other ancestors had taken to the hill country to live in miserable poverty with their only pleasures, fornicating, corn likker, shoutin' and rollin' and an occasional "nigger hunt." They never owned any slaves. They just hated the Negro, perhaps because somehow, in spite of a poverty and ignorance as abject as their own, the Negro had a better life—because he ate better and had more fun out of the whole sorry thing. There wasn't any reason for Homer's folks to think themselves better than their Negro neighbors, except a fancied reason that had no logic in it—that their skins were white instead of black, and that was only an accident. I wondered how many of them there were like Homer, whether all the community in which he lived back there was a community merely of Homers.

He was "underprivileged" all right, but what did you do about him and all his kind? I doubted that anything could be done about Homer, and I doubted that anything could be done about his wretched offspring unless they were taken away from Homer and his folks altogether. What did you do about someone who could not be brought out of his own particular wilderness into the world, because the world instinctively looked upon him with loathing and contempt? How else could you look on somebody like Homer?

It occurred to me that it was the tendency of our times to label and pigeonhole everything, people most of all. Perhaps it was a mixture of sentimentality and of the bureaucratic mind which likes to have its statistics straight and everything adding up to two times two. But "underprivileged" was a silly convenient term for the sloppy thinkers and the demagogic politicians. If they meant the simple or the humble as Christ used those words, they had some meaning, for humbleness and simplicity are virtues and not economic labels. Homer certainly fitted neither the category of the humble nor the simple. There must certainly be some good in every man, but neither the Sergeant nor myself had ever been able to find any good in Homer, try as we would from the beginning. He wasn't the only such specimen I had encountered in the Army, but he was probably the worst. He was the sort the reformers proposed to "level up" while they leveled down the intelligent, the able, the virtuous to his level, all, of course, in terms of economics.

"Well," I thought, "let them try to level Homer upward. All

he wants is his gun, a houn' dog, some corn likker, fornication, and an occasional 'nigger hunt.' Let them give him the vote to be exercised for the first cheap politician who comes along and talks down to his level of lynchings and ignorance and insane religion and prejudice. Let them try to level up Homer . . . and see how far they get."

Homer didn't want to be leveled unless it was in terms of cash given to him without the demand for anything in return. He just wanted to be let alone. How did you expect to get anything out of the dark, inbred, suppressed ancestry which had produced him. Sure, he'd be great in a mob, great in a revolution, for he'd be free to express the only talent he had—for bullying and tearing down and destroying everything, for murdering and torturing and burning anybody who was a little more intelligent or a grain kindlier or more human than himself. Underprivileged, hell!

I went back to writing, and presently the distant racket of the Sergeant's radio was shut off and there were only the sounds of the night and the jungle which had an extraordinary variety and often resembled human sounds although you knew there was no one there. It was as if spirits returned to haunt the night. It showered now and then, and presently I no longer heard even the sounds of the jungle and felt sleepy, and as I was undressing slowly, the noisy wet stillness was shattered by a shot and then another and another in rapid succession until several had been fired.

I thought first of the Sergeant's theory of the stray Japs and pulled on my pants and picked up my service revolver and an electric torch. The sound came from the direction of the huts and I made my way through the darkness toward them. There was a light on in the Sergeant's quarters, and in the luminous darkness outside I presently came upon his heavy figure, highly visible because he was clad only in white shorts and singlet. He carried an electric torch, flashing it spasmodically so as not to provide a fixed aim for any attacker. Quickly I caught up with him, calling out my name so that I might not get a pot shot in my belly during the excitement.

"It's over here, I think!" he said.

Then abruptly we came upon Homer in the darkness. He was standing flattened out against the side of one of the Quonset huts.

"What's up?" asked the Sergeant, and Homer said, "It's them Japs. I seen 'em!"

"What Japs?" asked the Sergeant.

"Them Japs that's been stealin' the cans." Then from the sounds I knew Homer was vomiting. Maybe it was the unaccustomed whisky I had given him and maybe it was because he was plain scared.

"Let's get out of here," said Homer and turned on his electric torch. The Sergeant grabbed it from him and said, "You damned fool! D'you want to get us all potted?" Then I said, "Better get under cover some place until we can find out what happened."

I led the way back through the darkness to the Sergeant's office. If it was only two or three Japs they were possibly unarmed and probably wouldn't try to harm us unless we came on them suddenly. If there were any Japs at all they simply wanted to keep out of our way and scrounge what food they could find even out of the garbage pit.

Once inside the hut we hung jackets over the two windows. Homer was still retching and his freckled face was a gray-green color. The Sergeant in his underwear looked like the bottom man of a strong-act team. In a corner Al, the farm boy, was pulling clothes onto his husky frame, with a curious dazed look on his face as if he were not yet quite awake. For the sake of space the two cots occupied by the Sergeant and Al had been pushed near to each other and were covered by a single canopy of mosquito netting.

The Sergeant said to Homer, "Now give us a line on what happened. Pull yourself together and talk."

"What about Meyer?" I asked and the Sergeant turned to Al. "Better go and bring him in here too. It looks like we've got trouble on our hands."

With a certain amount of absurdity Al pulled a comb through his tousled curly hair and then started off for the other hut. At the same time Homer said, "I was patrollin' the huts and all at once when I come round the corner of the hut that was broke into I run onto a Jap, almost fell over him."

"How'd you know he was a Jap? It might have been one of them fuzzy-wuzzies."

Homer seemed to have lost some of his fear and the color began to come back into his face. "I turned my flashlight on him just as he was gittin' away into the brush. I seen he was a Jap."

"But how?" persisted the Sergeant.

"I know the little sonsofbitches," said Homer. "I seen lots of 'em at Maloyka when they brung 'em as prisoners—short bow-legged yellow bastards. They ain't the same color and they ain't built the same as the fuzzy-wuzzies. They got short thick legs and the fuzzy-wuzzies is long and skinny."

The Sergeant looked at me. "Well, what are we gonna do?" But before I could answer him he turned again to Homer. "When you shot did you hit him?"

"I kinda think I did," said Homer. "Just as he hit the brush he let out a yell and jumped into the air. It was just like hittin' a rabbit."

Then Al returned bringing Meyer with him. The dark little fellow hadn't even wakened up and he said nothing now. He just came in and stood there watching us with his great dark beautiful eyes. It was a funny assembly.

The Sergeant turned to Homer. "You'd better go back out there and go on watching. There ain't any use in letting 'em come up and plump grenades in the window."

At first Homer didn't answer, but the lower lip of the big loose mouth was thrust out suddenly. Then he said, "I ain't agoin' outside just to be a pot shot for no goddamn Jap."

The Sergeant moved instinctively toward him to give him a good going-over. I said, "Wait a minute. Better all three of you go out—you and Al and Meyer. You can make up sleep tomorrow. The Sergeant and I will have to work out some strategy." I turned to the two others. "Go ahead, boys. Keep your eyes open. Don't get between the bushes and the sky and don't use your torches unless you want to get a shot . . . and don't shoot each other."

"It's only fair," said Homer.

Al and Meyer were both awake now and you could see that both of them kind of liked the excitement, what with nothing going on for so long. Al picked up his Tommy gun and slung it on. Then the three of them went out.

When they had gone the Sergeant turned and said, "What d'you think of that damned wool-hat sonofabitch?"

I grinned. "What did you expect?"

"Not very damned much."

"Maybe there was only one Jap and maybe Homer hit him."

"It ain't likely either way," said the Sergeant. "What are we gonna do now?"

He sat down on a packing case, and I said, "I guess we'll just have to keep our eyes open and work out some plan of doubled guard duty."

"With only three of them," he said, "it ain't goin' to be easy. I'll take over myself for three or four nights anyway. We sure can't run the Japs outa that jungle. A whole division couldn't do it."

Then we were silent for a time and a brilliant idea came to me. "Tell you what we could do, Sergeant. We could feed them."

"What d'you mean . . . feed 'em?"

"We could leave out some food every night for them to come and get."

He looked at me with astonishment. "That wouldn't be Army regulations—feedin' the enemy. No, that wouldn't be accordin' to regulations."

I grinned. "What the hell? Which do you prefer—feeding them or letting them blow us all up and kill us off one by one like sitting ducks. We could put out so many cans of stuff every night where they'd find it. Just let 'em come and get it. Maybe they haven't got any guns. If they swam over here the chances are they're unarmed. But maybe they have. And a starving man is likely to kill anybody. Feed 'em and probably they'll let us alone."

"Unless they're nuts like a lot of 'em are. You know . . . what they call fanatic . . . them Banzai charges."

"That could be."

"And what about the reports and if they come to check up on the stores?"

"Nobody's going to check up. They've damned near forgotten us already, and if they do come to get us the order will be to destroy all the supplies. We might just as well buy protection for ourselves."

The Sergeant scratched his bristly head. "Somehow it don't seem right—givin' aid and comfort to the enemy."

"Well," I said, "that's what we're going to do. I haven't got any intention of getting myself or any of you guys killed just because it's against Army regulations to feed a few godforsaken starving Japs. We'll just see how it works anyway. Maybe they'll even come in and surrender and then they can do the washing and kitchen police."

At this the troubled look went off the Sergeant's big red face. He even grinned. "You've got something there. Could be."

"Tell you what," I said. "Tomorrow have the boys rake the sand all smooth for about ten feet out from the huts and tell them to keep off it. Then if we get any footprints we'll know whether they're Japs or not. Maybe they're just fuzzy-wuzzies."

The idea appealed to his detective-story tastes. "That's great," he said. "That's great! Robinson Crusoe."

I turned to the door. "I'll go out and make the rounds now and then go to bed. Better keep an eye on the boys till morning and in a couple of nights I think we can get back to the one-man guard. And tomorrow before dark put out a half-dozen cans of feed . . . make it an assortment, you know—beans, corn, and soup. The more tasty you make it, the more they'll let us alone."

He was all for the idea now and grinning about it. "Better put out a can opener too. The poor bastards probably have to smash the cans to get 'em open."

I started for the door and the Sergeant said, "Jeez. You ought to be a general."

"No," I said. "Diplomat is the word."

Outside it was raining again. I found the three soldiers together. Everything seemed to be quiet and I said to Homer, "I want to speak to you for a minute. You other fellows go along with your patrol."

The other two went off leaving Homer standing there. I could not see him in the thick darkness but I knew how he looked, the lower lip thrust out, the narrow face sullen and pinched.

"You know what you did, Homer?"

"No, what?"

"You refused to obey orders and you know what the penalty is. You could be sent up for years or you might even be shot."

"To hell with that!" he said suddenly and with equal suddenness I lost my temper. "So that's what you think," I said. "Now I'm going to tell *you* something. If I wanted to I could shut you up right now and put you on bread and water and keep you there till somebody came along and picked you up and took you back for trial. You're no damned good and you never have been any good to anybody any place. You make trouble. You won't work. You're a coward and a bully. In fact you're about the worst sonofabitch I've ever known. Have you got anything to say for yourself?"

"I ain't gonna get killed savin' the rest of you. That's what you'd all like—to get me killed and out of the way. I'm always gettin' the dirty work shoved off on me."

I could see it wasn't any good going on in that vein. It didn't make any impression. I said, "I'm not going to put you under arrest and I'm not going to send in any report. Now it's up to you to behave yourself. I don't want any more trouble. Okay?"

Out of the darkness came the answer—"Okay"—but it was an answer heavy with hate and resentment.

I waited till the watch came round again and Homer joined them, and then went back toward my own hut. On the way I passed the Sergeant dressed now, bustling, and on the job.

I said, "Everything seems to be quiet. I think it'll be all right now . . . especially if Homer did get that Jap."

"He never did," said the Sergeant. "The truth ain't in him. If he gets scared he'll just blast away at anything. I'm more scared of bein' shot by him than I am of the Japs. Go on to bed, Captain. I'll keep on the job."

Back in the hut I put out the light and undressed but I didn't sleep. I kept thinking how easy it would be for a Jap to pitch a grenade in the window. But it wasn't really that which kept me awake. I kept thinking of other things . . . what a silly situation this was—five of us sitting out here guarding a lot of food that nobody was ever going to use. And all around us were the half-starved natives full of lice and disease living in a jungle so rich and dense that you couldn't get through it without hacking your way. And it grew right up again behind as you went through. And crawling around in that jungle were Japs, maybe one, maybe two, maybe a dozen starving to death in the midst of all that rich rank vegetation and maybe plotting to clean us all out, poor ignorant little bastards fighting to hang onto a life which was hardly worth hanging onto. What were we all doing here? What the hell was it all about?

At last I got up and hung a canvas over the door and a coat over the window and went about writing down all this, and suddenly it came over me that in essence and spirit the life here wasn't much different from the life back in Oakdale. In both places I had been marking time . . . until I began to write all this. Probably nobody will read it. Probably in my heart I never meant it to be read by anybody, but whatever happens I am beginning to feel that I am really doing something for the first time in my life, really doing something in which my mind works and I can take satisfaction.

Note: There are more Japs around. In the morning the cans of food were gone and on the clean-swept sands there were naked footprints. They were not the prints of the long splay feet of the fuzzy-wuzzies. They were those of unmistakably Jap feet, short, thick, and flat and smaller than any of ours. The poor devils must really be starving to risk being shot at. Again my only fear is that trigger-happy Homer will shoot one of them or even one of us.

IX Oakdale

THE LAST NIGHT OR TWO I HAVE BEEN READING OVER WHAT I have written up to now and I felt a sudden profound wave of discouragement and failure. I have been trying to set down everything and I have failed. It all seems curiously unsatisfactory for it seems to give the picture of a sullen, unpopular, morose introvert, yet that is only a part of the *whole* picture. There was another side, almost wholly contradictory, as if I were two persons. The Greeks had a saying that every man is three persons— the person people thought he was, the person he thought he was, and the person he really was. It seems to me that up to now I have been writing only about the person I think I am and paying no attention to the person other people think I am. And I am aware that somewhere along the line there must be a great difference, else the story would not be so complex and difficult. The person I really am no one can describe except God, but certainly it must be a very confused, changeable, and unstable creature ... which indeed is probably true of all of us.

Tonight I decided to attempt seeing myself as I must appear to others, not only to the friends and the acquaintances back in Oakdale, but to strangers I might meet on the street or on a train. When I attempt it I begin to understand that a great many of my troubles come from a divided personality, that even many of the misconceptions shared by our friends concerning Enid and me and our life together arise from that fact. People have *not* seen the truth, not because they were unperceptive, but because it was only possible to judge from appearances.

I wonder how many men and women suffer from the same division of personality and the same outward deception. Perhaps in my own way I have been as great a fraud as Enid. It occurs to me that she is able to judge only from my outside personality because she has never been allowed to see or to share what might be called the inside personality which I seem to have been writing about.

Let's pretend that you met me in the club car on a streamlined train. You would think me at once to be a prosperous, conservative, contented businessman on the verge of middle age. What you would see would be a fairly good-looking fellow with a little gray in his hair and a few lines on his face, with a healthy skin, smooth-shaven with well-kept, rather beautiful hands—neither the hands of a working man nor the long thin hand of the nervous, oversensitive type. You would see a man with a youthful figure, thickening only a little around the middle, dressed in a conservative plain or pin-striped blue suit. You would see a man who did not wear hand-painted ties or any of the vulgar imitations of them but a plain blue or maroon tie or one of foulard with tiny figures on it. There would be an expensive wrist watch and a clean good handkerchief tucked negligently into the breast pocket. Very likely you would say, "There is a successful and happy fellow, well adjusted, looking probably younger than his years—a fellow who has been to one of the better colleges and already is on boards of directors and interested in the good of his community."

You might make some remark about the train being late or how badly things were going in Washington, and presently there would be a conversation punctuated by a drink or two and one or two stories, not the dirty bathroom jokes of the traveling salesman in the smoking room, but funny stories, a little strong but with a point. And presently the talk might turn to families and education and children, and the fellow (me) would tell you about his own family. It would come out that he was happily married and that his wife was very active in public affairs without neglecting her household, that his two children (a boy and a girl) were healthy and went to excellent schools. You would find out that the fellow lived in a nice suburb called

Oakdale, and had a very prosperous insurance business which he hoped his boy would take over a little later so that he could ease off a bit and enjoy himself more. You would discover that the fellow played golf in the eighties and raised roses for a hobby. (That might be the only weak, betraying spot.) But when at last the train arrived or one of you went to bed, you parted thinking you had met a very fortunate and prosperous fellow. You had exchanged addresses and promised to let each other know if either of you ever visited the home town of the other. You might even, in your pleasure at making a new friend, think, "There's a sample of what America can produce. That's what you might call the average middle-class American. No country produces a finer product."

Or at home in Oakdale you would find that the man known as Wolcott Ferris living at 818 Bosquet Road was one of the finest fellows you had ever met. He played a good game of golf. He could drink with the best. He had plenty of brains and was a good businessman. He had one of the soundest wives in the community, good-looking and a good dresser and a good housekeeper who was active in the P.T.A., the League of Woman Voters, the Red Cross, and other social activities. He was a fellow who was generous with his contributions and knew how to have a good time when away with the boys at a convention—nothing priggish about him. And he "had class"—that meaning the neat well-cut clothes, the conservative ties, and the college education. Lately he had become perhaps a little less convivial, drinking less, going to the club less frequently, and sometimes absenting himself from the usual businessmen's lunches on the excuse of overwork. But there was nothing unusual about that. Anybody growing older was likely to slow down a little. A smart businessman too!

That I imagine is as I must seem to others, both strangers and friends. I am not sure how much the division of personality is my own doing and how much of it is the result of the pressures of early background and the kind of world and community in which I live. Certainly the division is a sharp one, painful at times and not in any sense healthy. It is the kind of thing which could lead to outright schizophrenia.

What satisfaction must be found in being a complete extrovert, in bellowing and shouting and showing off, in playing the fool, with never a thought of any depth, never a thought which could bite and sear until at last the tissue built up by fearful and cowardly men to conceal truth is burned or cut away and truth lies naked, blinding and sometimes bitter but beautiful. Only the strong can survive such a spectacle. Only the strong can understand truth and perhaps, armed with it, defend himself against the society in which he is forced to live and even to strike back with blows which, accumulated, may some day liberate all men, strong and weak alike.

Some extroverts, like the Sergeant, are simply born that way, with a set of glands operating furiously so that a kind of fierce physical activity leaves no time save for sleep which recharges the glands so that in the morning light they begin to operate furiously all over again. These are driven men and women, perhaps superficially happier than others but perpetually ignorant of any subtle or profound satisfaction. They are the clowns, the boisterous, whose emptiness echoes and re-echoes with a booming sound through a hollow cavern. And they contribute nothing. They bring nothing into the world. And they take nothing from it in experience. They are, I suppose, happy. They can suffer, but it is only a physical suffering like that of the Sergeant deprived for a long period not of the love of one woman but of the mechanical sensual satisfaction of women—who become in time a kind of mechanical apparatus like that used in the artificial insemination of cattle.

And there are others, extroverts of a different sort, who become so out of fear and cowardice, who will not be alone out of terror of the thoughts that constantly creep up behind them and threaten them—the ones who spend all their lives in turning away, in deceiving themselves. What happens to them in the still of the night when they waken and are alone? What happens must be horrible, so horrible that they remain incapable of ever revealing the experience.

It seems to me that the sickness of our society is that it has become a society either of stupid or of contrived and cowardly extrovert individuals who frequent the clubs, the pool parlors, the whorehouses, the night clubs, or the bars out of sheer terror. They give themselves over to talking pictures, to radio, to television, to comics, to sports because, inherently and instinctively, they are afraid. Of what?

One might try to take one of the polls which are an evil symptom of our times, but the pollster would not get one honest answer because an honest answer would be a shamed answer and because so many would not even know why they are afraid. It is a fear much worse and more desperate than the terror of warfare by disease or of great bombs that destroy whole cities. Those are merely physical fears and do not particularly terrify any healthy or decent person. But the fears which drive us to live in crowds, to pursue amusements and diversions beyond the ultimate limits of boredom, to contrive drinking parties and clubs and organizations and meetings in order not to be alone, not to think, and never to see ourselves, are fears infinitely worse. They possess at once the hair-raising nameless terror of ghosts and the ultimate terror of utter emptiness, which Poe might well have dissected. And so the victims mark time in a limbo of agitation, swirling round and round, until at last death releases them from the necessity of ever having a thought and from the perpetual flight from the pitiable spectacle of their own emptiness.

Such an extrovert society can create a great furor and hubbub; it can raise great anthills with the deadening and uninspired muddy efficiency and mediocrity of the Socialist; it can even amass and expand and devalue money in its self-deception, but it will never contribute much to civilization and in the end can create only a society of morons who work for themselves and others, like the workers of a hive, merely to keep alive without ever knowing quite why they are working or why they want to live at all.

All this creates more and more a society and a race of men who live only by some cosmic force which compels them to go on living and working, without plan, without ambition, without vision, without any of those gifts or potentialities which slowly, over millions of years, have raised man above the level of animals. Could it be that we are slipping backward while we seem to be surging forward? Could it be that all the things science has discovered to keep alive those who should have died are merely the cynical manifestation of wise and all-knowing God and nature slapping down the pretensions of insignificant and pompous little man, permitting him to destroy not only his "civilization" but eventually himself? Are we not, by emphasis on all material things, upon "security," upon the leveling upward and downward of all men to a single plane of mediocrity, merely destroying that element, that core, which has since the beginning lifted civilized man slowly and painfully upward from the level of barbarism?

An extrovert society which works only for material rewards and spends all its time at the games in the arena and whose only goal is a leveled mediocrity is a doomed society.

Perhaps all of us are in one degree or another schizophrenics. Only the simplest and most primitive of men living in a simple tribal community with a minumum of taboos escapes those pressures which split and divide us, which force us into suppressions and hypocrisies and snobberies and pretense. Sometimes sitting in the bar at the country club I have slipped out of the general conversation for a moment and across my glass have watched men whom I knew well and yet did not know at all and have wondered what was *the other side of them*. What was it they did not tell? What was it they refused to face? What was it, besides age and too many Bourbons, that brought the tired harsh lines into their middle-aged faces?

What would happen if I said suddenly to one of them, "Let's talk about ourselves. Let's abolish all rules and habits and just dig down inside and spill everything!"

If such a fantastic thing were possible. I know what would

happen. There would be first a sudden astonished silence and then a suspicious glance such as one might give suddenly to a person who had been talking along normally and suddenly said, "Go and report to Maréchal Ney. I am Napoleon," and then probably an exclamation of astonishment, "What the hell are you talking about?"

It occurs to me that there has been in my existence only one person who ever has seen the other, inward side of me and that was Mary Raeburn. She is probably the only one living to whom I have ever talked about myself. She might have saved me, but in the end she only brought disaster.

In order to understand many things it is necessary to go into Mary's background which wasn't at all the ordinary one. Indeed it was rather exceptional and even peculiar. Mary was the granddaughter of one of the first men to see the great possibilities of a place like Crescent City in the midst of a wild country that was rapidly being tamed. He spent all of his time trying to build up the community and in the process acquired a great deal of land in what is now the heart of a big industrial city. His own efforts and the efforts of other people in time brought an immense value to this land so that by the time he died he was many times a millionaire.

He left a rather fantastic will leaving all of the fortune to an only son but with every kind of restriction. The land was never to be sold until the third generation, which was as far ahead as he was able to tie up the fortune. He had never sold any land himself; he had only acquired more and more, and he did not want the fortune squandered or broken up. The whole of the properties were run in a kind of corporation with a board of directors which included his own son, whose judgment he apparently did not hold in great esteem. Already before he died he had seen fortunes made in the new country squandered and he had seen the inheritors leave Crescent City and go to live in New York or in Europe, drawing their incomes from Crescent City and spending them elsewhere. So he made another provision —that the inheritors through the second generation could not have the income unless they spent at least six months of every year in residence in Crescent City itself. That is how Mary Raeburn came to spend part of each year there.

The old man's distrust of the ability and interests of his only child, a son, may have been well founded for the son showed no interest whatever in business. With the passion of the pioneer's determination that his children should be well educated, the old man sent his son East to school and there something happened to him. After four years in Harvard and three summers in Europe, the son, who was Mary's father, returned a stranger to Crescent City, and when the old man died the son no longer made any effort to conceal his preference for the East and for Europe. He married a rather colorless New England woman, and from then on Europe was their home. They only came to Crescent City for the period necessary to keep the big income which increased every year, and even while they were residing officially in Crescent City they spent most of the six-month period traveling within the borders of the United States or visiting rich and somewhat fashionable friends in the East and the South.

Mary was born about three years after me in Europe. I never saw much of her until about a year before I came out here to this South Pacific island and I never really knew her until then. The society of a place like Crescent City is more complex than appears on the surface. Those of us who lived in Oakdale and belong to the country-club set appeared to many people, especially those who lived in less rich suburbs, to be what might be called "hot stuff" socially, yet there was a circle, very small and very unstandardized, which occupied a situation still higher.

The people in this set existed a little apart not because they were necessarily wealthier—some of the Oakdale families were very rich indeed—but because of something almost intangible which it was difficult to explain. They *knew* more and they took an interest in a great many things which were ignored or went unheeded and even unheard of in our Oakdale world. They did not believe the world ended at the borders of Oakdale or even Crescent City or even of the state itself. Whether they traveled or stayed at home, they *lived* everywhere. Some of them included businessmen important enough to be a part of the society of the whole nation, who came and went, with interests in Texas or California or South Carolina or where you will. None of them might have been called "Mr. Smith" or "Mr. Jones." Most of them were nice and kindly people, frequently very friendly and generous, but all of them were busy people. A few of them were almost like Frank Saunders' family. They were not snobbish. If they appeared infrequently at the country club or rarely played golf and seldom gave cocktail parties, it was only because they were too busy . . . busy with what? That too is difficult to answer.

There was old Mrs. Sidell who would rather sit at home in one of the finest of gardens and work on her needlepoint while she talked endlessly about things which Enid, even with her college education, would never have understood. Mrs. Sidell's needlework was known to connoisseurs all over the states and all over the world. When she died most of what she had done would become museum material, for they were real works of art. She was a great lady, simple, kindly, and warm. There was Tom Worthington, one of the world's greatest chemists, and Alice Mackaye who had been a very fine actress and finally came back to live on a big farm with her sister and her sister's family. Her sister was a great horse and cattle breeder. And the Birdwells. Harry Birdwell had a share in a family factory in which he took some interest, but most of his time was spent with his wife in research concerning the lesser-known Elizabethan poets. Scholars in every part of the world knew them both and what they had accomplished and sometimes came to Crescent City to see the books and papers he had collected. And there was Ernest Lawton, as fine a lawyer as you could find anywhere.

These people did not live together in a small community like our own. They lived where they chose in Crescent City and they stayed in Crescent City because that is where their roots were and because they liked it—Alice Mackaye and her sister on a big farm, the Birdwells in a rather gloomy big house in the center of town on a street which had long since gone to filling stations and faith-healer's offices and the churches of hysterical splinter religious sects. Tom Worthington and his wife lived in an apartment near the center of town.

There were many others who "belonged" to no set yet among themselves lived in a separate world. They were scattered and saw each other infrequently yet there was a surprising intimacy among them. None of them was perhaps busier than most of us in Oakdale, but their business had a purpose, a design, and a fire. They were not busy merely killing time. There was no "clubbiness," no groups and cliques who saw each other seven days a week. They were all about us and yet in no way a part of us. It was as if each one lived in a world of his own which was in some way related to all the other worlds. But all of us in Enid's circle were excluded from *all* those worlds.

It was among these people that Mary Raeburn belonged and among them that she had lived during all of the years in which she spent part of her time in Crescent City.

While we were growing up and until after Enid and I were married, Mary sometimes came to the parties when in Crescent City where the young people met, but she always seemed a little apart, which was possibly only natural since she did not spend enough time among us to know all the gossip and indulge in the somewhat feeble talk and giggling that passed among the girls of our world for conversation. I know that one year she went for a time to the Oakdale High School (it was new then and the teaching good and the children of all the better families went there without any thought of boarding school), but she did not have a happy time since she was always an outsider and "different." Her parents never attempted the experiment again after that first year.

She was never the flashy sort of girl that the boys ran after. At that time she was rather plain and too plump. Like many such girls, as she grew older and fined down a bit, her figure improved and the fine bone structure in her face became evident and she acquired a look of distinction that at times approached actual beauty. After the time she was twenty-two or -three we rarely saw her. Now and then she appeared at the country club to play golf with someone who was visiting her, or we encountered her at a charity ball or some other more or less public function. She was always pleasant and agreeable, but somehow she didn't fit in with the women of Enid's set, I think because neither side could find anything to talk about.

When she was twenty-two or -three her father died and Mary came into an immense income, predicated always upon the condition that she spend so much of every year in Crescent City. A year or two later she married a man from the East called Herbert Raeburn. I saw him once or twice and he seemed to be all right, dark, older than Mary, and rather handsome. But something went wrong with the marriage and after four years they were divorced. After that her contacts with the people of Oakdale and most of those in Crescent City became even more tenuous and broken. There were always visitors at her big strange house, but we rarely saw them, and she spent a good deal of time on week ends in the Kentucky horse country and, after planes came in, even as far away as Virginia.

The house in which she lived had been built in the Eighties by her grandfather and by the standards of a generation or two later it was considered ugly, although by now it has acquired a certain antique beauty which was always there unnoticed in the scale and proportion of the porches, the windows, and the doorways. It was built in the period when iron dogs and stags were familiar ornaments on the huge lawns beneath great elms and maples. The porches were enormous and wide and very high, with complicated columns supporting the roofs, and at one side there was a kind of tower, square in shape, with a magnificent view over the whole of the great river valley. Inside there was a huge hallway with a wide winding stairway. The ceilings were high, perhaps as high as fifteen feet, with windows on the ground floor, running from floor to ceiling, which opened outward onto the porches or directly into the garden. Behind the house there were big stables and a great carriage barn where the dogcarts and phaetons and victorias of the grandfather's time are still preserved.

There was a curious sadness about the house as if it had been built for a great family with children running about. But in two generations there were only two children to grow up in the big house—Mary's father and then Mary herself. It was certainly in our time a very expensive house to run. Heating it alone must have cost a small fortune, and there was the endless problem of cleaning it and keeping it in repair. People were always saying they could not see why Mary spent so much money and took so much trouble to keep up such a vast old-fashioned house when she could have lived so much more pleasantly in a smaller more convenient one. But Mary had plenty of money—no one but the trustees ever really knew how much, and until the times of huge taxes it is likely that she could not possibly spend her income and the money continued to pile up. Still, even money could not make the problems of servants and cleaning and repairs anything less than a trouble and a worry.

My grandfather, the German ironmonger, and Mary's father had been friends and they were both fond of music, and while my grandfather was still alive I went there a few times with him after supper in the evening. Usually I ran about the stables where there were five or six colored men in charge of the horses and carriages, but I did come to know as well the inside of the house.

It was what might have been called "richly furnished" with heavy dark furniture and heavy curtains of brocade or velvet running from floor to ceiling with carved and gilded baldachins at the tops of the windows. There were splendid gilt console tables with marble tops and huge fireplaces in which as a small boy I could stand upright without touching my head. The stair rail or banister of the great stairway was made of heavy dark wood, very broad and very slippery, and one of my childhood frustrations arose from the fact that there were no children there to play with who might have slid down it and I never had courage enough to attempt it on my own. Mary herself was three years younger than I, and even when she was at home there was no contact between us beyond a mere childish how-do-you-do. At that age the fact that she was a girl kept us apart and at that age three years' difference in age makes an enormous obstacle even to communication. All I remember about her at that period was that she seemed shy and fat and rather overdressed and a little sad.

When my grandfather died I did not see the house again until I was nearly twenty when twice during the summer of that year Mary's mother made a rather listless effort to bring Mary more closely together with the young people of Crescent City and twice gave dinner parties which were much grander than anything most of us had ever seen, with a real English butler and two or three colored menservants wearing white cotton gloves and with wonderful silver and crystal on the table. After that summer the mother's health grew worse and she became what was known in an earlier generation as an invalid. When Mary was twenty-six, two years after the marriage which did not last, she died.

I have put all this down because it helps to explain why Mary and I did not get together when we were young. We might have married each other then. On my side I might have rescued her from the great sad house and the ailing mother and an unhappy marriage and on her side she might have opened up for me a world which she did open up many years later when we were both on the edge of middle age. It didn't happen. To the young men of Crescent City Mary seemed not to have much reality. She was somewhat like an enchanted princess in a tower, isolated not only by the different manners of a life she had known away from Crescent City but by the concrete fact of her great fortune, for everybody knew how rich she was and whenever any young man showed her any attention it was whispered at once that he was after her money.

I met her again at what for me was a dangerous time. I had been reading and reading and in a vicarious way I had been growing, as you might say, from the inside out, and the dreariness of my life with Enid had become very nearly insupportable

—so insupportable that when I went to New Orleans along with some of the men from Crescent City on a convention I flung myself into what might be described as debauchery out of sheer despair.

Five of us went together. Their names are unimportant to all of this and I would not want them hurt if ever what I am writing came into the wrong hands. Let us call them Tom, Dick, Harry, and Ernest. Tom was a prosperous manufacturer with a wife and three children, about forty-five years old. Dick was a widower of fifty-five, a businessman who was one of our best drinkers. Harry held the agency for one of the most popular of automobiles which was a gold mine. He and his wife had no children and led a strange life of quarrels and reconciliations, now together, now apart. Ernest was the most conventional of all—a very respected lawyer, conventionally and apparently happily married, the kind of man who appears almost ascetic, handsome, grayish, and even thin-lipped. All of them had worked hard for their money and were still working hard, save in the rare times when they took a few days off. Then they relaxed too violently, too desperately, as if to make up for lost time. Although I had made many a similar trip in similar company, I can remember very little concerning them. But this trip still remains clear as a brilliant photograph, perhaps because of Ernest's death and because it marked the end of something in my life.

The train had scarcely left the station when Ernest began ordering old-fashioneds, and from then on the drinking rarely stopped until the tragic end of the trip. We had several before lunch and then ate a quick meal, and three of the five of us retired to the bedrooms to sleep off the first fine flush of intoxication. It was not so much, I think, that they were actually in need of sleep but that the drinking made it possible to sleep. It did many things for them . . . and indeed for myself. . . . In the haze of alcohol the world seemed brighter and the constant small worries and unhappinesses and annoyance seemed to fade out or to take on their proper scale of importance in the business of living, becoming suddenly small and insignificant to the point where presently they were forgotten altogether in a warm sense of well-being which was physical as well as mental.

Ernest, who outwardly was the most respectable of us all, had a bad heart—a heart which at fifty-three was merely tired as muscles become tired following some effort of immense and prolonged physical exertion. When he drank I think it actually improved for the time being not only his sense of physical well-being but released a brilliance and clarity of mind which always had been there but which long ago had become obscured simply through the weariness of the physical machine. Back in Crescent City, in his office or at home or at the country club, one had at times the impression of a man dragging his way along. At times in the very midst of a conversation his eyes would close suddenly and his thin nervous hand would go of itself to his forehead and for a little while he would not be there at all. And one could understand that. He had worked very hard all his life with long hours and the immense concentration and detail, which go into the making of any brilliant, successful lawyer. And he had given money and what was vastly more important, much of his time and energy to the good works of the community. He was certainly a scholar and a gentleman, but there were times when, I think, he actually thirsted, with some of the agonies, almost physical, which accompany the slow persistent misery of thirst, for earthiness, for low and common things. In short there were times when, in order to restore himself, there came over him a physical urge to wallow, to debase himself and his somewhat ascetic ideals, to get back to earth, the earth from which all of us come and to which all of us return. In this it might be said that he resembled many a saint in ecclesiastical history.

Outwardly at least his marriage was a happy one, although his wife always seemed a bit rarefied for my taste. She was the daughter of a bishop of the Episcopal church, and there was an air of delicacy, even of fragility, about her, as if she had grown up in the rather damp stained-glass dusk of an Episcopal palace. She was extremely intelligent and cultivated, and on the intellectual side I am certain that she was a satisfactory partner.

I do not believe they quarreled or even had any serious disagreement. There was in both of them a gentleness and an intelligence which made quarreling seem vulgar and futile. Yet it was, I think, that very lack of violence together with his wife's fragility and delicacy which made all that was male in him cry out at times for the violence and earthiness and passion of a wholly different life. His own must at times have seemed made up wholly of wraiths and shadows and drifting mist. I think any man will know what I mean.

In his own life Ernest had a satisfaction which none of the others of us really knew. He liked his work. He *liked* being a lawyer. The history and the intricacies of the law fascinated him. The rest of us never knew these satisfactions. We were all doing something or other, however successfully, which had simply happened to fall in our paths. Everything seemed to be all right for Ernest but it wasn't. There were these times when he had to go away and plunge deeply into another kind of life, hard, physical, physiological, even, according to some standards, depraved. I had heard rumors of these excursions but had never come across him during one of them. Whether his wife knew of them I do not know, but I suspect that she had heard rumors. It was as if he had at times to cry out from the depths of an ordered, overcivilized life the violent, even the coarse words and expressions of brutal passion. These strange, wild excursions into the depths may have made a better man and a better husband of him, and it is not impossible that his ethereal wife knew and understood this.

But, with all of us, a trip like this brought a certain relaxation and refreshment. It made us feel young again, and physiologically at least such a trip was probably a good thing for us. The others, save perhaps Ernest, indulged themselves far more frequently than I did, and on the few occasions when I had taken part in what might be simply described as a three- or four-day orgy, I never went as far as the others. The odd thing is that, almost without knowing it, each one of us was always hoping that something marvelous would happen, that there would be a gleam of excitement or even of romance or of something which we had never known and very likely would never know. Only in the case of Ernest was the attitude perhaps a different one. In his intellectual aloofness I think these debauches were regarded by him actually as regenerative activities, as if in some way they recharged his batteries, as if wallowing for a time in the dregs cleared his mind and body and restored his perspective. I think that perhaps he entered them with a certain deliberateness and even calculation as one takes a purge when one feels a bilious attack coming on. In his case respectability itself in too large doses had given him periodically what might be described as a bilious attack of the spirit and the mind. As he took drink after drink something happened to the rather lean ascetic face. The rather tight look about the lips softened and at last disappeared. Into the rather cold but very clear blue eyes there came a twinkle. Not everybody noticed the change, and perhaps I flatter myself when I say that I think he credited me with understanding, that he looked upon me as a little above the others in intellect and comprehension. I only say this because now and then, on the occasion of some particularly commonplace or hypocritical observation made in our circle, he would give me a swift, concealed glance of understanding.

As for myself I had never enjoyed these outings much beyond the point where I had had enough to drink to make everything seem rosy and all that I said seem brilliant or humorous or witty. There were always women involved and now and then I experimented. But I had never found anything satisfactory for a great variety of reasons. Such women were usually stupid and all too often they were avaricious. I learned a few things from them but afterward I always felt the worse for such encounters, occasionally repentant and sometimes filled with a sense of sordidness, but usually with disappointment that the whole thing had been merely rather cheap and insignificant and transient and without meaning.

But on the occasion of this New Orleans excursion there was a difference. I think that perhaps I approached a little the feeling which affected Ernest—that somehow in order to restore myself I must be washed free and clean, rather like a ship hauled up in dry dock to be cleared of the barnacles and seaweed which had accumulated in great quantities on the hull. I felt as do the members of some obscure religious sects—that there can be no repentance without sin and that it is necessary periodically to sin violently in order to repent and be cleansed. I felt the need of being cleared of all the barnacles and seaweed of respectability, of hypocrisy, of monotony or falseness and boredom, of the particular sea in which I was sailing out my life without ever coming into any port. Perhaps if I could get clear I might arrive somewhere or at least have the force to go on sailing. I was prepared with coldness and calculation for any debauchery whatever, looking upon it as a good purge.

It would not have been so and perhaps I would never have gone on the trip at all but for the fact that two days earlier Enid and I had had a monumental quarrel, the greatest and perhaps the only genuinely violent quarrel we had had up until then.

Whenever I went away on a trip alone she was resentful for days in advance. It was the old thing, I believe—that if I went off alone I was escaping her. I honestly do not believe that she would have minded any of the casual coarse infidelities, even if she had known of them, nearly so much as the fact that I was out of reach, that she could not for three or four days "share" everything with me. I doubt that suspicion or physical jealousy troubled her very much. She was jealous of my "freedom," although it was something she herself neither understood nor desired.

Immediately she scented that there was a possibility of my making a trip, she would begin finagling to arrange it so that she could go with me. In the beginning this worked, but presently I learned to devise reasons why it was impossible for her to go—that the trip was too expensive or that I should be for the whole of the time engaged in business and would not even be free for lunch or for dinner. On the occasions when I did let her accompany me, I found that she became incapable of leading any life of her own even for a moment or two during the day. She would ride with me in the taxi to any appointment I had or she would plan to come and fetch me. The rest of the time she would sit in the hotel room, doing what I was never able to discover, for she was not a reader and she rarely knitted or sewed. The subtle and curious thing is that she did not do any of this to protect me from attack by other women or to thwart any secret rendezvous I might have had but because she did not want me to escape her. At times she became a great nuisance by insisting that she be as important as myself in any gathering where women were admitted. She would insist on attracting and holding the attention of others and interrupt or correct what I was saying. She was one of those who habitually interrupt you in the midst of a story with some remark such as, "No, dear, it wasn't Monday. I remember it was Tuesday because it was the day the cook left us." If she had been a mistress or a wife passionately in love with me, all this might have been understandable, but this was not true. She behaved thus and indeed her behavior became exaggerated long after we had ceased to have any physical relationship.

She began this particular violent quarrel by saying, "I can't see why you have to go all the way to New Orleans at this time. It's nothing but a convention and you won't even go to the meetings."

Beginning on the old well-worn tack I said, "It will be good for business and good for me. You're always telling me that I don't pay enough attention to business and that you and the children are going to starve."

"You know perfectly well that the drunks you're going with already take out all their insurance with you and they'll go on doing it."

"Ernest is hardly a drunk. He's one of the finest lawyers in the whole country."

"I wouldn't trust Ernest Lawton from here to there."

This was one of the horrible remarks she used over and over again until they became threadbare. They meant nothing whatever, but whenever she could not find any answer she injected something like that which made no direct assertion but left a cloud of suspicions, insinuations, and implications.

I turned to her and said, "Isn't it enough that I simply want to get away for a while?" and added desperately, "Just for a change!"

"No," she said flatly. "It isn't. Change! Change! That's all I hear! All wives would like a change sometimes too!"

"Then why in hell don't you all go away and take a change on your own? There's nothing to stop you. The children are old enough to take care of themselves. It would probably do you all good."

She didn't answer this but as usual veered elsewhere. "All you do is go away and get drunk and God knows what else . . . and then come home sick and full of remorse."

"Okay!" I said. "Even that sometimes does a man good."

"I don't know what you do and I don't care. Only I'd like a change too sometimes. It might do *me* good."

We were getting into one of those hopeless snarls which at times made me feel that the inside of my head was like a clock in which the mainspring has suddenly broken loose and everything has begun to whirr about without sense, meaning, or discipline. What she meant by "a change" was that I should take her to New York and spend every minute of the twenty-four hours with her, going shopping, to the theater, to bars and restaurants she'd read about in the gossip columns and where she knew no one. We did do that occasionally, for I felt that she deserved it, but it was no change. Change, in essence, is not related to a difference in furniture, in background, or even climate. It is related to people as indeed are all situations of importance to people of any depth. For me, or indeed for her, there was no change. For me the whole thing was much worse because at home at least there were the hours when I was more or less alone at the office.

The whirring in my head got beyond endurance and I said, "Look, Enid, there's one thing you don't understand and never will because you won't let yourself understand it. It's a very simple fact, psychological and physiological, that men and women are different—or should be if they're any way normal. A man gets fed up with the order which a woman loves. She wants security and solidity and everything going on every day just as it has the day before. She's got a man who's given her children and a home and pays the grocery bills and she doesn't want any change. A man isn't like that. Every now and then he's got to cut loose. You can't fit him into a woman's pattern. The average man, until he's too old to care, always wants changes. . . . Maybe it's fishing or hunting or conventions or . . ." She attempted to interrupt me but again I said, "Shut up! For just one moment." Then I continued, "I never made you any trouble with other women and I don't want to particularly, but by God now and then I've got to get away for a time."

"I don't know why it's the men who have to have all the change."

"You could go away any time you like and stay as long as you like. The children and I will get on very well. Why don't you? I'll tell you! Because you don't want to. You'd rather go every day to the country club and the garden clubs and yackety-yack with all the other women who don't want to go away unless it means their husbands are going with them."

I heard a door opening somewhere and Enid said, "Shh! I don't want the children to hear us quarreling."

"Christ!" I said. "I don't consider this a quarrel. I could really show you a quarrel if I wanted to let go."

She began to cry. "The trouble is you really hate me!"

Then the whirring in my head became unendurable. I heard myself shouting, "You're goddamn right I hate you and for only one reason—that I can never get away from you for one minute of the day . . . not even when I go to bed at night." I shouted louder, "And I'll tell you something else. Beginning tonight I'm going to move into the guest room and I'm going to keep the door locked so at least for a little time in my own house I can get away and be myself without having a goddamn blood-drinking octopus devouring me, morning, noon, and night."

At that she gave a scream as if I had struck her (which I know now would probably have suited her better and even pleased her since it would have made her seem more important). Then she screamed a second time, crying out, "A goddamn blood-drinking octopus! Oh! Oh!" and dramatically struck her forehead with her hand.

I felt an overwhelming desire to laugh, loudly and hysterically, but checked it and then saw Esther standing in the doorway. On her child's face was no expression of horror or of terror. On the contrary, she looked perfectly calm and extremely interested, as if she were watching a stirring domestic drama taking place in a second-rate movie. There was no doubt whatever that Esther was enjoying the scene which she regarded as an exciting double-bill spectacle.

Then Enid spied her and, rushing toward her, sobbing loudly and gathering the child into her arms, "You poor, poor child!" she cried. "To hear your own father calling your mother such names."

In a perfectly flat voice the child said, "What's the matter?"

"I can't tell you now," sobbed Enid. "I'll tell you some day. You must forgive your father, darling. Forgive him, you understand, he doesn't know what he's doing."

Esther looked at me with an expression of bewilderment and then suddenly, overcome by Enid's caterwauling and hysteria, opened her own mouth in cold blood and began to squawl.

That was enough. I went out of the house, slamming the door behind me, and as I went to the garage a decision came to me. I thought, "I'm going to New Orleans and I'm going to wallow in the gutter. That's the only way I can feel clean again after this one."

Until then I hadn't much cared whether I went with the boys to the convention or not, but after that scene the trip became a necessity. It had to be done as much as if I had been told by a doctor that such treatment was the only thing which could save me.

And so there we were on the train bound for New Orleans,

four prosperous middle-aged or near middle-aged men, respected as respectability goes nowadays. We were tired, and each one in his own way was suffering from bad nerves and the frustrations of lives which, in spite of every effort, seemed unsatisfactory when we were not engaged in drinking or in physical exercise. Youth was gone and with it hope, and none of us was as yet reconciled to inaction, to the business of sitting back and reflecting even if any of us save Ernest possessed the capacity for reflection. But the most fearsome thing was that all of us, again with the possible exception of Ernest, would have, when that time came, damned little to reflect upon. If any of us lived into old age, which seemed unlikely considering the strains and the premature weariness from which all of us suffered, we should simply be cantankerous and idle and unsatisfied old men.

What had wearied us? That is the thing I am trying to get at as I write all of this but fail continually to discover. We were wearied of many things—of taxes and financial anxieties, of rushing about always at top speed, of being persecuted by the telephone and the automobile, of being unable to spend even a single evening at home doing nothing but sitting with our families and reading and talking. We were wearied by the politicians and wearied of constant regulations and of filling in forms for this and for that, of an almost total remoteness, even in the case of Ernest, from those enjoyments which derive from one's natural environment, . . . of that refreshment which comes of smelling the fresh still air of the early morning and noticing the aroma of freshly turned earth or sitting still to watch a sunset or the water of a stream flowing swiftly along its willow-bordered course. We were wearied of listening to radios interrupted by vulgar clamorous commercials, bored by the monotonous dull-witted movies in which we occasionally tried to lose ourselves. We were tired of keeping up with the next-door neighbor, of raising the money to send our children to the right schools, to pay for fur coats and the new bathroom, tired of seeing each other, of talking back and forth perpetually over the same ground. I think, very possibly, we were sick of middle-class

American life which at the age of all of us had become merely a treadmill on which we ran endlessly day after day without ever arriving anywhere. And we were getting old. Although we tried never to think of it, the thought was always there. We were getting old, but the true horror lay in the fact that we were getting old without anything having ever happened to us. It would be over presently . . . and so what!

The sleep that followed quickly the heavy drinking was an escape. It was the kind of sleep, induced by alcohol, which was not interrupted by the fitful dreams and the wakefulness which we struggled desperately to escape, trying to drive ourselves back into unconsciousness because consciousness and reality had become for the time being unbearable to us. If you drank enough you were simply overcome and fell into a state of utter blankness and void which was next to death. I doubt that any of the group, save perhaps Ernest and myself, ever had such thoughts as these, but the same will was there—the will from time to time to black out, to fall into that same intoxicated trance which was next to death.

Yet we were envied. We were successful. We had everything. Oh! Hell! What we had could be measured in terms of banknotes or automobiles or expensive radio sets or tiled bathrooms or fur coats. So what!

But we were on our way to New Orleans, the gayest city outside Paris, to a convention to raise hell! And death was riding with us!

About four in the afternoon the three who had blacked out wakened and, a little foggy-eyed, came into the drawing room I shared with Ernest. Tom, Dick, Harry, and myself started a rummy game with Ernest watching, and the drinking began again at once. Ernest, I noticed, drank more than any of us. He said it raised his low blood pressure and made him feel better, and it is true that I never saw him in a condition which could even vaguely be described as intoxication. It was as if he soaked it up after long periods of drought.

We were all drinking of course to set ourselves free and in the end to bring about that drunkenness which was near to death. The bad jokes and the great laughs at nothing continued and grew more and more noisy. We had dinner, and after dinner we settled down again to cards, playing poker this time with Ernest taking a hand together with an automobile agency man from Louisville with whom Harry had struck up an acquaintance in the club car. Now and then other acquaintances bound like ourselves for New Orleans looked in at the doorway and stood for a time kibitzing with drinks in their hands.

God! It was all dreary!

X   The Jungle

Homer, the wool-hat, was right about his having hit a Jap that night when he fired into the jungle. We discovered it today when I was returning with Al from the beach. It is not a very good beach, being made up of rather sharp coral and you can't swim very far for fear of sharks. I never know about them. You hear so many stories out here in the East. Some say that they will attack on sight and others that unless there is blood in the water, which rouses their appetites and tends to infuriate them, they will not bother you at all. What I do know is that there are plenty of them about and that I'm not taking any chances or allowing any of the men to take chances.

As a rule I go down with them in the morning for a swim merely to keep an eye on them. We don't only have sharks but we usually have a large audience of fuzzy-wuzzies as well. They have discovered the swimming hour and come down every day about that time, men, women, and children, to watch us. Homer, who has managed, during his amorous adventures, some means of communicating with them, and Solomon, a black boy who worked once at Port Moresby, say that it is our white skins that amuse them. They never seem able to get used to the whiteness, and they even bring friends through the thick jungle from the next village to watch us and especially to comment upon the extreme hairiness of the Sergeant and the milky-white streak of skin around the middle of Homer who never tans but only turns shrimp pink. At first their presence embarrassed us and we took to wearing shorts, but after a time we abandoned all coverings and took to swimming naked again which is much more pleasurable. I must say I have no feelings of modesty left. It's a little as if that string of dark-skinned people covered with grease and yaws, lined up on the edge of the jungle laughing and making what are clearly dirty remarks, were no more than a bunch of animals.

Al, the Kansas boy, and I came up from the beach today together, and as we passed through the jagged coral that makes a kind of barrier between the jungle and the beach, we caught a whiff downwind of a stench concerning which there could be no doubts. It was sweetish and sickly and repulsive. It was the smell of a dead man in a hot climate, a smell which I had encountered on the other islands once or twice before I was buried away here in this bloody hole. Al had never smelled it before since he has not been in action, but when I looked at him I saw that he understood.

"Something dead around here," he said, adding that all dead animals smelled alike. But the odd thing was that the big strapping Kansas farm boy had turned a little pale.

"We'd better go and investigate it," I said. "It'll only get worse."

So cautiously—for the coral could cut through the canvas of our sneakers—we worked our way upwind toward the smell. We were on the right track because the further we went the stronger became the repulsive odor. And then suddenly behind a clump of bushes we came upon the Jap.

He was lying on his back with one hand clutched at a gunshot wound in his abdomen, and the body had begun to swell so that the whole abdomen was hideously inflated. The lips, as in such cases, were drawn back to expose the projecting teeth, as if at the very end he had been grinning hideously. There was another hole in the chest just below where the ribs are joined, so Homer, the wool-hat, shooting blindly in the dark, must have gotten him in two places.

Death, the quiet death of old age or after a long illness when it comes as a relief, or even the death of a suicide, is not in itself distressing, since it seems to carry a certain sense of release and of naturalness. It is in the order of things, or someone has taken his own life because it has become unbearable. But I have never succeeded in reconciling myself to the death of the young who wanted to live and had a pattern of experience and achievement yet before them to fulfill. There is a shocking sense of unfulfillment in the death of the young in battle. To me, that is what makes the idea of war insupportable and irreconcilable, particularly in the somewhat meaningless wars of our time which are caused by the confusion of man and of his machines, and men no longer die fighting hand to hand but are more often than not killed by some projectile coming from a wholly unseen point of departure or by stepping on some hidden explosive monstrosity against which there is no defense with not even the satisfaction of combat spirit roused by the proper functioning of glands. Today men die not with a spirit of fury or gallantry or even any longer in the sense that they are crusaders. The only emotion they know is a humiliating fear, without relief or compensation, since one cannot have a hand-to-hand struggle with a mortar shell or a mine.

I once saw a dead general but he left me unmoved because it seemed to me that, despite the fact that he had been blown up in a jeep, he had got what he wanted and what was coming to him. He who lives by the sword . . . I confess that I was more moved by the sight of this dead, swollen, wretched little Jap than at the sight of the shattered body of the dead general. It seems to me that at the sight of death one must, provided he has any brains or humanity, ask, "Why?" and so as I stood there looking down, I could not help asking myself why this poor dead little yellow man should have been transported thousands of miles from his home to be killed while trying to steal piled-up, slowly rotting food out of an Army warehouse which had been virtually forgotten.

As near as one could judge he had probably been little more than a boy and undoubtedly he had no idea why he was fighting or what it was all about. But in that he was no different from Homer, the wool-hat, or a great many other common soldiers I have talked to in our own Army. But here he was, dead, in a world which made no sense at all.

To Al I said, "Poor bastard! We'll have to bury him quickly before he stinks up the whole camp," and then I saw that Al's face had turned from gray to white. A moment later he began to retch and vomit. The effect of the corpse on Al, who was a farm boy, surprised me, but I felt sorry for him. I said, "Come along. I'll send Homer and Meyer back to bury him. If Homer can stand the smell of these fuzzy-wuzzies, he won't mind this."

But Al said, "If you don't mind, Captain, I want to go back to the beach."

For a moment while he continued retching I was puzzled. Then I said, "Okay," and he went off across the white coral and plunged again into the brilliant blue sea and I understood what he was doing. He was young. He was washing the smell of death off him.

Back at the camp I found Meyer washing his clothes and Homer just sitting with his backside against the shady wall of the hut. He was chewing tobacco and playing a game of seeing how far he could spit. I called them together and said, "There's a dead Jap down there by the beach. You two fellows get a couple of shovels and cover him up—deep or he's likely to smell. Dig the grave up leeward side, and when it's dug you can take the jeep and a cable and drag him into it."

A gleam of pleasure came into Homer's weak blue eyes. "So I got him, did I?" he said.

"Yes, you got him in two places—right through the middle."

"I gotta see that!" he said. "Come on, Meyer." It was the first time I had ever seen him move quickly. Meyer simply stood there, a look of fear in his big deer eyes. "There must be others around, Captain," he said. "He wouldn't be alone."

"Sure there are," I said. "You saw their footprints. But as long as we feed 'em, they'll let us alone."

Then Homer came back carrying two shovels and called out, "Come on, Meyer. I want to see the sonofabitch!" and they went off together in the direction I indicated.

A little later I saw Al coming back, a towel wrapped about his tanned naked body, and I called out. "Come in for a minute. A drink'll make you feel better."

He came in looking rather shamefaced and said, "I don't drink usually but I'll take one this time."

The clear salt water had brought back his color, but he still seemed a little shaky. "I'm sorry, Captain," he said sheepishly. "I don't know what happened to me. I wasn't scared. It wasn't that. I only saw one dead person before and that was my grandfather and he looked kind of peaceful . . . in his coffin . . . and right. I didn't get sick like this at all."

I laughed. "It's nothing. It often affects people like that. Some people can't even stand the sight of blood. Sometimes they get used to it and sometimes they don't."

He took the drink, swallowed, and coughed. "Maybe," he said, "it would be a good idea for me to go back there and bury the Jap alone . . . just to get over this."

"You don't need to worry. Homer will enjoy it. He vomited the other night because he was scared but this kind of thing won't bother him." I grinned. "Knowing Homer, he may even enjoy it."

"Don't think it was because I was scared."

"Sure I don't think that."

"It was just like I'd eaten something that made me throw up."

"You feel better now?"

"Yes." Then he looked directly at me and said, "Excuse me, Captain, if I ask you something?"

"Sure . . . go ahead."

"When do you think we'll get out of here if we ever do?"

"I don't know."

"I'd like to get out," the boy said. "On active service. I'm not afraid of fighting but this is hell. I'm twenty-two and I've been out here already almost three years wasting my time, wasting my life. It wouldn't be so bad if I felt I was getting anywhere or that any of this meant anything." He looked down at his empty glass. "But it won't get anywhere. It'll just begin all over again."

"What makes you think that?"

"If it isn't Germany or Japan it'll be somebody else unless . . ."

"Unless what?"

"Unless we finish the job right and *tell* the others what they've got to do."

I didn't answer him for a moment and then I said, "You seem to have been doing a lot of thinking."

He grinned. "What else is there to do in this hellhole?"

A look almost of excitement came into his face, and I realized suddenly that all along he had wanted to talk to me but was too shy. Now with the hot, unaccustomed whisky in his stomach he had courage.

He said, "You know, I look at these fuzzy-wuzzies or that poor dead Jap and wonder what it's all about. And sometimes I think about the farm and the way things are there. You know a farm is awfully close to the way nature operates. It's a kind of pattern. It's pretty complex too—a lot more complex than most people realize. It's complex, but it's got to have direction and some kind of orderly pattern. You don't just say to all the animals, 'Now we'll have democracy. You take over. . . .' I mean the hogs and chickens and cattle. . . . 'You take over and run things. Make up a government for yourself and take over.' That would be a hell of a mess. The cattle would eat up everything so there wasn't any forage when winter came. The hogs would eat the ducks and chickens and there'd be yackety-yack and arguments about everything. No, a farm, which is as good a pattern as any, has to be managed and it has to be managed by the smartest animal on it or everything goes to hell. And who's the smartest animal? Why, the farmer of course. He's what holds it together and makes it possible for all the animals to live at all."

There was a light in his eye and I did not interrupt him. "I look at these fuzzy-wuzzies. Why, they're no smarter than our collie dog or one of our brood sows . . . maybe they aren't as smart as a sow who's the smartest animal on a farm. What I can't get into my head is that a lot of damned fools want to set the fuzzy-wuzzies free and tell them that now they must practice democracy. And that poor Jap—what the hell did he know about anything? He just went on breeding when he shouldn't have bred, until there got to be too many people and all of 'em were living half like animals. And they were used just like animals—sent out to be slaughtered just the way we'd send steers to market." He put down his glass and scratched his blond curly head in a puzzled fashion. "Sometimes I think we've gotten a long way . . . too long a way . . . from such things as natural law. We get sentimental about people and we keep alive a lot of people to breed who nature would eliminate for the good of everybody. And we talk about making people free who don't want to be free and about giving democracy to people who have never heard of it and couldn't understand it." He stood up suddenly and said, "We're just goddamn muddles. That's all. That's why it'll happen all over again until somebody like us Americans says, 'Listen, you! This is what you're going to do for your own damned good and the good of the rest of the world!' Then maybe we'll have peace and order and there won't be any more wars."

He hitched the towel tighter around his narrow waist.

I said, "There's something in what you say. God knows there's too many people in the world, and most of 'em don't care much whether they live or die, and some of them aren't much above the level of animals. That poor little yellow bastard with the holes in him was probably like that. Eat and breed and make Banzai charges when somebody . . . some sonofabitch told him to."

Evidently the boy didn't want to talk any more. He said, "Thanks, Captain, for the drink. I feel a lot better. Excuse me if I talked too much. I think till my head aches. I want to get out of here before I go nuts. When I think of all I might be doing back home instead of sitting here rotting away, guarding a lot of spoiled food, I damned near go crazy!" He looked at me suddenly. "It's a waste you know . . . a waste people and the world can't afford when you multiply it by millions. Hell!" he added. "Sometimes I get sick of the lousy reformers!"

I watched him cross the brilliant sun-drenched strip of white coral and I thought, "There's something in what he says and they'll be back after him when it happens all over again." Because I knew that he was right. Germany and England and France were probably finished. There was only one nation strong enough to bring order to the world, if it played its cards right. What would happen if all the young people in the world rose up and said, "We've had enough. We won't go on with this damned nonsense. Let us alone to work and create and build"? But that, of course, would never happen. They'd simply go on being killed or rotting away in the abysmal deadly brutishness of a soldier's life.

Anyway, Al had a chance to let off a little steam. If he lived and went back he'd be a good citizen, for at least he was one of those who think things out. He didn't live by emotion and cheap slogans and millenniums.

A little before eating time the Sergeant came across the white sand to my hut. He said, "I just heard something over the radio. They've used something called an atomic bomb on the Japs. It seems they blew up a whole big town—old men, women, children, and everything with one bomb."

"I suppose it was bound to come some day."

"Well, it's something I wouldn't want on *my* conscience. It's something I wouldn't want anything to do with. I'd be ashamed before my own children . . . if I had any that I knew of."

"It's just bigger than any other bomb. That's the only difference."

"No, it ain't," said the Sergeant.

"What do you mean?"

"It's because *we* done it first. We hadn't any right to do it . . . at least not to be the first ones. It's horrible! It makes me kind of ashamed of being an American."

"Take it easy."

Then suddenly he burst out. "I *am* takin' it easy. I never had any proper schooling like a lot of these here scientists and I ain't never been President of the United States. I've been an immoral sonofabitch all my life but there are some things I wouldn't do. Whoever decided to do that is a cheap ignorant sonofabitch. Somebody's got to have standards."

Then as if I had been responsible for the bomb he turned his back and stalked out of the hut and across the blinding white sand. After he had gone I lay down on my Army cot and lay there for a long time thinking . . . so long indeed that I forgot all about eating. I kept piecing together what Al and the Sergeant had said and, fitted into a pattern, it made great sense. They were both ashamed in their ways of being American and neither one knew quite why. I kept thinking back to Jefferson and his faith in the common people who never got very far away from the realities or from the same pattern Al had described in talking about his family farm. They never had their common sense or their moral sense distorted by ambitions and glory and egotism or science and intrigue and vanity . . . or, worst of all, by the feeling that they were the saviors of mankind. They never felt that warm, almost sexual glow of sanctimony which afflicts the frustrated perverted false Christers. The common man! Hell! There wasn't any such thing. There were apes like Homer, the wool-hat, but you didn't shed tears and sanctify them for being apes.

XI Oakdale

I HAVE NEVER BEEN ABLE TO REMEMBER MUCH ABOUT THE three days in New Orleans. It is a town which has been designed for just such excursions as that on which Ernest, Tom, Dick, Harry, and myself were bound. They advertise it as a "convention city" and that means that they make everything easy in the way of drink and gambling and women for tired and bored middle-aged men who are trying to escape from something and purify themselves of boredom and despair by a thorough, good bath of debauchery. Everything is made easy. The taxicab driver, the stray passer-by, even the bellhop, can "fix you up." You can have anything you want. The restaurants are supposed to be good and sometimes they are and sometimes they aren't. The joints are filled with a backwash of human beings who will provide you with any sort of goings-on you prefer, no matter what. There are plenty of other "convention cities" like New Orleans. It is more satisfactory perhaps than the others only because it seems more foreign and therefore farther away from all the things the conventioneers are trying to escape.

When I think back on that trip it always seems to me that the whole impression is like one of these surrealist pictures in which the whole place is a maze of narrow streets, dazzling with neon lights that spell out "The Oyster Girl" and "The Cat Girl" and hands and arms attached to nothing, mere phantoms, which reach out from narrow alleys and doorways to drag you in off the sidewalks. It certainly seems like that after you've had plenty to drink.

I remember that we registered at the hotel for rooms which we never used except to store our luggage and we registered at the convention desk where we received badges with our names on which we put into our pockets and forgot and I remember some place where we had a pretty good meal and then everything dissolved into the phantasmagoria which resembled the surrealist picture. Most of all I remember my own state of mind. I didn't care what happened. I was ready for anything at all. I no longer had left the shallowest vestige of an inhibition. It was a wonderful, almost voluptuous feeling.

Late that first night after we had made a round of bars and joints we found ourselves toward morning in a big parlor with an enormous shiny jukebox. The furniture was expensive but bad—a lot of overstuffed and ugly junk—and the room was full of women. They were of all ages from perhaps eighteen or nineteen to one or two, highly recommended by the madam, who were probably over forty. Most of them were overweight and had rather stupid faces, although two or three of them were quite pretty and well dressed, and the madam told me that these were not regular girls but came in occasionally from the outside. Nearly all of them were in evening dress in an obvious attempt at elegance which misfired because there was too much of everything on the dresses they wore.

The madam was in appearance exactly what you did not expect a madam to be. She was tall and thin and dark and rather spinsterish in appearance with perhaps a strain of Oriental blood in her. She was "refined" but also tough. Tom had lost his hat somewhere during the long night and was wearing a paper cap he had picked up in one of the joints. He was inclined to be noisy and now and then broke out into singing loudly "Mademoiselle from Armentières." He had enjoyed the First World War, and when he got a little drunk he always went back to it the way another type of man goes back regularly to college reunions. The war had been a great event in his life. He had been decorated for heroism and nothing had ever happened to him since then.

The madam didn't like his noisiness and said that the place was a refined place and that if he didn't calm down she'd have him thrown out. She wanted everybody to have a good time but in a gentlemanly way.

The oddest of all of us perhaps was Ernest. With his thin distinguished face he looked out of place in such an establishment. Although he had drunk quite as much as the rest of us in the course of the evening, he did not seem drunk at all, or at least he gave no sign of it, but there had come into his blue eyes a look of singular intensity and into his manner an urgency and even an enthusiasm which seemed almost obscene. I had again the impression that he, the only one of us who might by any stretch of the imagination be considered an intellectual, had come here deliberately and with a purpose which he meant to carry out. The odd thing was that somehow the purpose and the passion behind it became translated as if by telepathy into the consciousness of the more sensual women in the room. He sat on a low sofa and there were always four or five women surrounding him. Most of them were broad-faced and stupid in appearance, but this fact seemed to please him, as if they were the kind of women he wanted—the fatter, the more stupid, the more vicious, the better.

It was evident that the madam regarded me as the one most capable of keeping order and making the arrangements. Ernest, although sober, seemed obsessed, like a thirsty man coming upon an oasis, and the others were too drunk and too gay to make much sense.

She said, "Do you all want to spend the night?"

"Yes. You'd better arrange for them to stay until they get enough and sober up."

"That will be expensive," she said.

"It won't matter. They'll all pay you. I'll be responsible for that."

"Could you give me your name and hotel?" she asked.

"Of course," I said and wrote out a false name and the name of a hotel where we were not registered. She took it without blinking an eye and said, "It's customary in the case of a high-class establishment like this."

"That's all right," I said. "I understand."

"What about some more drinks?"

"Yes, a round for everybody!"

It did not matter any more to me or to the others. Indeed, it did not matter at that moment whether any of us ever left the house at all. Certainly it did not matter now how much it cost.

One of the "outside" girls had taken me over, and I did not object to this for she seemed quieter and nicer than most of the others. She was small and neat and dressed in a perfectly plain black dress and she wasn't noisy. Indeed, she looked singularly out of place. Quite simply she asked, "Do I please you?" and thrust her hand into mine. It was a small warm yielding hand.

"Yes," I said. "I like you very much."

"You won't be disappointed," she said. "I like you. Do you know why?"

"No. Tell me."

"You're very like someone I loved once . . . the way your hair grows, your mouth and eyes." She held up my hand and looked at it. "Even the back of your hands. Hands," she said, "can be very good-looking. They tell a lot."

"Yes. That's right."

I was beginning to reach that point where drink no longer brought any satisfaction and when even the taste or smell of it seemed repulsive. I had enjoyed drinking up until now, but now there wasn't any more release to be found in mere alcohol.

"Do you want to go to bed?" I whispered.

"Yes, honey, if you're tired."

"I'm not tired. I just want to get out of this room and away from all this noise."

"So do I."

She did not wait. She went over to the madam and spoke to her for a moment and then returned and said, "Come," and led me out of the room and up a stairway to a room furnished with a large double bed and some gilt chairs and tables. Clearly this was an "elegant" establishment. Oddly enough, it was Ernest who had known where it was and led us to it.

The next forty-eight hours passed quickly and in a kind of blur. I was very lucky in the girl who chose me. She was passionate and expert and yet quiet and rather gentle with it all. She told me that she was a widow and that she worked at times as a filing clerk but that she could not make enough money at it to take care of her child as well as she liked. The child was a boy about three years old. Sometimes she came to this place to pick up some extra money, but she also came because her life as a widow was insupportable and she had never found any man she liked or could endure permanently who was willing to keep or to marry her.

"Some day," she said simply, "I will find someone I want to marry and who wants to marry me and then things will be all right again."

Once she looked at me and said, "You've been very nice to me. You're a proper gentleman. You're very good too in other ways." She was a rather simple child, like Manon. I had heard such stories as she told me before now, but for once I had no reason to disbelieve what I was told. She showed me a picture of her boy. He was a nice-looking kid. The picture was a snapshot taken somewhere on the quay because there was a river boat in the background.

For two days I never left the room. We had our meals there, brought in by a very fat Negro woman and very good meals they were. Those two days were very peaceful ones. From the windows you could see up a narrow street with the high river levee at the end. The ships seemed to be floating in space, for you could not see the river at all but only the high banks with the ships moving slowly along at the top. There was no night or day, for I slept when I felt like it. In a way it was like a long, curiously refreshing and voluptuous dream from which all the world was shut out. It was all very simple and direct and without barriers. There was in the whole experience a curious direct quality of children playing and it made me feel wonderfully relaxed and rested. And after the quarrel with Enid, it made me feel clean. There was a kind of peace which I had not known for a very long time.

It had to come to an end sometime, but it came to an end in a tragic brutal fashion when, just before noon on the third day, there was a knock at the door, and when I had put a towel round my middle and stepped outside I found the tall, dark, rather forbidding madam.

She said, in an almost elegant fashion, "I'm sorry to disturb you, sir, but something serious has happened. One of your friends died a few minutes ago."

"Died?" I repeated. "Are you sure?"

"I'm very sure."

"Which one?" I asked, although I already knew.

"The tall one with the blue eyes and the gray hair. He said his name was Barrett, but of course that wasn't his real name. Such a thing is very serious for a house like this. You understand it means inquests and investigations and all that kind of thing."

"Of course."

"And it might mean scandal for his family."

"Yes—where is he?"

"In the room down the hall. The girl is downstairs. She's hysterical. You understand how it happened . . . a heart attack, I suppose."

"Yes. What shall we do?"

"I have a plan worked out which I think will be satisfactory," she said. "We have a small hotel half a block from here. It can be reached by a back alley. It takes in couples, but of course it's not a recognized house like this one. It's a hotel. If he could be found dead there in bed, everything would be all right and respectable."

She looked at me searchingly as if demanding that I volunteer as an accomplice rather than merely to accept her invitation.

"How can we manage that?"

"It's not too difficult," she said. "I've had it happen twice before in my experience before I came here. You understand . . . these middle-aged men sometimes . . ."

"Yes."

"I'll need your help and that of one of your friends. You understand the gentleman has been dead only a short while. We can still get him dressed. You and your friend can take him between you and walk him down the alley to the hotel. Everything will be ready. You can get him up the stairs to a bedroom and leave him on the bed. There will be someone to help you up the stairs. If you meet anyone who is curious you can pretend that he's dead drunk. But it isn't likely you'll meet anyone. After you've left the proprietor will knock on the door and when he gets no answer will go in and find the gentleman dead in bed of a heart attack. He'll notify the police and the doctor and everything will be in order. You can then come back to the hotel to meet him as if you didn't know anything and learn the news and make the arrangements quietly and legally."

I listened, I confess, with a certain fascination, impressed not only by the efficiency with which the operation was planned but also by the calmness with which the madam related the details. Love and death, I thought, all in the day's work! Poor Ernest!

"I'll come at once," I said. "In which room is the dark heavy-set man?" I chose Tom quickly because he was the strongest and the least likely to talk when he got back home.

She considered for a moment and then said, "I know where he is."

"He's the one to help us. Better tell him the story while I get dressed and tell him I expect him to help."

"I want to thank you, sir," she said. "You're being very helpful. The whole thing is very awkward, but I think this is the best way . . . especially for his own family."

"You're quite right," I said. "I won't be long. Where shall I find you?"

"I'll be waiting in the hallway."

As I dressed I told the girl—her name, she said, was Ernestine—that I had had a sudden emergency message and had to leave. She was to remain there in the room until the madam arranged her account. But all the time I was thinking about the madam. She spoke extraordinarily good English and made a nice choice of words. Obviously she had been well educated at some time and place. Why was she a madam? Thinking of her standing there in the hall waiting for me, she seemed an omen or a warning, of what I did not know. And I kept thinking, "Poor Ernest!" and asking myself, "Why do I say *poor* Ernest? He's probably very satisfied." In the first shock everything seemed clear and simple and real with no nonsense of any kind. In a way, this is what Ernest had come for. This was what he was seeking in his weariness and boredom.

The madam was standing just outside my door, and together we went down the hallway to find Tom who was putting on his coat. He looked at me with an odd frightened look in his eye. I don't think he had the resiliency which came to me out of the long hours when I thought about things. He didn't think at all. It struck him as the blow of a hammer might fell an ox. He was curiously excited.

At sight of me he said, "This is a hell of a note!"

"We'll have to do the best we can," I said. "I think she has the proper idea." I called the madam "she" because I didn't know her name.

Very politely she said, "My name is Miss Del Campo."

Together the three of us got Ernest dressed. It wasn't easy. If you're not an undertaker or you've never tried to get clothes on a dead man, you can't imagine how difficult it is. And it was very difficult to make the clothes look right on him as if he had been wearing them instead of as if they had just been put on a dead man.

Have you ever tried to dress a man freshly dead who is a friend? The limbs have not yet stiffened and the body is still warm, but the heart no longer beats and if you scratched the eyeballs they would not respond. The eyes are dead. Yet you want him to speak, to respond to your request to get on his feet and walk. Only a little while before you were talking to him and now he is gone as if a light bulb had flashed brilliantly for a moment and then died, burnt out and finished. It makes you think of many things, of why we should want so earnestly to go on living. If it was as easy as this, why do so many of us struggle to go on, why is there anything so terrible in death? Certainly nothing as terrible as the suffering which sometimes precedes it? Certainly nothing so sordid and wretched as the sordid unceasing material worries of daily existence?

To me it seemed, as I helped to pull the clothes onto the tired thin body, that Ernest had simply gone to sleep for good. Even the manner of his going was satisfactory if he found any pleasure in it. I remembered suddenly the bitter comment of someone—that the body caused us so much anxiety and suffering that it in turn owed us a great debt in pleasure and sensuality. But from all of this was Ernest gone, escaped, perhaps to another life, perhaps not. He would not have to drink any more.

In the shock and awe which had come over me, all the business of morality, as preached by most Christian churches and by the more ignorant and backward Protestant most of all, seemed suddenly insignificant in comparison with birth and death and even life for that matter. What tripe! What rubbish! What mattered was that man should live to fulfillment of himself and his possibilities. All else was insignificant. The world in which Ernest lived had twisted and distorted his existence. In the end he had been killed by it as much as if it had put him against a wall and shot him, for he had died in reaction against it, fighting its mediocrity, its conformity, its ignorance, its total lack of all the splendor which God had put into this world for us to enjoy.

When at last he appeared presentable the madam helped us raise him from the bed and get him between us. His arms were put over our shoulders and we held him by the hands. We pulled the hat far down over the dead eyes. This way we carried him down the stairs and out into the alley—as if he were dead drunk and we were helping him. Such a sight was not unusual in this part of New Orleans.

As the madam had promised, there was a man waiting for us at the back entrance of the little hotel. If I remember rightly, there was a sign over the door which read Hotel du Bayou. He helped us up the stairs and led us to a bedroom where we laid the body on the bed. Then we went back to the house to settle up everything. I said good-by to Ernestine and thanked her and she wrote her name and telephone number on a slip of paper in case I ever came back again.

"It's a bakery," she said. "I live above it and I help the owner with his books. He'll always call me or take a message."

Then Tom and I routed out the others and told them the news, and Tom and I went back to the Hotel du Bayou where we were told officially that our friend had been found dead in bed.

The other three went home the next day but Tom stayed loyally by me to help with all the tiresome details which were more troublesome than we had expected. Together we brought the body home, and Tom wished upon me the unwelcome task of calling on Ernest's wife.

She had been crying and her grief made her seem even more fragile and ascetic than usual. She gave me a drink of Ernest's whisky—it was always the best in town—and then said quietly, "Tell me what happened. The telegrams didn't seem very clear."

So I simply told a story—that we had had an excellent dinner and plenty of cocktails and wine and had stayed out quite late seeing the sights of the Latin Quarter. About four in the morning we had all gone to bed and the next day about noon I was wakened by the proprietor who told me that Ernest had been found dead.

"He must have died in his sleep," I said. "If it had to be, it was a good way to go."

"Yes," she said. "I suppose it was what he would have wanted. His heart was very tired. He never saved himself. Sometimes it seemed to me as if he was driven by something which never gave him any peace. He was a good man. I was never good enough for him."

"You mustn't feel that way about it," I said. "Ernest loved you more than any man I know loves his wife."

She was thoughtful for a moment and then very quietly she said, "Yes, I think that's true. The only thing is . . ." She appeared to search for words and then said, "I wasn't enough for him. You understand what I mean. I should have been stronger and more violent and more . . . more fleshly."

The use of the word shocked me at first and then I understood that in her own shock and grief it was as if she were talking to herself. "Men are strange things," she said. "The stronger and greater they are, the stranger they are. I'm very grateful to have been Ernest's wife . . . no matter what he did. I couldn't have stuck it out with most of the men I ever knew." And it dawned upon me that very quietly she was letting me know the truth and that she had known the truth all along. She said, "I always liked Ernest to go away on trips like this. He didn't do it often enough. If he had, I think he might still be alive. He never had much fun with me . . . except with things like books and music. He couldn't find much of those things anywhere else around here."

When I left her house I didn't go directly home. I drove around for a while thinking about the things she had said, not being quite sure whether I had read into them things which were not there. But after a time it became clear that she had, in her delicate, restrained fashion, told me the story of their lives, and I understood suddenly that what I had heard was a very beautiful story.

When at last I drove the car into the garage Enid called out the side door, "Supper has been ready for half an hour," and when I came in she kissed me as usual, as if nothing had happened. She had not "let the sun set on her anger." When later in the evening she said what she had been waiting all along to say, I decided the sun had set on mine, once and for all, and that I no longer owed her anything or even liked her. I did not care enough even to be angry at her. She said, "I hope what happened will be a lesson to you. You're not so young yourself any more. Some day you'll probably die the same way as that dirty old man."

Somehow she had found out already.

About the time of the New Orleans episode I had begun again to drink steadily. I am sure of some of the reasons but not perhaps of all of them. At the root it was the old despair coming back. For a little time I had escaped in reading and in the exploration of worlds which were wholly new to me and of whose very existence I had been completely unaware. And then there arrived the time of confusion.

When the first excitement over the mere discovery of reading and the new worlds it opened up had abated a little, I began to see that perhaps I should never have opened a book at all. There was no one with whom I could discuss what I read or learned. Before Ernest's death we sometimes touched upon these things, but I always had the feeling that he found me naïve, as if I was discovering things I should have discovered and learned at the age of twenty. I was also aware that on the occasions when we were together his mind was tired and he was unwilling to talk to me in words of one syllable about things which he had long ago discovered, absorbed, and made an integral part of his very mind and spirit. That knowledge made me increasingly shy. And now of course Ernest was dead and there was no one to talk to.

Because there was no outlet for the churned-up, congested ideas and thoughts I gradually acquired, I began to suffer from a kind of intellectual indigestion. It is difficult to describe—this indigestion—but it was as if my head ached from being so crammed with new and unabsorbed impressions. Added to this was the confusion of a mind which, however ambitious, however hungry, had never been taught either in school or in college to *think,* and thinking, I suppose, is merely the process of using the imagination and the mind in an orderly manner so that a creative process takes place and a subsequent process of growth. But with me there was no growth. There was no creation. In all my life there had never been, until I was near to middle age, either the necessity or the desire to think. *Really* to *think* is not a simple thing. It cannot easily be taught, and learning by experience requires time and a steadily growing maturity. I had already lost nearly twenty years which should have been employed in thinking, and because those years had been wasted I had never attained any degree of maturity. I had merely grown older, and like those men who constantly cling to their youth or return to it at college reunions and Legion conventions, I had merely withered.

I remember once having heard Ernest describe a common acquaintance as "a man who had passed from adolescence to senile decay with nothing in between." The description haunted me, for it seemed to fit not only myself but all the people in the world in which I lived. Some did not shrivel; they grew fat. But the effect and the result was the same. Nothing—either ethical, moral, or intellectual—had occurred to us since we left college, and very little of change or inspiration occurred during those days in college when we should have been learning to think and become mature. I am quite certain that much of the weariness which affected the body and spirit of Ernest arose from a feeling of frustration—that whatever intellectual life he had was always confined to the interior of his own head and the only sympathy which he received was from his fragile wife.

Even now I have no feeling of maturity. I am concerned with things which long ago should have been understood and put in order in the general pattern of my existence, and even as I write I am aware that I am putting many things on paper which should belong properly in a college theme. I began too late after too many wasted years, and I have attempted to grow in an ill-watered and sterile desert.

Something of all of this went into the renewal of my heavy drinking. When I try to find out why I came to drink more and more, I can, from this distance in time and space, see it all a little more clearly. My life with Enid was becoming steadily more insufferable for a million reasons, but worst of all I had begun to hate my own home, to dread returning to it, to sleep badly when I was in it. I had begun to feel indifferent even toward my own children, perhaps because they seemed merely to be growing into small copies of Enid, stamped and molded by her ideas and her ideals. In one sense they were the most normal of healthy children, but in another they were becoming mere monsters of "normality," performing on their level all the banalities of which she had become for me the symbol.

I wakened in the morning not only tired but, what was much worse, bored. I certainly had small interest in my business which ran itself and I had no real interests elsewhere save in the reading which had led me merely into confusion and frustration. I was reluctant about starting the day and could see no reason for doing so. A drink always helped. First it provided a physical reaction of warmth and stimulation which got me on my feet, and whenever during the day that sensation of false well-being began to waver, I took another drink to preserve and increase it, and presently I had enough to make everything seem blurred and endurable if not pleasant and happy. From then on until I fell asleep at last because my blood was filled with alcohol, the world seemed a fairly agreeable place.

For a time the drinking grew so bad that friends began to talk of it, as if I were one of those congenital drunkards whose systems cannot accept and absorb alcohol even in small quantities without intoxication. There are many of these—indeed I think most drunkards fall into this category—but I was not one of them. I was always what was called "a good drinker." I could absorb vast quantities of alcohol without becoming drunk, and never in all my life have I been able to attain the kind of drunkenness which becomes noisy and violent and offensive. As during the episode in New Orleans, I finally reach a point where alcohol no longer has any effect and becomes for the time being merely repulsive. I was never the violent sort of drunk. I drank not because of the weakness of the body but from a sickness of the mind, and I was aware that this kind of drinking can become the worst of all since it becomes an escape and a refuge and, as in the case of Tom, Dick, and Harry, it is closely related to what certain psychologists call the "death wish."

This "death wish" is a curious thing, and I am certain that many more people experience it than any psychologists can estimate. I am sure that there are ten thousand people who have contemplated suicide seriously to everyone who has carried the contemplation through into action. Drunkenness and drugs are all too often the expression of the death wish among those who lack the desperation or the courage to achieve the total and permanent oblivion. I know that this is why I drank. It was the desire to escape, wholly, entirely, without any reservation whatever.

Just as I planned on two occasions the murder of Enid but lacked the will to carry through the plans, so I planned suicide many times but always rejected the idea, each time because there arose at the last moment in my heart a desperate hope that if I stayed alive there might still lie before me experiences that were new and perhaps satisfying. It is hope which keeps many people alive. Sometimes too I thought that suicide might be messy for the children and that I had no right to embarrass or distress them. It would indeed be a horrible punishment for Enid, perhaps worse than if I killed her, for suicide was in her mind the greatest of all scandals. It would have humiliated and disgraced her and of course, I would have escaped her for good, for once and all with the finality of death itself. Drink, I shortly discovered, could provide the escape for a good part of each day, and in the end, if the process continued long enough and intensely enough, it would mean final and total escape, though the process might be slow and painful and degrading.

It was worth noting that among my friends I was regarded as a congenital physiological potential drunk, for there seemed to be no other reason. They always said, "Why should Wolly Ferris take to drink? He has everything!" and this, I must say, was reasonable enough, on the exterior. I doubt that any of them, with the exception of dead Ernest, ever had the faintest idea of the reasons for my drinking or had the power to understand those reasons. This is ironic, in view of the fact that many of them sought the same "short death" for reasons which were similar.

I know as I write that whoever reads this may inevitably ask, "But had you no faith in God? Could not the church have helped you?" And I answer, "Perhaps," but somehow the circumstances never made it possible either for God or for the church to help me.

Let me say that I believe in God as a force which somehow has brought an orderly universe out of chaos. Whether He is an impersonal, vague, and powerful set of laws still far beyond our understanding, whether He is the vengeful Jahveh of the Jew or the Santa Claus God of the Italian peasant, who represents all that is good and nothing that is evil, I do not know, nor do I believe that anyone else knows any better than myself. God, to me, has always been, I suppose, the Great Mystery which I must accept without understanding, since I have no other choice. There is no very great comfort in this, nor can one blame one's own weaknesses or faults on something as vague as a Great Mystery nor go to it for help in distress.

The few times I have prayed I have always found myself in the final analysis praying to myself—reminding myself that I was weak or stupid or lazy or that I had done an ungenerous or selfish thing and so violated rules which I knew and understood perfectly well and which were as rigid and exact as the laws of chemistry. After all, God is to a very great degree the Sermon on the Mount and the Ten Commandments, and these we can touch and understand and practice, and virtually all the evils in the world arise from the fact that too many of us ignore this conception of God and seek instead a bearded old man who will excuse us our derelictions if we merely pray to him and recognize him. That kind of God seems to me execrable and little more than a concoction in the minds of those who are either too weak or too cowardly or too unintelligent to live properly and decently ... as you might say, on a level with God Himself.

Certainly I have never made any great pretensions in that direction. I have been as weak and as "sinful" as the next fellow, and usually I have recognized the fact and it has depressed me, which is probably a great handicap in the worldly sense, for it has withered all capacity for ruthlessness. It has reduced me to the level of those who only question without being able to find an answer or to believe in one. And that perhaps is the great sickness of my own small world and perhaps of all Christian civilization. Perhaps it would be far better to be ignorant and superstitious like my Sergeant, living only in the flesh and by the flesh whose sins are easily forgiven and comparatively unimportant. Then I could have accepted a God who was like a benevolent but sometimes angry father who bestowed favor and dealt out chastisements. Certainly it would have simplified my life and perhaps the lives of those nearest to me.

The trouble is that I, like so many of us, have been educated to the point where a belief in such a God is no longer possible yet we have not been educated to the point, either ethically or intellectually, where we have the force and the courage to stand upon our own, each as an integral part of God Himself. We are merely lost and at the same time somewhat pretentious without reason. In short, middle-class contemporary man is a mess of pottage and confusion, save in the realm of materialism out of which he has created the porcelain water closet, the automobile, and the atom bomb.

My hostility to churches and theology began when I was still a small boy. It began when I was forced each Sunday to dress myself in stiff clothes, polish my black Sunday shoes—"my good shoes"—and set off for the Presbyterian Sunday School to pass two hours and a half of misery until at last I could run down the steps of the church after the morning service and escape into my old clothes and the neighboring woods and fields. When I was very small the "infant class" meant little except marching about and seeing great colored posters of remarkably clean and sentimental and beautiful people entering the Promised Land or strewing palms before Christ on a donkey. But that was much better than when, as I grew up, I went on into an older class "led" by a local prosperous shoe merchant named Wesley Downes.

Elder Downes had a great reputation as a Sunday School teacher in Crescent City and throughout church circles in the state. He was a good enough fellow, plump, pink-faced, and gray-haired, who found great pleasure in expounding the stories of the Bible. This he did, I suppose, rather well, but even at the age of thirteen or fourteen I found it difficult to swallow either a great many of these stories or his special versions of them. He was, I suppose, what might be called a Fundamentalist. At least he professed to believe everything that was written in the sacred book and took all of it with complete literalness, even to such legends as that of Jonah and the Whale which I once attempted to dispute with him only to be humiliated by accusations of lack of faith in God because I did not believe that a whale could swallow Jonah, carry him around for a long time in his stomach, and finally disgorge him intact and in good health.

Elder Downes believed absolutely that God had sent angels to visit Sodom and Gomorrah and warn the bawdy inhabitants, and he believed that, when the angels had to flee from worse than death, God actually poured fire and brimstone upon the evil cities of the plain. It was apparently inconceivable to him that such a magnificent story could have been a legend based upon some actual disaster and worked into dramatic form by an Hebraic Old Testament Billy Sunday.

I doubt that he understood at all the full implications of the story or the peculiar forms of depravity involved which were perhaps common enough in those times and still are today among certain Semitic and Moslem peoples. If he did understand even faintly the implications, he never touched upon them for such wickedness was something you did not talk about. For Elder Downes the debauchery of Sodom and Gomorrah was, I am sure, something like the "orgies" depicted in the films of D. W. Griffith or C. B. DeMille—vast expensively produced spectacles in which ladies waved bunches of grapes and bearded gentlemen reclining on couches responded by waving empty papier-mâché goblets to indicate drunkenness. As I see it now, the innocence of Elder Downes was colossal, but so was his vindictiveness. I do not think he was ever much troubled by fleshly temptations. He was the plump eunuch gland type. He took it all out in his performance as a minor prophet interpreting the Bible to less inspired boys and businessmen.

Neither my father nor mother was very religious, and I am certain that neither of them sent me to Sunday School or church for the good of my soul or in the belief that I should find there spiritual regeneration. They did it because sending one's children to Sunday School was the thing to do. My own children go regularly to Sunday School, and I doubt that they like it any better than I did, although today all kinds of inducements, including even movies, have been introduced to lure children to Sunday School classes. They would still rather be at home in their old clothes playing with the dog. But that, of course, would be heathen goings-on and Enid would permit no such thing.

The church in Oakdale to which they go has a wonderful new parish house equipped with the finest in modern plumbing. It has a basketball floor, and as soon as the war ends and building becomes possible once more they are constructing a swimming pool. There are three pool tables and three ping-pong tables and periodically there are dances for the young. I think this is all fine as a means of keeping the young distracted and the Devil from getting hold of idle hands, but I do not know how much it has to do with God or faith or an understanding of the universe.

With my father and mother it was their "duty" to send their children to the Presbyterian Sunday School. My father attended church regularly and dozed more often than not, and my mother went to church on the Sundays when she was not traveling and uplifting the world. She saw her friends and received a kind of homage at the church door as a woman well known in circles outside Crescent City, but I am in grave doubts as to any spiritual comfort she or my father received.

Indeed it was, I think, difficult for anyone to derive much spiritual comfort from the ugliness of the old downtown First Presbyterian Church which, even considering the peculiar hideousness of the churches built in its period, was exceptionally ugly. It resembled neither the ornate beauties of an ancient Catholic church nor the austere beauties of the New England meeting house. Architecturally it was a mess which had cost a great deal of money and required nearly twenty-five years to pay for. The seats were placed like those in a theater beneath two monstrous brass chandeliers with a pipe organ and choir loft at one end. The windows were enormous and filled with what could only be described as monstrous concoctions of painted, not stained, glass which resembled something which had been spewed up or removed during an operation. If there was nothing beautiful in it, neither was there anything which inspired faith or religion. If it manifested anything it was the sound incomes of a middle-class world in a rich, partly civilized, and growing community.

Throughout most of my youth we had the same preacher. He remained for so long a time because he managed never to displease or alienate anyone in the congregation and managed somehow to please most of them. Probably he was popular because he never disturbed his congregation either collectively or individually. But this fact did not make for inspiration or good sermons or even faith. I think that he bought most of his sermons already written for him, and he never diverged from them even by a single gleam of originality. The only ritual concerned with the church was the fundamental ritual of attending services. After many years my only impression of it was one of fabulous aridity and boredom. I cannot imagine ever going to that particular preacher for solace, advice, or comfort.

And so as soon as I could escape I did escape, and I have never gone back, even to the handsome new church with its "modern" clergyman, its pool room and basketball court and its ping-pong tables. The old church had nothing to give me in a spiritual sense and I see no prospect of change in the new and modern version which has supplanted it. Of poetry, of mysticism, of beauty, even of faith there are few manifestations. It is as if the "new" church were concerned with the body and its functions and had no concern whatever for the spirit. The older church had concern neither for the body nor the spirit.

All of this is no special criticism of any Protestant sect or denomination. Many of them are worse than the churches I have described and some perhaps are better.

It is possible that the Roman Catholic church might have brought me something approaching strength and salvation, but I never came close enough to it to understand or appreciate it or to feel any special or irresistible attraction. Between me and the Roman church there were many obstacles, not the least of which was the long childhood indoctrination of Calvinist Protestantism. The Jesuits themselves, I believe, are credited with saying that they need train a child only during the first six years of his life to claim him for the church forever. Whether the Jesuits ever really said such a thing or not I do not know, but I believe there is much truth in the saying. During my childhood there was built up within me a profound and instinctive mistrust of the Roman church, indeed so profound that it came to seem a foreign and even a Godless institution in which all sorts of evil took place.

Certainly it played a small part in the world in which I lived. It was wholly a Protestant world with two or three Catholic families who, by the mere fact of being Catholics, always seemed a little strange and never quite an integral part of our society. Otherwise the Roman church in Crescent City was represented by the immigrant population or the first generation of immigrants, and between them and the world of Oakdale there was little contact or sympathy. Among the women of my world there was a feeling, subconscious at its mildest and aggressive at its strongest, that being a Roman Catholic was actually a social disadvantage. It was a tight world, a Protestant world, and consequently a materialist and middle-class world.

It was only after I came to know Mary Raeburn again that I began to understand a little that I might have found some of the things I was seeking within the Roman world. It was only then that I began to understand how closely that world was rooted in the whole history of Western civilization and culture. It was only then that I began to understand the profundity of the meaning lying beneath the outward symbols and rites which until then had seemed meaningless and to a Calvinist mind so much claptrap. Until then I did not understand that in those very symbols and rites there lay an appeal to the intelligent and cultivated mind and the roots of mysticism and beauty which many of us were seeking hungrily without ever finding.

Yet even all of this was confused in my mind for it seemed to me that there were in Crescent City, at least, only two kinds of Catholics—the immigrant element which, through ignorance and fear, was bound to the church without reason and by no more than a vague instinctive realization of the beauty and the roots, and, on the other hand, those with intelligent and logical but formal minds which accepted certain things which I could not accept or laid them at one side for the sake of consolations more profound.

But in all of this there was largely only a confusion of mind and a groping for something in which there was a form and a faith as there might be form in a beautiful sculpture or picture, and faith of the sort which I sometimes felt as a child in the country at sunrise when my heart cried out, "This is a wonderful and beautiful world and I am grateful for being alive!"

I know that I was not alone in my confusion and my groping in the darkness. There was the same sensation of being lost among many of those about me, even among the four men who went with me on the tragic trip to New Orleans. Three of us on that trip did not know or suspect the sources of that doubt and dissatisfaction bordering upon despair which drove them toward the "little death" of drinking. But Ernest *knew* and I knew, although with his trained and superior mind he understood the aridity of his life better than I, and perhaps that very knowledge and understanding drove him toward the grotesque ending of that life.

When I am writing of these men I am not writing of Babbitts. There are no more Babbitts. They belonged to a certain phase of American life and that phase has passed. Babbitt, with his bumptiousness, his good nature, his extreme extroversion, the noisiness which covered up his ignorance, is today a curiosity and in many ways an outcast. All his qualities, his very problem, have been supplanted by a kind of sickness and confusion unrecognized by the victims who seek escape in materialism, in a supercharged activity, and in drinking. Babbitt in his way was crude but healthy. The sickness of which I write and which spreads and grows constantly is quite different. I know of what I am speaking; and I am frightened for a whole nation and a whole people.

This then was my state of mind on the return from New Orleans. All this is why I was drinking again. I knew on my return that, while I should probably go on living with Enid for the sake of the children, it would be a kind of life in death in which we both hated each other, although hatred would not end her passion for possession and "sharing" but only intensify it because she was one of those who could not accept defeat. She would not even admit to herself that hatred had supplanted whatever love there had been. It would only be worse than before and more ugly. Perhaps it would have been better if I had run away or smashed things altogether, but there something intervened. Call it decency or conservatism or habit or Calvinist ethics and morality or what you will, I do not know. Perhaps it was a mixture of all of these things. Something still held me fast in the pattern in which I had lived for nearly half my life. I do not know whether it was for better or for worse. I cannot, honestly, either praise or blame myself. I do sometimes think that both Enid and I were victims of all the combined forces which made each of us what we were—the forces I have tried so hard to trace back to the very beginning. I find myself as I write coming back again and again to that apparently unanswerable question of why as a free and healthy individual I did not simply walk out on the whole thing. Even now I do not know.

And then one Saturday afternoon I came upon Mary Raeburn standing beside her car on the road from the country club. A tire on the front wheel had burst and thrown the car off the road into the ditch and she was waiting for someone to come along. At a distance I did not recognize her, perhaps because it had been a long time since I had seen her and the image I kept in my mind was that of the rather plumpish young woman I had known in my early twenties. If I had never seen her before I would have been attracted. Meeting her under other circumstances, perhaps only in passing her on the street, I would have turned for a second look, not because she was beautiful or even very young, but because there was something about her which I as a man would have found appealing.

It is not easy to say what that something was since it was compounded of many things, of the look of quiet serenity that was in her face, the way she moved, not tottering along on over-high heels, her buttocks shaking as she walked, but moving surely and with a certain swift grace. Perhaps it was the way she dressed, quietly but with a sudden flash of color at the throat or on her hat, or perhaps it was the cut of her clothes, simple yet perfect, and the way she wore them. There are some women whom you could dress in the most expensive and beautifully cut clothes who would still look dowdy and others who would make a Mother Hubbard appear beautiful and smart. After we came to be intimate there were a hundred little things I noticed about her, perhaps most of all a certain fastidiousness. There was never lipstick on her teeth. Her hands and nails were always perfectly done. There was a kind of art in the way she fastened a scarf with a pin. Her hair seemed always perfectly in control. And she never wore too much of anything. The fastidiousness and perfection gave her an air of coolness which I discovered later was wholly deceptive, but it also gave her an air of calm and of order as if she had everything under control which at that moment perhaps was the thing I desired most in all the world.

XII The Jungle

Last night an ugly thing happened. Homer, the wool-hat, shot another Jap and I do not know now what will happen. We had had peace for many weeks with one or two of the Japs coming out of the jungle in the middle of the night to take the food we left out for them. I suspect they understood the truce and the arrangement and were willing to let it stand so long as we were here, all of us together, on this godforsaken island.

The second poor Jap Homer got right through the heart so that he was only able to run a few steps before he fell on his face and died. The shot roused me and I was the first to find him lying face down in the moonlight on the white sand darkened by a small pool of blood. Scattered around him lay some three-year-old tins of soup and baked beans. He was about the same age as the first Jap, and having been alive only a moment or two before, he did not have the horrible, grinning, half-decayed, inhuman look of the other. The Sergeant turned him over, and as he did so a great and weary sigh seemed to emerge from the dead body as the air was pressed out of the lungs. Under the flashlight the face seemed like that of a little boy, like those Japanese babies with cropped hair, or like a cheap Japanese doll. He had the long body and the short strong muscular legs of a peasant.

The Sergeant said, "He's dead all right!" Then he turned to Homer. "What'd you shoot him for? The poor bastard wasn't doing anybody any harm."

Homer said, "He ran at me and hit me! I shot him in self-defense."

The Sergeant said, "What'd he hit you with—a can of soup?"

"He tried to jump on my back. I was smart and shook him off."

The Sergeant scowled and I knew that suddenly the ferocious temper was about to give way. It was only a question of seconds.

"I suppose," the Sergeant said, "he climbed you with his arms full of canned goods." He kicked away one of the scattered cans.

Homer, the wool-hat, began to whine. "What are you pickin' on me for? You ought to be thankful I kin shoot. He mighta killed all of us."

"That poor little bastard with nothin' to kill us with but Campbell's soup!" Then a sudden thought occurred to him. "Wait a minute," he said and bent down and turned the flashlight full on the shattered chest of the dead Jap. After a second he straightened up and said, "You shot him in the back, you white trash sonofabitch! You shot that poor starving little bastard in the back when he was goin' away with his arms full of groceries. He was trustin' us and you shot him in the back. I oughta kill you . . . that's what I ought to do . . . you and your goddamn squirrel shootin'. I suppose you learned that on one of your famous nigger hunts. I can't kill you but I'm sure gonna beat hell outa you."

With that he smashed his fist straight into Homer's face and Homer began to yell. It didn't last long for Al and I, with the help of Meyer, managed to drag the Sergeant off and quiet him. If we hadn't been there he might have killed Homer. I knew it wasn't only the fact that he had shot a defenseless man in the back which enraged the Sergeant. It was much more than that. It was all the things Homer was, the way he thought, his evil stupid prejudiced mind, his physical dirtiness. The whole flood welled up and burst.

The blood was streaming down Homer's face and he was blubbering again and whining, "Jeez! I'll get you for that! I'll get you if it's the last thing I do . . . you goddamn nigger lover!"

"Shut up," I said. "Go and wash your face. I'll take care of this later."

The Sergeant ignored him and ordered Al and Meyer to go and get a shovel and the jeep. None of us wanted the dead Jap lying around there all night. Left alone with me, the Sergeant said suddenly, "What a bunch of damned fools we are—standin' out here in the moonlight. If there is any more Japs and they've got a grenade or a gun they could fix us all and quick like sittin' birds!"

But if they hadn't fixed us by now it wasn't likely they'd fix us before we got the body down on the beach sand and buried, so we went along with our work. Maybe there weren't any more Japs. Maybe there had been only two of them and after the first was killed this poor little bastard had been left alone, hiding in the jungle by day and coming out by night to pick up what we left out for him, living off the handouts we gave him. On the sand where we left the canned goods there had never been more than one set of footprints, very neat, coming and going. The sky was turning pink over the lagoon by the time the boys had finished their task and I fell asleep at last.

The tacit truce with the hidden Japs had been a helpful thing for our nerves, but it had served to soften very little the tension and monotony which grew steadily worse. The "going-over" of Homer by the Sergeant had indicated how quickly violence and hatred and perhaps even murder could flare up. And now the truce with the Japs had been violated and we could not know what to expect.

In the morning the Sergeant came to me and said, "Maybe we'd better take the guns away from Homer altogether. He's a nasty piece of goods. He'll always find an excuse for what he wants to do."

We talked of such a procedure for a time, but I pointed out that if we did that, it would increase the guard duty for the other boys. This would be unfair, and it may have been that this was exactly what Homer was playing for. . . . If you couldn't put him on guard duty he could sleep all night. You couldn't punish him by putting him on kitchen police or making him permanent cook because nobody would eat after him. You always kept thinking of the black women and their yaws which you couldn't keep him away from. He was crafty enough. I sometimes wondered why he had not managed long before now to get himself thrown out of the Army altogether. Certainly if there had been any way of throwing him off the island we would have done so long ago.

In the end we agreed that by constantly threatening him with punishment we might keep him in order and make him pull his own weight—something he avoided doing whenever possible. That appeared to be the only kind of treatment he understood.

Just as we finished talking, an Army plane buzzed us and dropped a bag of mail, the first we had had in nearly a month. There were two books for me sent by Enid and a letter. It was not very interesting, mostly gossip and household matters, but for the first time it seemed to me to come out of a strange, remote, and utterly foreign world, and at first this alarmed me. Perhaps I thought, "I'm becoming a beachcomber." On consideration the prospect did not displease me. It might even be a solution—to go on when the war was over, wandering from island to island in the Pacific. I could even be quite a luxurious beachcomber with the money I could arrange to have sent me. I discovered suddenly that I actually did not dislike even this lonely forgotten existence I was leading. It was monotonous, but there was more peace in it than I had ever known and in a negative sense I was happy, perhaps because the writing has occupied so much of my time and given me a sense of satisfaction.

When I had torn up Enid's letter—there was no reason to preserve its emptiness—I left the hut to walk down to the beach for a late-morning swim, and as I passed one of the great clumps of dying mangrove isolated by the coral sand, I heard the sound of sobbing. It was a desperate heartbreaking kind of sobbing and I felt forced to investigate it.

In the midst of the mangrove clump I found Meyer lying on his face. I bent down to him, thinking that at last his nerves had broken, and asked him what the matter was and whether I could help him in any way, but he could not answer me at first. After a little he sat up, looking ashamed, and rubbed the sleeve of his shirt across his eyes, but he still could not speak. His body was shaking like that of a child who has been crying violently and cannot stop sobbing.

I persuaded him to return to my hut, and there, seated on my bed, he managed to get control of himself and talk with some degree of coherence.

He had had a letter from home telling him that his mother was dying of cancer and could not live until he could get back. She had been ill for a long time but would do nothing about it until it was too late. His sister had written at once, but she said the doctor did not expect the mother to live more than a few days and the letter had already been two weeks on the way. That was all, and now Meyer sat on the edge of my bed staring into space and answering me politely enough if I asked him a question but otherwise behaving as if he were dazed.

I did manage to find out some things of importance—that he was an only son. The only other child was a sister older than himself. And I discovered how profound is the Jewish sense of family and how closely knit are the ties among orthodox Jews like himself. And I came to understand why it was that he was always so silent. Here on this island, surrounded only by Gentiles, he felt completely uprooted and perhaps more lonely than any of us, for it was not only America or even Brooklyn for which he was homesick but for the close tight little circle of Jewish relatives and friends—a citadel from which he had seldom made a sortie into the world outside. So closed had it been, so conventional in its ancient ghetto traditions and its religious orthodoxy, that he was in truth a foreigner not only to Brooklyn but to everything which was commonplace in American life to the rest of us. I had lived all my life in the world of Crescent City and Oakdale and Al, the big farm boy, in the open country of Kansas. The Sergeant was at home anywhere save in circles which socially or intellectually were above him. Even Homer, the woolhat, had some traditions in common with the rest of us. But poor Meyer was a stranger. There had never been anyone to whom he could turn, no one who would understand his world or what he felt about his family. With Homer and even at times with the Sergeant he was constantly reminded that he was not only a stranger but a Jew. And now this tragic news. He had every reason for hiding in the jungle to sob his heart out.

I tried to get through to him, but I am afraid I was not very successful. I shall go on working at it, for if I can only get him to talk it will make things easier. It is one of the tragedies of the Jew, perhaps the greatest of the many tragedies which the Jew has borne, that persecution and segregation have exaggerated his human traits out of all proportion and often to the point of caricature. It has made too many Jews into extreme introverts or extreme extroverts. It has made neurotics and psychiatrists or kibitzers and gangsters. Meyer was the extreme introvert who in order to exist needed that familiar small world in which his wife and his mother and his baby possessed an importance which few Gentiles will ever understand.

I said to him, "Look, Meyer, whenever you want to talk, come in here and talk . . . about anything at all. I always have time. I haven't got anything else to do."

He answered me without looking up from the floor. "Yes, sir. Thank you."

"I'll make a superhuman effort to get a plane for you, but there's no use kidding ourselves. There isn't enough time and it would have to be an amphibious number. You understand that, don't you?"

His thin little body shook suddenly with a sob beyond his control. "Yes, sir. I understand it." Then he sat up and looked at me for the first time out of the great brown liquid eyes, speaking with the grotesque accent that comes out of some parts of Brooklyn. "It don't make things any easier." His body shook again and he said, "You see, I was a baby when my mother came from Poland. They had a hard time. She used to do any kind of work and go without food for my sake. She wanted to get ahead. She made me go on to school when I could have gone to work to help her. And now . . . she'll be gone. . . ." His voice trailed off and his head slipped down between his hands and he stared at the floor.

Presently I said, "Look. You don't want to go back to the barracks now. You stay here. Lie down on the cot. Cry your heart out if it does you any good and try to go to sleep. Sleep can do wonderful things. It's like morphine. I'll go and try to get a radio message through. You've a right to go home even if it's too late. I'll do everything I can."

He sat up erect once more but looking down at the bed in a strange way as if he could not bring himself to be so presumptuous as to lie on the bed of an officer.

"Go on," I said. "I'm going to get the Sergeant to try and send a message." Then I left because I knew that as long as I was there he would not lie down.

As I walked across the white sands to the Sergeant's hut I felt depressed and frustrated that I could not get through to a fellow human being, that there should be so many intangible but impassable barriers between us. I was troubled too because the radio had been working badly for a long time and the parts which the Sergeant had requested had not been forwarded or had not arrived. It was the kind of thing which happens in the Army to forgotten men like ourselves.

When I walked into the Sergeant's hut I found him tinkering with the transmitter.

"Got it working?" I asked him.

He answered me without looking up. "Hell, no!" he said. "This time I think it's out for good. I've patched it up for the last time."

I grinned. "That kind of leaves us isolated," I said.

He slammed the coil of wire he had in his hands on the floor and began to swear. It was a magnificent performance in which he employed about every four-letter word known to the English vocabulary of filth. Because it was so passionate and magnificent, the words he used did not seem dirty. He finished up by saying, "Once I get out of this —— Army, I'll stay away from it as far as possible."

"The trouble is," I said, "that wars and armies are out of date."

Then I told him about Meyer, and as he listened he seemed to melt. When I finished he said, "The poor little sonofabitch!" and after a moment's silence he said, "He's a funny little guy. I can't like or dislike him. He don't seem human sometimes . . . he's so goddamn quiet," adding, "We'll have to get the —— transmitter fixed somehow and try and get a plane down here."

I was thinking ahead of him and said, "If he gets out you know what it means, don't you?"

"No, what?"

"The chances are they wouldn't let any of the rest of us off for weeks or months. They won't send any replacements out here and they won't let us cut down the post to three men."

A deep scowl came over his face. "Hell, I never thought of that! Hell!" This time he had not enough profanity left to relieve his feeling. He picked up the tool kit that was lying beside him and threw it, with all his immense strength against the side of the hut. The case smashed apart and the tools flew in all directions.

I said, "Do you think you can fix the thing up for a last time?"

He was silent for a moment and then in a very quiet voice he said, "I can do my best. That poor little bastard hasn't got anything in the world but his mother, his wife, and his kid!" Then slowly he began to pick up the scattered tools, saying, "I'll get Al in to help. Sometimes he's got smart ideas. He's smarter with tools than I am."

"Thanks," I said. "You're a good boy."

As I went out the door I heard him saying, "Tell that to the —— marines!"

I went into the jungle along the path that led toward the fuzzy-wuzzy village. I didn't want to disturb Meyer and there wasn't anywhere to go but down to the beach or along the path. The air smelled of growth and desolation, of dampness, of birth and decay and of growth feeding upon decay. I wondered whether the Sergeant would really try to repair the transmitter and get to the outside world. If they could send a plane in, it meant that Meyer would go out and the Sergeant would be left behind, denied what he wanted most in all the world—escape and some women and some excitement. There were many things he could do. If he allowed the transmitter to go unrepaired for a few days it would be too late to do any good so far as Meyer was concerned. The Army didn't send you halfway round the world simply to attend a funeral or to get consolation from the surviving relatives. The only hope of getting leave for Meyer was that we could get through quickly enough while there was still, by some miracle, a chance of sending him home while his mother was alive. Even then it would depend on the kind of man the officer at Kinoko was. But, of course, the whole thing really depended upon the Sergeant himself. It was for him to choose to sacrifice the thing he wanted most in life at the moment.

I walked nearly as far as the jungle village, near enough to see the huts raised high on stilts with the skinny pigs and mangy dogs foraging underneath among the garbage and excrement. I could smell it from a great distance, a smell of filth and heat and disease that was perhaps worse than the smell of the dead Jap. Then I turned back.

On my return I went instinctively down to the beach for a swim, as if to rid myself of any trace of that horrible smell, and then returned to my own hut.

Meyer was lying on his back, his head a little on one side. The dark skin of his cheeks was wet with tears, but he was asleep. Leaving him undisturbed I went over to the Sergeant's hut, and as I reached the door I heard him testing the transmitter. Al was beside him. Both of them were dripping with sweat. I stood in the doorway listening, and presently my shadow, falling across the floor, attracted the Sergeant's attention. He went on sending out his signal and listening and without speaking he grinned and nodded his head, and then presently it came clear and he called me.

We had managed to get Kinoko, but both transmission and reception were weak and blurred. When I got the commanding officer I managed with great difficulty to tell him the whole story. It was a maddening business. I believed that if I could have talked to him directly or even clearly over the transmitter I could have fixed things for Meyer, but how can you make a case to a strange officer you have never seen when you are five hundred miles away talking in waves which alternately roar and recede into silence interrupted by a steady crackle of explosions?

Finally I did get the story across and presently I got back the answer through the maddening silences and static uproar.

It was no good. They hadn't seen a seaplane at Kinoko in three weeks and did not know when they would see another. That was the end of it.

All the time I had been talking, the Sergeant and Al listened with strained faces, and before I cut off communications they had already divined the answer. When I turned to them the Sergeant said, "It's a goddamn shame!"

I wanted to hug him, but I only put my hand on the huge shoulders and said, "Well, anyway, you did all you could." He looked up at me and I added, "And that was plenty!"

And plenty it was. It had been his first turn at leave from this maddening godforsaken spot and he had been willing to sacrifice it although he need never have done so. A leave meant nothing much to me one way or another. In fact I didn't want it until I'd finished the writing I was doing and even after that I felt no strong desire to go back into the world, but the Sergeant was different. He lived by his senses—to eat and drink and make love. As I walked back to my own hut I felt better than I had felt for a long time, for I had witnessed self-sacrifice and something approaching heroism.

Meyer slept until nearly dark, and when finally he awakened I told him as gently as possible the bad news. When he heard it he did not cry. Behind him for generations there was a kind of stoicism which manifested itself once the first anguish had passed.

Quietly he said, "Thank you, Captain. I know you've done everything you could."

"It's the Sergeant you must thank," I said. "He was willing to give up his leave for you."

"I know that, sir," said Meyer. "Maybe some day I can do something for him."

"You'd better get something to eat," I said. "Al is cooking tonight. Usually he has something good."

"I don't feel hungry."

"Try to eat anyway." I put my arm around his shoulders. "There isn't any use saying anything except maybe that we're all for you."

"Thanks, sir."

I watched him walk across the sand and it was the walk of a man moving in a trance, and suddenly a fantastic thought came into my mind—"What if it had been *my* mother?"—but the thought left me numb and without reaction. I knew that at first I would feel a shock and perhaps remember one or two happy moments in my youth which were connected with her and after that I would feel nothing at all save perhaps the relief that I should not have to see her again. It would be like hearing the news that a public institution had collapsed and died. For a second I felt an anguish of envy for poor little Meyer—that he had a humble Jewish mother instead of a prominent do-gooding public character.

That night Meyer did not come to mess but lay on his cot in the darkness of the hut he shared with Homer, the wool-hat. On hearing the news the latter made no comment at all or even displayed any interest.

After supper the Sergeant and Al and I went down to the beach with the net the two of them had made of unraveled rope and caught a few small fish which we cooked when we returned after dark, and after that I left them and came back to my typewriter to set down in my journal what had happened during the day. When that was finished I turned back again to the biography, working late because I was writing about Mary Raeburn whom I had loved and who had taught me what love could be, and for a little time I managed to recapture in memory something of that glow which had illuminated all that brief part of my existence.

Very late—it must have been nearly one in the morning—the sound of a footstep in the doorway startled me and I thought at once of the Japs that Homer might have stirred up. But in the moonlight I saw that it was Homer himself, his gun slung across his shoulder.

The sight of him always depressed me, but I managed to say, "Yes, Homer."

He said, "Kin you come with me, Captain? I wanta show you something."

"What?"

"I cain't tell you. I gotta show you."

"Is it important?"

"Uh-huh."

It might be important or it might not and with Homer you could never tell. His standards of importance were peculiar. I had finished writing for the night and so I went with him. He led the way, walking a little in advance of me across the white sand that sparkled in the moonlight, in the direction of the Sergeant's hut. There he stopped by the open doorway and motioned with one hand. The moonlight was brilliant and I suddenly saw the swollen eye the Sergeant had given him the night before for killing the poor Jap. As I stepped up beside him he turned on the electric torch, throwing the beam against the roof of the hut so that the inside was illuminated by a diffuse light.

"Look," he whispered, pointing toward the mosquito netting that covered the two Army cots placed side by side on which slept the Sergeant and Al. "Look," he repeated in a low voice, "kin you see?"

What I saw was the Sergeant's heavy figure on one cot and the tall body of the Kansas farm boy on the other. I couldn't understand what Homer, the wool-hat, was talking about until he snickered and then I noticed that one of the Sergeant's arms was thrown outward and across the body of Al.

I turned quickly away from the doorway lest one of them should waken and see me there as if I had been spying on them.

"Come," I said sharply to the wool-hat, and when we were a good distance from the doorway I said, "What were you trying to show me? Are you crazy?"

He didn't answer but merely snickered again and I have seldom heard a filthier sound.

"What the hell are you talking about?"

He snickered a third time and said, "I tried to tell you a long time ago something was goin' on."

For a moment I could not find words and then when I found them I managed somehow to hold them in, for if I had spoken I would have said worse things than I said to him on the night he vomited after shooting at the first Jap. As an officer I could not say to him what I wanted to, nor as an officer could I beat him up. Presently when I had gained control of myself I said, "I think I know what you're trying to say . . . I think I know what you're trying to do. You're a damned nasty piece of goods and don't ever do anything like that again. You'd damned well better behave yourself from here on out!"

He muttered, "I thought I was doin' what was right."

Again a wave of rage swept over me and again I held my tongue and my fists. I said, "Those are two of the best guys in the world. You keep your filth and your dirty black women to yourself." Then he snickered again and I felt as if suddenly I had been contaminated by the mere sound, as if he had smirched me with some of his own physical filth. I managed to say, "Now get back to your post and don't do any more shooting or I'll take that damned gun away from you for good." He stood there silent in the moonlight. "You heard me," I repeated. "Get going!"

He looked toward me, suddenly thrusting out his thin neck

in a gesture which seemed like the peck of an angry buzzard. His back was to the moon and his face in the shadow so that I could not see his expression, but I knew that it was one of murderous hatred for the Sergeant, for Al, but most of all for myself.

When he had gone I thought, "We've all got to get out of here before something terrible happens!"

Back in my hut I lay awake for a long time, disturbed and worrying about many things, among them the tragedy of Meyer, which was only one among thousands caused by an idiotic war, and the tragedy of Homer and his hatreds. What did they come from? Why should he be burdened by this intangible mess of perverted ideas and hatreds and standards? What could you do to help someone like him? Nothing that I could discover, lying there awake in the moonlit darkness. And the Sergeant and Al. What Homer had tried to pin on them seemed immensely unimportant, perhaps even touching. There were limits by which the starved affection or even the starved sensuality of people should not and could not be tested. Half asleep I seemed to see a balance. On the one side were the Sergeant and Al, sweating their hearts out to repair the radio transmitter so that Meyer had one chance in a thousand of seeing his mother alive, and on the other was the dead Jap shot in the back by Homer to sharpen his eye in practice as a squirrel shooter. As I fell asleep one thought posed itself in my fading consciousness—that ignorance and the cruelty arising from it were the most evil of all the evil manifestations of man.

XIII Oakdale

Although I did not recognize Mary at first sight that day on the road, she knew me at once. This seemed odd because in Crescent City she was a fairly mysterious and spectacular person about whom people talked a great deal and whose very appearance on the streets caused people to turn and look and make comments. On the other hand I myself was simply "Mr. Smith," a typical citizen, almost a kind of impersonal symbol.

She smiled and said, "Oh, hello, Wolcott! Thank God somebody came along!"

I got down from the car and said, "You aren't hurt, are you?"

"No, at least I don't think so . . . nothing that shows." She was astonishingly calm to have just come through an upsetting experience and one which might have been disastrous.

"Will you take me home?" she said. "I'll get someone to send for the car."

That was the beginning—as simple as that. There is always a point in the relations between a man or a woman when one or both can see what is coming, perhaps foresee the hurt or the disaster that lies ahead, and turn aside before it is too late. Sometimes of course one senses the disaster and rushes toward it, perhaps because the driving force of desire is so great that the achievement of the end seems worth any misery or disaster, and with some, I suppose, the unhappiness, the disaster, is of no consequence because it is in reality a part of the whole and complete experience. I can only speculate about these things since of course I cannot answer for others and no one really knows the heart of any other person. Certainly at that time I was unaware of what was to happen, and even though I had divined something of the unhappiness that was finally to come, I might not have turned aside, for at that moment I was ready for any experience, no matter what. Inwardly and secretly, in the spirit, I was both sick and desperate. As for Mary, she may have known all along. Certainly of the two she was the more experienced.

On the drive back to Mary's house we made the most conventional and trivial conversation. I noticed only one thing—once or twice I found her regarding intently my profile, so intently that I could *feel* her regard.

I had not been on the grounds of the big Victorian house for more than twenty years and doubt that I had been even in Mary's part of town more than once or twice since that time, and I was surprised that the house and grounds had changed so little. The neighborhood had become greatly altered and the near-by houses, once more or less pretentious, had fallen upon shabby days and turned into boarding houses and tourist "homes," but like an expensive luxurious island in a sea of shabbiness, the old house stood proud and well kept. The iron grillwork of the tall barrier which surrounded all the lawn and garden was freshly painted with black paint. The same iron deer and dogs, freshly whitewashed, stood on the lawns among the ordered, circular, and crescent-shaped beds of geraniums, kohlias, salvia, and lobelia. The driveway must have been freshly raked only a little while earlier, for there were no automobile tracks or even a footprint on the blue-gray limestone gravel. The whole place was a museum piece out of the past.

As we drove under the great high porte-cochere Mary said, "Better come in and have a cocktail."

"Delighted," I said, shut off the motor, and followed her into the great cross-hallway which led from the porte-cochere into the main hall of the house.

At the foot of the great stairway the old desire to slide down the long wide rail returned to me and I spoke of it. Mary laughed and said, "I used to think of it sometimes, but I never did any sliding. There were never any children about to join in the game. Sliding alone wouldn't have been much fun. The impulse always died."

Then she raised her voice and called, "Nicole! Nicole!" and a voice from above stairs answered, "*Oui, cherie,*" and Mary called again, "We have a visitor. Come down!" and then incongruously the voice called back, "Okay. I'll be right down."

Then Mary turned to me and said, "Would you like to have a look around? You remember the house. I haven't changed anything," and I became aware of the music which filled the whole of the place. It seemed to pervade every room, coming from some invisible source. It was pleasant music and I commented on it and Mary said, "Yes. It's a ballet—called 'Giselle.' I'm very fond of the ballet. Do you like it?"

"I've never seen a ballet," I said.

"No, I suppose you haven't. It's a great art," and with that she appeared to dismiss the whole subject.

It was true. She had changed nothing in the big old house. There was the same old heavy furniture and the great gilded baldachins capping the high windows with their curtains of red velvet, the same marble-topped tables and consoles, and the same thick heavy dark carpets which must have been renewed since my day. It was as if she had sought to arrest the corroding flight of time and change. The odd thing was that the furnishings and the decorations which in my youth had been considered old-fashioned and ugly—and indeed I myself had considered them so—had somehow changed and were now beautiful. They had, it is certain, a great look of richness and even dignity as compared with the houses of my own world, all decorated in mud colors by Mr. Banville, so alike that you could not tell them apart.

She said, "Do you like it this way?"

"Yes." And then Nicole came into the room.

She was a small thin dark woman with black hair in which there was a streak of white. Her eyes were small and intensely bright and intelligent. She moved in a small quick bird-like way, like a song sparrow. I almost expected a flick of a tail. She might have been forty or sixty. It was difficult to make a certain estimate.

Mary said, "This is Nicole Villon, a great friend of mine."

The little dark woman shook hands with me and said, "Delighted, Mr. Ferris." She pronounced my name with a distinct hiss at the end.

Mary said, "Tell Alexander I'm home and to bring the cocktail things to the veranda . . . and thanks a lot."

When she had gone out Mary said, "Nicole is a very old friend. She sometimes travels with me. She is part French and part Rumanian. She is very clever. She writes for the French journals," and I was aware that Mary had sent Nicole for the cocktails because she wanted time to explain her and I was also aware that Nicole knew why she was sent out of the room and approved.

Then Mary led us to the veranda on the north side of the

[217]

house where it was cool. Here I discovered the only change. The north veranda had been screened in and was furnished with comfortable wicker furniture upholstered in bright-colored chintz. From the veranda there was a wide view of the whole of Crescent City. I had not seen this view for twenty years and I was struck suddenly by how much the landscape had altered during that time. Here and there rose the towers of new tall buildings. The familiar roofs of whole streets of houses had disappeared and in their place were the broad wide roofs and sheds of factories and warehouses with the late afternoon sun painting whole sheets of their windows the color of fresh blood. The hills beyond the river, which once were covered with trees and only a scattering of houses, were now bare of trees. Where the virgin forest had been in my grandfather's time there were rows of streets lined with houses all exactly alike. The change had been going on steadily and so gradually that I had not noticed the complete transformation until now when I saw it all at once from the same angle after almost a generation.

It was no longer the town it had been in my grandfather's day or even the town it had been in my own boyhood. This town which I saw from the veranda of Mary's house, this town in which I had spent the whole of my life, was a stranger. It was not even a town but a great city in which, in a way, all of us were lost. It was quite beyond control, spreading out, crossing the river, climbing the once wooded hills on the far side, growing here, dying and rotting there, but it was a living thing possessed of a colossal vitality. It had neither remained static nor had it begun to die. It was possessed of an empty dynamism which forced it to grow and change but without order or direction in a kind of cancerous fashion in the midst of the once rural, almost primitive landscape. And somewhere in the midst of it I, and many others like me, was lost and confused, belonging neither to the old strong dominant generations which had cleared the way out of a desert wilderness nor to a new generation which might, if God willed it, dominate and channel and bring to real fruitfulness all the violent and dynamic forces which were loose, growing, expanding, spreading aimlessly like the growth of a cancer, a growth which did not know where it was going, unguided by any ideal or philosophy save that of bigness and speed and material wealth. Perhaps it was more like a plant growing on an unbalanced diet, rapidly and aimlessly until at last, without order or support, it collapsed to earth once more.

I had had enough to drink not to mind standing there in silence looking at the spectacle, permitting my soft, ambitious, undisciplined mind to wander and to speculate. All this and the things which had grown out of it were a long way from the day of my two immediate grandfathers. How in such a world was a man to be strong, to have character, to dominate his surroundings, to find the way out for himself, his children, or his friends? Suddenly it seemed like a tower of Babel which one day would collapse because of its very pretentiousness and pride.

For a moment I fancied that I divined why Mary had kept this immense and flamboyant old house exactly as it had always been. It was a monument, a museum, a rock, past which had swept the torrent of mediocrity and uniformity, a torrent of ranch-type and bungalow houses, and picture windows and scatter rugs and dull conforming minds, of universities like ant heaps turning out clod-brained athletes and hordes of uneducated and mediocre drones, and clubs and government bureaus and do-gooding and taxes, worse than those of the ruined and decayed Roman Empire.

Out of such a torrent no civilization was ever built, for it was a torrent in which there was nothing of taste or individuality, or respect for the mind or the spirit, or even ethics and morality, in which even science was largely dedicated to destruction. In some ways it was uglier than the rotting desert of the Dark Ages when man lived again by his own wits and civilization, burning with a brilliant enduring light, took refuge in monasteries and fortified farms. In such a world there would at least be some satisfaction. A man could be a man.

I heard Mary saying suddenly, "You're thinking how much it has changed since we were children," and I started at the fashion in which she had read my thoughts. It was a trick she had, as I was to learn later on.

"It's almost unbelievable," I said. "I'd never noticed it before."

"I would notice it more than you because I'm away for at least half the time. I could keep this place as it was, but I couldn't control the whole of the city."

Suddenly I asked, "Do you like it here?"

She smiled. "I don't really know. I needn't tell you why I have to come back. Everybody knows why. That makes a difference. If I came back by choice I'd probably like it more . . . or perhaps I wouldn't come back at all. I don't really know. I like it because my father loved it here in this house."

She moved to the table as Nicole returned followed by Alexander, an ancient colored servant from her father's day, who came in bringing ice and glasses and the things for making martinis. She looked at me with a quizzical look. "I suppose that surprises you. Most people never thought of him as liking Crescent City and particularly this house, but he did. He loved it much more than my mother. He didn't go out much, but he had some very good friends in the town and he was always happy here. My mother was restless—and trivial. If there were not crowds of people about her she was lost. He said once that our life in Europe made this place seem more attractive and that each time he came here it made him value more the life we had over there. He was a very civilized man and because he was very rich he could devote all his time to being civilized. I suppose he was a kind of parasite in his way. It's because of him I've kept this place exactly as it was. Even the books in his library are in the same order they were in on the day he died."

Then she laughed. "Well, well. That was a long speech, but I thought I'd explain. I know a lot of people in Crescent City think I'm a good deal of a mystery or a little crazy. It's only that this is a good place to rest."

She started to mix the martinis and almost at once Nicole began to chatter, very rapidly like a bird, about the heat, about the countryside and the beauties of the road along the river.

"It's as beautiful as any river in the world and the farms are so rich and prosperous. The houses and the barns are different, but otherwise the country is like the *Valois en France*."

Mary said, "Nicole is writing a book of poems called *Paysages*! It is about the difference and likeness of landscapes the world over."

I started to express my doubts that such a book would have a big public and then checked myself.

The martinis were made and Mary passed them. An unexpected animation seemed to have come over her. Her eyes seemed brighter and there was more color in her face. I made an effort to help her with the cocktails, but she said, "No, I like waiting on people. Sit still and relax. I don't imagine you have much opportunity in Crescent City. Everybody is always running about."

When she sat down I noticed that she did not take a cocktail but poured herself a glass of sherry. She said, "I'll tell you something, but it's a secret. My lawyers are trying to break the conditions concerning the estate which force me to spend half of every year here. I don't know whether they'll succeed or not and I don't suppose it would make much difference in the way I live. I'd still keep the house the way it is and I'd probably come back just the same. Legally I can still go about and visit friends while I'm here. But I hate the idea of being pinned down to something."

"How right you are, *cherie*," said Nicole. "Don't you think so, Mr. Ferris?"

The martini had acted quickly on top of all the whisky I had had at the club and the feeling of strangeness began to go away. I think the presence of Nicole had something to do with the change as well. She was so completely trivial and friendly and *un*shy.

The music inside the house continued softly, and in the fading twilight the view over the familiar city which in the full sun had been sharp and garish and ugly began to soften and take on a dull color as the cool of the evening chilled the mist arising from the river so that it hung low, blurring and softening the harsh outlines of factories and warehouses and shabby houses. Across the river the coke ovens and blast furnaces were turning slowly from black and sooty ugliness into a kind of glowing illuminated beauty. I had another martini and then another and another until I was feeling very well indeed. My tongue was loosened, and although I do not remember what it was we talked about, we must have talked a great deal. I remember that something happened which made us no longer strangers and I remember that I began to feel a growing confidence in myself, perhaps because I did not seem a bore to two women of so much experience and knowledge of the world.

Once Mary said, "Oh, my God! I've forgotten all about the car! I'll go and tell Alexander to call about it. I'll be back in a moment."

When she had gone Nicole said, "She is a charming woman, Mary," and I answered, "Yes. We haven't seen each other for a long time. It was almost like two strangers meeting."

"Very warm in personality she is," said Nicole, "and impetuous. We're very old friends. We've seen a great deal together."

It was odd that in describing Mary she should use two words that would never have occurred to me in connection with her. But perhaps she was right. I had never really known Mary at all and certainly she seemed friendly enough on this occasion. Certainly the Mary I had encountered on the road was a very different person from the shy, rather plump girl I had known so casually a long time ago.

When Mary returned she said, "Why don't you stay to dinner? There's only Nicole and myself. We'd love it."

"Thanks, it's already past my dinner hour and I haven't even called home."

I wanted to stay but something restrained me. I think perhaps it was the feeling that I didn't quite belong—as yet. I knew that at home Enid and the children would probably already have finished dinner. I was not particularly concerned about this because since our open quarrel I had told her that if I did not arrive home at the expected hour she should not wait for me, and she had been forced to accept the arrangement since I really did not care whether she accepted it or not.

Then Mary said, "I dislike being personal, but did it ever occur to you, Wolcott, that you have remarkably beautiful hands?"

I laughed. "I've never thought about it one way or the other. I just thought of them as hands." I was suddenly embarrassed as I have always been when I am paid a compliment, especially if the compliment comes from a woman. She moved forward a little in her chair and leaned toward me. "May I look at them?"

I extended my hands palms upward, still embarrassed and uncertain. She said, "No, one at a time. Your right hand first," and laughing she said, "I'm interested in palmistry." Her eyes seemed suddenly very bright and her habitual rather quiet manner seemed completely changed although she had taken only part of the sherry in her glass.

As she leaned toward me the blouse of thin transparent stuff fell away from her body and I was aware that she had very beautiful breasts. Then as she took my hand in both hers something happened which was the beginning of everything. Her hands were small and beautifully kept and warm and—how shall I describe it?—vibrant, I suppose, to use a banal word, and on contact with them a kind of current ran through the whole of my body and something inside me said, "Here's your chance! Here's experience! Here's everything! Here's escape! Now something may happen to you."

She squeezed the palm gently and said, "Look, Nicole! It's an interesting hand!" She looked up at me very frankly and in the friendliest way. "It's a tortured hand," she said, looking directly at me. "What is it that tortures you?"

"I don't know," I said. "I didn't know that I was tortured," but I confess that I was a little scared and uneasy. I felt the color coming into my face and found myself avoiding her gaze.

"Are you happy?" she asked.

"I suppose as happy as anybody."

Then she laughed in an excited way. "In any case it's none of my business. Let's forget it. Have one more for the road." She dropped my hand quickly and rose to make a final cocktail.

"I must say," she said, "that my accident was really very lucky. This has been a pleasant couple of hours. We must do it again."

"There's nothing I'd like better," I said with the sudden boldness of alcohol. "Whenever you like. How about tomorrow?"

"Fine," she said, pouring the one for the road.

"About the same time?"

"Okay. It's been great fun for Nicole and me. We don't see many people. Nicole works and I do a great deal of reading when we aren't in Virginia or Kentucky."

A little later she said, "You must have noticed me staring at you this afternoon driving home."

"Yes," I said. "I did notice it."

"It was for a special reason. It struck me suddenly how much you looked like my father. I never noticed it before, but of course I hardly knew you at all and when you were younger your face was softer. It's sharpened now and the likeness is really extraordinary. Do you notice it, Nicole? In the throat and in the sharp clean angle of the jaw and chin . . . like the Sargent portrait in the house in the Rue de la Pompe."

"Yes," said Nicole. "*Extraordinaire . . . même le nez.*"

Then Mary rose quickly and said, "Wait, I'll fetch a picture of him. You probably don't remember him very well."

I confessed that I did not. In my memory there was no image of him at all.

She came back in a moment with a photograph of the Sargent, a painting which must have been done of her father when he was about my age. The painter had given his subject a certain dash which the man may or may not have had. The head was turned a little to the right with the chin tilted a little as if in pride. In the picture the man was certainly handsome, more handsome, I am sure, than I have ever been. I knew my own face from shaving (God knows only too well—that was what started all the trouble), and I had seen it a thousand times from just the angle shown in the picture with the chin tilted a little so as to shave clean that part of me where the line of the throat joined that of the jaw, I saw what she meant. There was a marked likeness. The man in the picture wore rather long and romantic sideburns.

I said, "I see what you mean. But your father was a much handsomer man."

"Not really," said Mary. "Sargent always made his subjects glorified—everyone he painted. He even made my mother seem pretty—even distinguished although she had no distinction." And after a moment she said, glancing from me to the picture and back again, "Really it is remarkable. The only difference is the sideburns. If you wore them you would be exactly like the portrait."

It did not seem to me that the likeness was quite that remarkable, but she seemed so intent upon the point that I did not press the argument.

Then somewhere in the depth of the house a bell rang. It must have been a big bell and the sound was exactly like that of the bell at Churchill Downs which means, "They're off!"

"You're sure you won't stay?" Mary said. "I'm sure Alexander has laid a place for you."

"No, I really can't."

Something told me that it was better to leave. I was quite drunk although probably I did not show it. I had need to pull myself together and try to precipitate my confusion as a cloud is precipitated into rain. Everything that had happened was so wholly unexpected, so completely different from what I had imagined, lazily and indifferently, on the way to the old house, would be the experience of having a cocktail with Mary Raeburn. I was aware that suddenly we seemed very old friends and that there was even a feeling of warmth between us, but I did not know why, and with that coldness and clarity of thought which has always stuck by me even after much drink, and with the caution which has dominated the whole of my life, I thought that perhaps after the martinis I had simply imagined all of these things and had better sober up a little before progressing any farther.

I rose and said, "I've had a lovely time. If you expect me tomorrow I'll be here."

Mary laughed. "Of course we expect you!"

"*Bien sûr*," said Nicole.

They both walked with me through the long hall to the porte-cochere and Mary said again, "It's been great fun," and then Alexander appeared and said, "Telephone, Miss Mary. It's long-distance from Warrenton. They're holding it."

"Good-by," said Mary and turned to follow him, but Nicole remained behind. As I stepped into my car she said, "You've been verree good for Mary. She doesn't see enough people. She doesn't like enough people. But with you . . . She *likes* you."

Then I drove off, still in a kind of fog, aware that something had happened of the greatest importance although I did not quite know what it was.

I did not go home, for I did not want to see Enid both because I felt I had had enough alcohol either to put me at a disadvantage with her or to precipitate a quarrel and because I wanted to clear my head a little, so I turned toward the road to Williamsport along the river. I thought, "To hell with Enid!" and at the same time I was aware that such an attitude was dangerous, for it always gave her the advantage over me in all her calculations.

I write about this in great detail as I remember it because it was the beginning of something that was at once the most wonderful and the most wretched period of my life, and everything about it seems to be etched in my memory like the lines on copper plate. The unhappiness with Enid was a dull and boring kind of misery which by now is almost wholly erased from my memory, especially since I have transferred much of it from my heart onto paper and so purged myself of it, but this other experience involves pain and a humiliation almost brilliant in its clarity, to which I cling as if I could not bear to give it up.

Even now I can remember small and insignificant things which occurred during that first meeting and in all the meetings which followed—the way she held her sherry glass and the way, toward the end of that afternoon when one blond lock detached itself and fell across her face until she thrust it back again into place, and a certain breathlessness which I had never expected in her and which excited me. And remember, in my mind there were no longer any inhibitions. I did not care what happened and I felt no responsibility toward anyone.

As I drove along the river the night air grew steadily cooler and presently I felt almost sober again and began examining carefully, detail by detail, what had happened and, because I was able to recreate everything with great clarity and the utmost sense of reality, I began to understand that it had all happened as it seemed to have happened and that nothing of it was an illusion born of alcohol. It really did happen and it had meaning. What it meant was that if things went well I could have Mary Raeburn and indeed that she could have me and that perhaps this would be a good thing for both. I remembered what she had said about the hand being that of a tortured person.

"Now," I thought, "is my chance!"

I was aware that for a moment I seemed to have entered again that distant glowing half-forgotten world of Frank Saunders and his family, yet it was not the same. They were both worlds in which people moved about, it seemed, on a different plane and with a freedom and ease which was strange yet pleasurable, a world in which the barriers and inhibitions, the limitations, the vulgar incessant concern with small things did not seem to exist. On this plane Mary and I had moved quickly and directly toward each other in the short space of a few hours. Yet I was aware of a difference between the world of Mary and the world of Frank which I could neither pin down nor understand.

I do not know whether at that moment I was in love with Mary or not. Certainly I was aware of a strong physical attraction and I was aware with a sensation of surprise and almost of shock that Mary was not at all what I had believed her to be, if indeed I had believed her to be anything at all, one way or another. It was not that she had thrown herself at my head, but I knew that if I chose I could have her and I knew even then that this was what she wanted and that she knew I was aware of her willingness. There had not been a word or even a gesture that could be interpreted as an invitation, yet we both *knew*. Those who have fallen in love at a mature age will understand what I mean.

The figure of Nicole disturbed me vaguely. Why was she there? Who was she? Her foreignness and the alien quality not only of her speech but of her manner and behavior seemed to envelop her in mystery. To be sure, I had never met a woman anything like her. She seemed unobtrusive and at times almost servile in her eagerness to agree with every opinion of Mary's. Apparently she was a friend and an equal, yet she seemed also to be a kind of servant to whom Mary gave orders.

Once during the drive home I experienced a sudden shadow of doubt and an impulse to withdraw from the whole thing while it was still possible, and I might have done so but for the belief that here was my chance to escape both in flesh and in spirit and that it might be my last chance. It was the only time doubt occurred until the very end of the affair.

I had had that earlier chance, long ago in my youth, when Frank Saunders had opened the door for a moment on a new and dazzling world and then closed it ruthlessly in my face. This chance was different, for it involved desire and the flesh which cannot quickly and ruthlessly be cast aside, which once the flame is lighted cannot be extinguished until at last desire is satisfied or burnt out. I was calculating enough to understand that in the case of Mary, once my foot was in the door, it must remain there for a least a little time. In the earlier experience the flesh was not involved except vaguely perhaps in the shadows of Frank's consciousness and of my own, in that realm in which we could not and would not at that age recognize or even admit the truth, although I think the flesh was the only explanation of the fashion in which he took me up quickly and warmly and apparently without reason and then abandoned me as if he understood that what he thought was friendship was not friendship at all but only a sudden emotional mistake and one which troubled him deeply.

Once I stopped at a roadhouse for a drink and by the time I arrived home it was after midnight. I put the car in the garage and went to the icebox and ate half a chicken I found there, knowing that in the morning I should hear complaints from Enid that I had upset the whole of her week's planning and budgeting. She must have heard me close the garage door but she did not appear. I did not care one way or another. On the drive back from Williamsport I had made my decision. Between Enid and me everything I knew now was finished. We might speak to each other in a civil fashion for the sake of the children, but beyond that there would not even be conversation.

In the morning Enid had breakfast with me as always. She seemed to be remarkably cheerful and talkative and more than usually filled with plans for redoing the living room, for putting a bird bath in the garden near the dogwoods. (She was never one of those who was willing to leave nature in peace. She was always for putting in concrete paths and garden globes and special benches she had seen advertised in some "home planning" magazine.)

She asked, "Did you have a good time last night?"

"Yes," I said, and easy as anything added, "Some of us went up to Williamsport bowling."

She poured me another cup of coffee and said, "I've been thinking over what you said once . . . about being more free, about doing things on your own occasionally. I think you were quite right. That's the trouble with a lot of our friends. I've come to believe there is such a thing as being *too* devoted. It can become morbid."

"Yes," I said without much interest. "I'm sure of that."

"I want you to feel as free as free, darling."

And then looking up from my paper I caught her watching me, and out of long experience I knew that she understood at last that she had lost me and she could not understand how it had happened and was trying a new tactic of throwing my freedom at my head. Probably she had read such advice in one of the modern psychiatry columns that were beginning to appear in the papers. ("All men are really boys at heart and want to *think* that they are free. This is something that it is easy for any clever wife to accomplish. Once a husband *thinks* he has his freedom he will want to stay at home every night.")

I thought, "Oh, yeah!"

"Will you be home for dinner tonight?" she asked. "I don't mind. If you won't be I'll just have a simple meal for me and the children."

"You know it's the monthly meeting of the Chamber," I said. "I'll just have dinner downtown and be home right after the meeting." She didn't of course know that it was the night of the monthly meeting, but it did happen to be and it came into my head as an inspiration.

"Okay," she said. "The children and I will just have a pick-up meal. Don't hurry to come home afterward. If you're not in early I'll just go to bed."

She was overdoing the freedom idea, thrusting it down my throat, forcing me to see how *free* she was permitting me to be, exaggerating it, rubbing my nose in it. It struck me that she was never able to let anything alone. She had to work at it, organize it, exploit it as if it were the Parent-Teacher Association or the League of Women Voters. Why were so many American women like that? What was the matter with them? What in hell weren't they getting and what did they want? Why couldn't they simply relax and be women?

I thought, "Okay, if you're going to force freedom down my throat it will make much easier what I am going to do."

What made American women think so much about "holding" their husbands or "winning them back" after they had lost them? It made everything, every relationship, seem phony and involved and tiresome.

I hurriedly finished my coffee before the children went off to school not because I had a bad conscience but simply because I did not want to be left alone with Enid to kiss me as if nothing had happened between us, to have her bring me my hat and stand watching me in the doorway when I got out the car and drove off. I simply wanted to be left alone. I simply wanted her not to bother me, not to go on assuming and indeed *imposing* on me the illusion that these small acts gave me any pleasure. I think I would have minded much less a nagging wife than one who behaved like Enid.

All day at the office and even at lunch with the boys I kept thinking of Mary Raeburn. Again and again I lived through all that had happened the evening before until I no longer doubted what lay ahead of both of us. I no longer had any doubts that she had made the way clear, and the more I considered the whole affair, the more desirable it seemed to be. And suddenly I realized that something wonderful had happened to me. I was no longer bored. There was something I wanted to do, something in which I was interested. It was like being very young again, almost like being born. There was at last an interest in my life. There was something I wanted to do.

In order not to appear too eager and arrive at Mary's house too soon I stopped at the hotel bar and had a couple of drinks with the boys. It was the first time in months, even years, when I enjoyed a drink instead of drinking mechanically to raise my spirits. It was after six o'clock when I drove through the big iron gateway of the big house and up the driveway which again had been freshly raked with no sign of a track or a footprint on it. It occurred to me that the place was like the palace of the sleeping beauty.

As I drove into the porte-cochere she was standing there, dressed in a lot of soft green stuff that trailed on the floor, with a curious high collar that gave her an old-fashioned look as if she were a ghost who had lingered on from the time when the house was new.

She said, "Hello! I'd been waiting for you."

I parked the car, and as I came up the steps and joined her she thrust her arm through mine and said, "I've got a perfect martini waiting for you and Hazel has got a wonderful dinner.

I told her eight o'clock so we wouldn't have to hurry," and almost coquettishly she added, "You're late."

The whole greeting may have been impulse or it may have been calculated, but the effect was not only sympathetic and warm but it skipped, as you might say, a lot of ground. It was as if we had known each other intimately for a long time or had been seeing each other constantly. Only an experienced woman, I think, could have conceived and contrived the whole thing. With one gesture she had taken me wholly into her world. My only doubt arose from the knowledge that once before it had happened like this with Frank and his family.

I noticed that since yesterday there were flowers in the house, huge bouquets of mixed flowers out of the garden for which she kept a gardener the year round. They were not simply like stuffy bouquets of zinnias or marigolds or garden-club flower arrangements; they were great flamboyant bouquets made up of huge dahlias and second-flowering delphinium and day lilies and gladioli, opulent, rich, and on scale with the size of the big rooms and the great height of the ceilings. They had, like the flowers which Frank's mother had arranged long ago, an architectural quality.

The house was filled again with music which seemed to be in every room.

On the veranda Nicole was sitting, dressed all in black lace with a lot of loose crimson lacy stuff wrapped about her throat. She wore tiny diamonds in her ears and looked even more foreign than she had looked the day before.

I think it was at dinner that I divined for the first time a hint of the unreality, even of the fantasy in which later I was to lose myself almost completely for a time.

The table was laid out much as it had been at that single dinner Mary's mother had given long ago in a feeble, rather muddled effort to bring her daughter closer to the young people of the town. The huge mahogany table carried a heavy old-fashioned silver epergne with many small compartments filled with flowers and fruit. And there were many silver dishes and two enormous silver candelabra with candles which threw the great height and size of the room into the shadows. We sat at one end of the table and were waited upon by old Alexander.

The dinner was excellent and as always there was music coming from some distant part of the big house.

I remember that I had a curious impression for an instant of having gone backward in time to another period, another perhaps happier if more ignorant and stupid time in my life. Even the dresses that Mary and Nicole Villon wore seemed to fit into this return into the past or at least they seemed timeless. Certainly Crescent City and Oakdale seemed immensely and pleasantly remote and even unreal.

I do not remember the conversation at dinner. What I remember most clearly was that the effect of cocktails followed by an excellent dinner with two kinds of wine and brandy brought on not the sense of depression which attacked me frequently enough when I had been drinking heavily but a sense of dreaminess and relaxation and contentment—something that was unaccustomed in my life. It was more and more as if the outside world had vanished, as if by some enchantment I had been transported backward into some more leisurely, pleasant time. What I did not comprehend was that the illusion was created very largely through money . . . and wealth, in such proportions as to be almost incomprehensible even to a prosperous fellow like myself. Out of money Mary had attempted to create a world as she would have liked it, and in a way she had succeeded. But money or not, it was extremely agreeable.

We had the brandy together with coffee on the big screened veranda, and by the time we were seated there again, the summer sun had sunk across the river and in the dark moonless night, soft and black as velvet, the fires of the blast furnaces and the coke ovens lighted the whole of the sky along the flat land across the river and high on the hills of the opposite shore. By night the city was a bejeweled and magical place with a canopy of crimson on the reflected clouds overhead. The old man, Mary's grandfather, had done well to build his house on this hill. When the house was new the view must have been wild and romantic with the river boats coming up from New Orleans and the barges slipping downstream with the current against the forested hills opposite. It was all changed now; the beauty was equally wild but different, far more savage than the beauty of the original wilderness.

Mary said, "I wonder what would have happened if things had been different . . . if this had really been my home instead of just a town where I visited . . . if, for example, we had married each other."

I laughed. "It's something to think about."

"*Quel romanticisme*," said Nicole. She had brought a piece of fine tapestry and was working on it as she sat without speaking.

"I used to think you were very good-looking when you were a boy in the twenties." She laughed. "I never told you that . . . but I liked your hair and your blue eyes and your high color. You always looked so clean."

"I hope I still do."

"You still do. My father liked you too. I think he'd have been pleased if we had got married. But in those days I was shy. I never really knew anybody very well here. When I had to go out and compete with the other girls it was agony."

I laughed again. "It was hard to get to know you. I never knew what to talk about. I always thought you considered us a bunch of hicks, and anyway if I'd tried to get acquainted with you people would have said, 'There's that Ferris boy, trying to marry Mary for her money. Probably his mother is behind it.' I was just as shy as you were."

"It might have been different save for my mother," said Mary. "I never really liked her and I don't think she liked me. She was a rather silly woman who chattered a great deal and never said anything. There were times when she drove my father crazy. And she couldn't bear to be alone. It didn't matter what kind of company surrounded her so long as someone was there to be talked at. Words just came out of her mouth without any thought behind them. Sometimes she was ludicrous, and she never learned that very often people were laughing at her rather than *with* her and this ignorance only incited her to more of the same silly talk. She always thought that she was having a great success. I think it was so because at heart she was supremely selfish. Everything, even the weather, was referred to her own ego and whether it pleased her or not. Needless to say, she dressed very fussily and extravagantly without taste. She was so feminine that she became nauseating—in her clothes, her manner, her self-confidence. For some time before he died my father scarcely talked with her at all. He was polite and answered her but avoided her company. She disliked me because as a child I was rather dumpy and never suited the lacy ribbony things in which she insisted on dressing me. The moment anyone came into a room when both of us were present, she at once began operating on me—straightening my dresses, tucking up my hair, rubbing smudge spots from my face with a lacy perfumed handkerchief. She always used the same perfume, rather heavy and sickening. It pervaded everything and hung in the room long after she had left it. I doubt that it's manufactured any more, but now and then I get a whiff of something which smells like it and suddenly I am sickened. Once or twice I have actually been sick." She lighted a cigarette and looked out over the glowing city. "You see," she added, "I really hated her. As a child I didn't know it because a child living as closely as I did with my parents, traveling with them everywhere, never having any close friends among other children . . . a child like that thinks the whole world is made up of people like his mother and father. I must have been a young woman before I discovered that all men were not like my father and all women not like my mother. But the experience made me dislike women. I have never been able to get on with them. I really hated my mother, but I didn't know it until I was nearly grown."

It was a very long speech and I wondered at the time why she made it. She was very quiet while she talked, as if she were very tired. It was almost as if she were talking to herself. Nicole went on working on her embroidery without looking up, perhaps because all of this was something the two women had discussed before many times.

I felt that I must say something so I said, "It's funny how

things happening in your childhood affect all the rest of your life."

She turned toward me, and for the first time I saw that some of the beauty which was in her eyes was the beauty of suffering. She said, "I know the girls here in town thought I had a wonderful life with all the money and the travel and Europe and New York. They envied me, but I'd have traded places then, and even now, with any of them. I was always lost and lonely, I never had any real home or any real roots. I just drifted about the world in luxury and I was about as shy and lonely as it was possible to be." She laughed again and a curious edge of hardness came into her voice. "But I learned to get over that. I learned the hard way by forcing myself. There are a lot of American women like me wandering around in Europe and in the East . . . the daughters of the second and third generations of great wealth who don't belong anywhere. They're the most unhappy people on earth. You've never asked me, but I know you've wondered like everybody else in the town why I keep this big house and spend so much money on it. It's because I'm still trying to grow roots and because the whole place is associated with my father whom I loved. When he died it was the worst thing that ever happened to me or that can ever happen. I got married at once because it seemed the only thing to do. And that was a mess. My God! What a mess! Herby was a suitable conventional man, not too bad in his way, but I scared him. In spite of the fact that I had never had any experience and only knew about sex through what I'd overheard as a child in the general gossip about mistresses, I scared him."

Suddenly she laughed. "It all makes me think of a story which happened to a Frenchwoman I know . . . a widow who married a second time at thirty-five a very handsome and desirable Englishman. Everyone thought the marriage ideal and believed her very fortunate, but after six months she appeared to be unhappy and looked very badly. Outwardly no one could see any reason for it. The husband was charming, considerate of her, and very much in love. At the end of a year a Frenchman, a cousin who had grown up with her, knew her very well, and loved her very much and was an experienced man, went to her and asked her to tell him frankly what the trouble was. She answered him quite as honestly. There was no physical satisfaction in her relation with her husband. He behaved as if the act were shameful and to be gotten over as rapidly as possible. Yet he was constantly driven to it.

"Forgive me for being so long-winded, but it's a good story with a great deal of significance. The French cousin approached the husband tactfully and suggested that he might give greater satisfaction, but the husband appeared bewildered and the Frenchman suggested that it might be a good thing for the husband to take a course in love-making. He even volunteered to provide the instructress—an attractive and experienced actress and courtesan of the better sort living in Paris. The ironic part of the story is that the English husband accepted the offer, in reality, because he loved his own wife so much and wanted to make her happy. He went to Paris on occasional visits and at length completed the course and was given a diploma for proficiency by the actress. But after months nothing seemed to change. The wife became more nervous and looked more and more drawn and ill, and when the cousin questioned her she told him that nothing had changed. It was all as bad as ever. So the cousin again approached the husband, telling him that the actress teacher had reported that he was charming, proficient, and satisfactory, yet his education appeared to be of no benefit to his wife who constantly grew more ill. Why, asked the cousin, had the husband not put into practice what he had been taught? But the husband only looked horrified and said, 'But, my dear fellow, a gentleman doesn't do such things with his wife!'"

Again she laughed. "I have told it fable fashion," she said, "but it explains why my marriage didn't last very long and why my husband was scared of me. He was a Harvard man and belonged to the best clubs, but he wasn't quite bright, and very conventional. There was never a chance of our being happily married and there wasn't any use in going on with it."

Then suddenly Nicole picked up her embroidery and stood up saying, "If you'll forgive me I'll go to bed. I've had a migraine all day and it's worse than ever." Then she turned to Mary and said, "Do you want to give me a moment to check over what I'm to do in New York?"

Mary got up and said, "Of course," and turning to me she said, "I'll only be five minutes. Nicole is going to New York in the morning, probably before I'm awake. You've got everything there on the table. Help yourself. I'll be back in a second."

The two women went out. I poured myself another brandy and lay back in the chair feeling relaxed, drowsy yet interested. I wondered why she had been so talkative and why she had revealed so much. There could only be one reason. I closed my eyes and lay back on the chaise longue.

She was gone for a longer time than she had promised, and when she returned I was not aware of her return until I felt the touch of her hand running through my hair. I opened my eyes and smiled at her saying, "Go on. That feels very pleasant."

She in turn smiled but said nothing. Her eyes seemed very brilliant and I knew then that both of us understood what it was we wanted. Then as if the gesture had never occurred at all she turned away from me and poured herself a glass of sherry and sat down.

"You've never told me anything about yourself," she said. "You're married and it seems to have lasted. Are you happy?"

I laughed. "As much as anybody is," I said. "Like most people I probably expected too much in the beginning. It didn't turn out that way."

"It seems to me that all of us are entitled to a share of happiness, even if we have to fight for it. Otherwise the world is a miserable gray place in which we just drag along until the end."

That was it! I suddenly saw the three of us—Mary and Enid and myself—each fighting for that little dole of happiness and satisfaction, each of us isolated, each of us wanting the other to conform to *his* terms. What was Enid's happiness was certainly not mine, nor mine hers. And Mary too probably wanted her happiness on her own terms. I began to see why the whole business of living must be a compromise. There might be moments or hours or even days when that satisfaction was achieved, but all the rest was compromise, a little here, a little there, until the whole thing lost its shape and purpose. But that was not what I wanted. I wanted the whole thing, as very clearly did Mary.

We began talking again about our childhoods and the past and it seemed to me that we had known each other intimately for much longer than a few hours. Perhaps, I thought, this is the thing called "understanding each other" which people were always talking about. And presently we found ourselves talking about her grandfather, the old Titan who had built this house which she cherished so carefully. Neither of us had ever known him very well and only as children, but on both of us he had left a tremendous memory and impression as dominant and forceful personalities do upon children. He had been shrewd and foresighted and sometimes extravagant but only in solid and material things which in the end paid him back for his extravagance—things like this huge old house overlooking the river which had become long ago a monument to his energy and wisdom that was known from one end to the other of the great river valley. In the old days it was pointed out on every river boat or barge that passed up or downstream.

He had had fine horses and a whole array of fine carriages, and when I spoke of them Mary said, "They're still there. They're kept like a museum." She sat up suddenly. "Would you like to see them?"

So we went out across the lawn. It was very dark under the great trees with only the distant light from the veranda to show us the way. We followed a great hedge of lilacs until we came to the courtyard of the stables, and there the lights from the blast furnaces and coke ovens, reflected downward from the low-lying clouds, illuminated the whole of the place. We crossed the open space, she switched on a light by which I found the key hanging on a nail and we went inside. There, ranged along the wall, polished and with all the metal shining, hung the harnesses of the horses long since dead, and on the floor itself there was in truth a museum collection of carriages, dogcarts, phaetons, cabriolets, an Irish jaunting cart, two governess' carts made to be drawn by ponies and donkeys, and even a sporting coach. They were all spotless and polished.

Mary seemed excited by the experience and even climbed into several of the carriages, but for me the whole exhibition of shining carriages was depressing, as depressing as the skeletons of animals exhibited in a museum of natural history. They were dead. They had no use. They belonged to another day.

"Once," said Mary, "the pony ran away with the governess' cart and dumped us all in a ditch. That's where I got the small scar over my left eye."

By now I knew what it was I wanted and that I wanted it now, tonight. It was the first time I had ever felt an emotion so strongly. The sensation was as much mental as physical. I could not leave her without its being satisfied. She divined, I think, that I was not much interested in the carriages and we left the place, and as we crossed the courtyard again I saw that she had not troubled to lift her long frock of flimsy stuff out of the dust. She walked very quickly, and as we reached the veranda she said. "While we're about it I'll show you my rooms upstairs."

I said, "I've never been upstairs in the house."

She said, "I'm rather fond of the place. I've made a kind of nest up there different from the rest of the house."

I followed her up the long high red-carpeted stairs with the heavy, polished balustrade, and at the top she turned to the left, opened a tall door, and after I had gone through it she closed it behind us and smiling at me she said, "Now?" and I took her in my arms and kissed her. It was a violent kiss. Her whole body was shaking. Her hands were tangled in my hair.

It was nearly daylight when I left. We agreed upon my leaving while it was still dark because of the old servants and because there was always a chance that someone might recognize me or my car.

What happened in the room was like nothing that had ever happened to me before. It was as if until then I had known nothing whatever of lovemaking and certainly nothing of what the response could be. It was beyond anything I had ever imagined. It is quite impossible for me with my poor gifts as a writer to put it on paper, even if I felt any desire to do so.

And now began a period of my life when, looking back upon it from the solitude and objectivity of this beautiful and wretched island, I seem to myself to be a stranger. It is very easy to see myself quite as if I had been at that time another person. The odd complex thing is that I like myself as I was then. I think I must have been quite attractive, physically. I was not quite forty, vigorous, with a good physique and at heart amiable if tormented. There is even, I think, a certain amount of narcissism in my feeling toward the stranger Wolcott Ferris of that brief and isolated period. I am proud even now of the vitality and the vigor I possessed in meeting the demands of Mary's curious obsession for me. I could take it and did, at least to the moment of the final break-up. How much longer I could have lasted physically I do not know. But for the time being I was quite a fellow.

I think that the real reason I seem a stranger is that for a time I was released from all worry or thought concerning myself and my life. I simply gave myself up to the whole thing. I became reckless, so reckless that, thinking of it now, it seems to me that it was all impossible and unbelievable. I slept marvelously well and wakened feeling young and wholly restored each morning, and I found that almost every hour of the day I was thinking of Mary and what had happened and how soon I could be with her again. Each moment away from her seemed wasted and lost. It did not matter to me very profoundly whether we were found out. My business ceased to be of any concern whatever, and it was fortunate that it was the kind of business which managed to run itself.

Certainly the people around me must have noticed a difference—that I was exceptionally good-humored and full of bad jokes, that in the office I was never ill-tempered and never criticized anyone or anything, that I enjoyed people again and enjoyed almost anything I did. Even conversation which had bored me to the point of hysterical deafness seemed all at once rather pleasant and agreeable.

And that brings us back again to what love is. I suppose this was real *amour* which I experienced, the thing French novelists write about better than any others, exploring it down to the finest of details. But again what is *amour* but a different thing for every individual, for every man and woman violently attracted to each other? So many things enter into it—background and tradition and environment, the condition of one's feeling and psychology at the moment, the so-called "chemical element of attraction," the compensation of two temperaments, the biological elements of glands and their stimulated activity which makes all people in love (even the ugly and the lout) appear to glow with an augmented vitality and even charm.

I had never thought of myself as especially passionate or demanding or driven where sex was concerned. The experiences I had had came about largely through boredom or the desire to become utterly lost for a time, as in the adventure with the girl in New Orleans who lived over the bakery shop. Now there was the element of sensuality, in my case an aroused sensuality which had never been touched during the mechanical embraces and tricks of the women whom I had taken up casually.

All this and much more went into this relationship with Mary. It was a powerful and overwhelming experience, and perhaps it was just as well that when it all ended suddenly and with violence I came out here to the South Pacific. Otherwise I might have gone on searching recklessly for something to replace it, something to carry along that sensation of lightness and delight which was always with me, that renewed interest in everything about me which I had known as a young man and which had come to die slowly during all the years in Oakdale. Out here there was nothing to explore, nothing to search for, with the only women for hundreds of miles around those black and greasy specimens with which Homer, the wool-hat, satisfies himself.

Probably such an adventure always seems unique to the man who has experienced it. While it lasts and even long afterward it must seem that this has never happened to any other man, and probably it has never happened in exactly the same fashion. But it is very likely something like it happens to many a man who is middle-aged or on the verge of middle age, especially in a world such as mine. It is doubtless the story of the preacher who elopes with the choir singer, the story of the solid businessman who suddenly abandons his wife and children and goes wild with a model or a female acrobat, the story of the mature and sedate lawyer who suddenly blasts the whole structure of his life for a girl working in the filing department.

It is often enough, I suppose, the story of Mr. Smith. It was different in my case only because Mary was very rich and because she never wanted to marry me or anyone else. It was different too in other ways which I did not understand until the very end, yet even then *amour* is compounded of so many things that with other Smiths there may have been similar complex psychological factors at once alike and different.

Crudely the fact is that I felt an animal delight in everything that was Mary, in the perfume she used which did not smell sweet and heavy like flowers but rather like a clean chemical, like a fresh, unscented, and delightful odor of fine soap. The lipstick which on Enid, and consequently with all other women, I abhorred, became an exciting element where Mary was concerned. Most of all perhaps was the fierce physical excitement of her body seen always in darkness or a half light. Even now the memory of it has a tremendous power to excite me, sometimes almost beyond endurance. There was nothing sentimental or spiritual about that. It was direct and primitive, yet I know that it was that which lent a kind of glow to every other element. And of course there was her own recklessness . . . that she held back nothing . . . nothing whatever to give me delight and satisfaction. Oh, I can understand well enough why it is that men at middle age and later suddenly throw all else recklessly to the winds for the sake even of a single night. If you have not known it there is no way of making you understand. It would not matter even if death brought down the curtain at the coming of the dawn.

For the first two weeks we saw each other every night in those rooms she had made over for herself on the second floor of the old house. At first I was so lost that I did not even see the rooms or the furniture, but gradually my consciousness became aware of the surroundings and I discovered that in all the house these were the only rooms which she had not kept as they had been in her father's time. They were furnished completely with the most feminine of French furniture. In reality what she had re-created there was, I suppose, the atmosphere of the boudoir and bedroom of a demimondaine. I do not know what men or how many men had been there before me, but it is unlikely that any will ever follow me there because Mary succeeded in breaking the rules of the trust and is no longer forced to return to Crescent City. There is a curious perverse satisfaction in such knowledge, even out here in the islands removed in both time and space from what happened there. I myself shall probably never see the rooms or the house again, and probably it is much better that way.

During much of those two weeks Nicole remained in New York. The old servants lived in a far wing of the house, and although they must have had suspicions when night after night I came to dinner, they could not know what went on afterward ... when each succeeding night we went at an earlier hour up the big empty stairway to the cocotte's boudoir, until presently we went there before dinner and returned again after we had had our brandy.

As a concession, or more perhaps out of long habit and because of the children, I returned each night to my own house an hour or two before daylight. Apparently Enid was always asleep in her own room, although when everything broke up I discovered that she always knew the hour at which I came in.

I took to sleeping late and usually got up about around ten or ten-thirty to find that at the sound of the footsteps overhead Enid had got my breakfast under way. After the first three or four times I came in late she no longer asked or even hinted for information as to where I had been. I think she discovered that I always had a quick lie ready for her, a lie which was difficult to run to earth and expose. Also she was still practicing the sob sister's advice of giving me my freedom until I was sick of it. But of course this wasn't simply a matter of freedom. It was infinitely more serious, and there was behind it all the years of slow corroding irritation, appeasement, and even hatred on my side which made the chances of my ever returning to her possession for good wholly out of the question.

This of course was something she could never understand since all her life, her thoughts, her calculations were upon a plane so false, so imaginary, so fictional that reality or truth could never touch them. In her world husbands and wives "shared" everything. Husbands were "lost" and "won back again." By the use of a new perfume or a little more effort at dressing attractively an erring husband could even be brought back to the conjugal bed. It was all formula and tricks which never once touched the tragic and passionate depths of reality or fact.

I sometimes think that during all this period she was at times actually happy because she saw herself playing a game, as she thought with great cleverness, bringing me back to submission without my knowing it—"the husband who after a fling always comes back to the fireside." Even after the gossip got around and people began talking I think she found satisfaction in the knowledge or at least in her own conviction that other women were saying, "Dear Enid, how well she is taking the whole thing!"

As I write it occurs to me that the whole of Enid's character and existence, all her motives and calculations might well be enclosed in quotation marks. And God knows that among American women she does not stand alone. It is a part of the whole dullness and unreality and confusion created by advertising hucksters and sob sisters and "he-man" novelists and preachers and interior decorators and perfume manufacturers and radio soap operas, as if a man could be tricked into or out of something which is stronger than any of us and over which in the end none of us but the unsexed or the weaklings have any control. It is a vicarious, synthetic, and pitiful world, indeed perhaps a whole civilization if it might be called that.

There are plenty of other men who have been subjected to the same maneuvers as those practiced by Enid and they will understand how incredibly maddening such tactics can be. I will never be sure that Enid herself was unaware of this and did not get some satisfactions out of the maneuvers and the peculiar torture they produced. She was always bright and cheerful, almost too much so, when she brought in my breakfast in the morning. Although the maid could have done it she never permitted this. She brought it "with her own hands." In the old days when I wanted desperately to read my newspaper undisturbed she was always interrupting me with questions and comments, but now she never interrupted me at all. She simply sat opposite me with her "extra cup of coffee," looking out of the window cheerfully, sometimes even half humming a tune. A little later she arranged it so that when I came downstairs the record player was playing music which she knew I especially liked (most of which I have never wanted to hear again). And when I went to the garage for the car she stood on the porch smiling and waving at me.

However rested and well I felt on waking up, my whole mood was destroyed by the time I left the house. Fortunately in my obsession the mood quickly vanished and I fell again to thinking of Mary to the exclusion of all else.

Of course it was inevitable that gossip should find us out. We had been lucky for a time in the fact that the big old house stood in a part of town where people we knew seldom came and that my car, parked there night after night, could not be seen from the street. It is probable that somehow the old servants came to talk, and once that pipeline was opened the news went quickly through every kitchen and laundry in Oakdale and thence upstairs to the women who were to so great an extent Oakdale itself. Who it was that tipped off Enid or when the revelation occurred I have never known, but there was never at any point any sign I could detect that she had discovered the whole of the truth.

In the meanwhile in the background Nicole Villon played a puzzling role. She remained in New York for several days, and when she returned she had dinner with us in the evening and then silently and without any explanation disappeared. Sometimes Mary went with her and was absent for a few moments. Nicole seemed more than ever like a small bright-eyed bird who came to dinner as a bird might come to a feeding shelf and then vanished. She never gave the faintest outward sign of knowing what was going on and none of us ever mentioned her trick of disappearing immediately after dinner. Outwardly, so far as the town was concerned, she served in a flimsy way as a "cover" or a chaperone for Mary.

Her presence and her relationship to Mary I found more and more puzzling. She seemed half friend and confidante and half servant, and I did not believe the story that she was writing a book of poetry. Presently I discovered that actually she also performed the duties of a lady's maid. She it was who pressed Mary's clothes and kept the rooms above stairs in order, yet there were moments when she could be disagreeable and even insolent to Mary. Obviously she had a good background with her languages and her knowledge of art and of music. It was Nicole who made the selections of the disks which kept the big house filled with music constantly and she who operated the expensive gramophone concealed in a room beneath the great stairway. Mary never took her anywhere in Crescent City and few people had ever seen her.

I came presently to get the impression that she was jealous of me or that she did not like me and that she talked against me to Mary. It was a curious impression which I could not analyze or justify, but when I suggested such a thing to Mary she only laughed and said, "You mustn't mind. It doesn't mean anything. She is always jealous of anyone who comes close to me. It's a very old story."

What puzzled me most was the bond between the two of

them. I could discover no reason for it save that, in traveling, such a woman as Nicole, who served as a companion, friend, secretary, and maid, might be useful. It is difficult to discover now why I experienced this growing reaction of mistrust and dislike of Nicole. There was nothing, no act, no insinuation, no word to which you could pin the feeling and explain it. It was, I think, a matter of instinct and intuition, of the male recognizing an element of hostility in the female, not toward any given individual but toward the whole of his sex. There are women like that, women who would be accounted "normal" (whatever that means) yet who experience and practice toward all men an attitude of actual hostility, who see any act, however trivial, of any man as a part of a general conspiracy against the whole of the female sex. It is not that they are involved personally; the whole thing is abstract, objective as you might say, "a matter of principle." They are suspicious of all men, suspecting them of calculated predation or at least of swindling and deceit. They are the most annoying of women and, of all neurotic types, the most unnatural.

Nicole was of that sort. The attitude may have been the result of unhappy experience in the past, and Mary did tell me that twice Nicole had been badly treated by men, once by a husband and once by a lover. As a clinical type she was neither masculine nor feminine but seemed wholly sexless—small, brisk, thin, with a quick if superficial intelligence.

I could not be rid of her. She was a third wheel in the affair, never really present and yet always there in the background, as if in some way she were an incarnation of fate, a symbol of the whole affair and its eventual sterility. There was no question of inducing Mary to be rid of her. When, after we had progressed beyond the first violence of passion into a degree of intimacy, I suggested that we, and especially myself, might be happier if Nicole went back to Europe, leaving us wholly free, Mary only laughed and said, "Don't be ridiculous. What difference does she make to us? In reality she is not here at all. She doesn't object to what we are doing. She hasn't even any interest in it and I can't do without her. She takes care of a million small things."

What troubled me most and what I suppose was nothing more than jealousy was the knowledge that when I was not with Mary her company was shared almost entirely by Nicole. And I felt that when they were together in the hours when I was absent they talked of me and of the whole affair, although Mary denied this when I once suggested my suspicion. I believed passionately that what went on between Mary and myself belonged to us alone and should be kept thus. And there was too the feeling, again wholly intuitive, that there was something at once cold and unclean about Nicole and that even her presence in some way defiled the whole of our relationship. In my obsession I wanted to share Mary with no one, and so I fell into the same error as Enid herself, consuming myself with a desire to absorb and devour Mary in the delusion that one person can *absorb* another. It is one of the greatest errors in love, whether it happens in the love between husband and wife, lover and mistress, or even mother and son. There is no such thing as complete possession. It cannot happen, and inevitably one of the partnership is hurt and in the end perhaps destroyed.

I know now that nothing could have been less possible with Mary than the attempt to *absorb* her for she was above all else independent. In a way she had a masculine mind and will within the most feminine and desirable of bodies. She wanted freedom and in the end she bought it, not only with all her money, but through the sacrifice of many other things, until she arrived at that point of instability which was her ruin.

It was, in other words, a nice mess in which I found myself— a rather simple, even naïve, inexperienced American approaching middle age. I saw and understood none of this until it was all finished and I had been used to the point of satiety. I am still trying to understand it all. It is possible that I shall never understand it although Mary in that final letter did her best to make me understand it—at least her side of it.

In the end there arrived a point at which it became impossible for us to carry on as we had been doing. Obviously I could not go on forever visiting her each night and returning home in the early morning in the face of the knowledge that by now almost everyone shared. I knew how thoroughly the whole thing was known, even by the way in which my friends and acquaintances looked at me. I knew that every time I bought something in the drug store the clerk knew why, that every time I ordered a drink in a bar the bartender would conceal in his eyes the knowledge he shared. I knew that every girl in my office watched me and once my back was turned began talking to the nearest companion about Mary and me. And there was always, I knew, the gossip that I was planning in the end to become Mary's husband and thus "feather my own nest."

But there was another element. Presently in our relationship there emerged a desire to give a curious kind of permanence to the affair, to make it in a way more "comfortable." And so we evolved a more sensible plan. It was that Mary should go away to stay in the East or in Virginia and that I should come there to meet her over week ends or even for a day or two in the middle of the week, and that is how it worked out. One concession I did achieve—that when I was with Mary, Nicole should be sent away.

As it turned out, the arrangement was more satisfactory than the old one because it meant that the old necessity for breaking off before morning no longer existed. I could remain with her as long as I liked. We could waken together, lazily, at any hour, have breakfast together, and share our waking hours. Even though it meant separation sometimes for several days, it was better than the old way. Indeed I think the arrangement even maintained our ardor and interest in each other at a higher pitch because during the periods apart I could think of nothing but the time when I should see her again. Each time we met it was a renewal. I returned fresh and excited and ardent. It has occurred to me that it might have continued thus for years had not the final crisis put a sudden end to the whole thing.

Sometimes we met at a hotel in New York when we rarely left the hotel bedroom-sitting room, and on several occasions we met in hotels at resort places, and twice she took me with her into the world of hunting and horses which she frequented from time to time. It was a pleasant world but to me a strange one in which people used what seemed almost a foreign tongue and in which I always felt an inferior outsider. And it was in that world that occurred the first warning, the first small spark of suspicion and disillusionment.

We had been staying at the hotel in Lexington and moving in a society which showed neither disapproval nor even very much interest in an affair carried on so openly. As in the world of Frank's family, these people had other interests. They regarded the romantic goings-on of individuals as their own affair. It was a long week end for us, from Thursday night to Tuesday morning, and on Saturday night, after the races, we went to the house of a man called Stacy who had a big stable of horses.

There were people there from all over the country and even from Europe, and I was both astonished and proud that nearly all of them seemed to know Mary and were glad to see her again. But most of all it seemed to me that Mary became almost another person. She appeared clever, gay, gregarious, and friendly. In the intensity of our relationship no one until now had ever come into it—no one save Nicole with her curious detached, almost clinical relationship. And for me this was a dashing attractive world in which everybody seemed to be a character. It was a world in which I would have liked to live, and during the week end I found myself calculating (for the first time since the affair had begun) on how this could be done and arrived at the conclusion that there were only two ways. One was to cut all ties with Crescent City and simply live and travel with Mary as her lover. The other of course was to have Enid divorce me and marry Mary, something which by now I divined would be virtually impossible. Enid would never divorce me, and Mary had a curious abhorrence of marriage, arising partly I think from the marital history of her parents and partly out of experience with her husband.

There were perhaps forty people at the big Stacy house for

cocktails and dinner, and many of them by the time dinner was served had had a great deal to drink.

At dinner Mary put me with two old friends of hers, a middle-aged and very horsy woman and a handsome younger woman who had come to dinner in jodhpurs and jacket. For me it was a sticky and uncomfortable position for they talked across me mostly of the ancestry, the build, and the records of horses, going far back into the England of the eighteenth century. So far as I was concerned they might have been talking Chinese, and I felt a worm.

Mary sat between two men to whom she had introduced me earlier, and because I was bored by my table companions and I was jealous I watched the two men. One was a thin, hard-bitten old man who must have been seventy. The other was a big man of perhaps my age, good-looking in a florid way with a very red face and very black hair. He had the physical softness about him that marks many a middle-aged heavy drinker, and from his manner and the loudness of his laughter it was evident that he had done very well by himself. It was clear that he found Mary attractive and that his attentions were annoying her, for more than once I observed her turn as if she would have moved away from him had it been possible. Once I saw anger flash in her blue eyes, and then presently I saw her excuse herself and go away from the table. The man looked after her and then rose and followed a little unsteadily.

I was aware of several things—that Mary wanted to escape from him, that he was obviously following her, and that my course of action was to go to her rescue. I was aware too that I must do this discreetly in order not to make the rescue evident or to risk an unpleasant scene of some sort. Jealousy did not enter into the picture, for it was clear that she wanted only to rid herself of the man.

When I felt that I could do so discreetly I excused myself to my two horsy companions and slipped away from the table, going in the direction of the hallway through which Mary had disappeared. It led, I discovered, to one of the huge verandas which surrounded the house, and I followed the veranda to the point where it turned a corner. The veranda where I stood was dimly lighted. Further on it lay in darkness.

As I reached the corner I heard Mary's voice, very cold now, saying, "Well, you wanted to talk to me, Basil. What is it you want to say?" and I hesitated, thinking that if he had followed at Mary's invitation I had no right to intervene. And again any jealousy I might have felt was extinguished by the peculiar hardness of Mary's voice. It indicated that she hated the man. I remained in case she might need help and because I was drawn by an almost ungovernable curiosity.

I heard the man called Basil say, "You know damned well what I want to say. I want you to come home with me for an hour."

Mary said, "That's all over and you know it. I'd as soon jump in the lake as go home with you. That goes even if you were sober. I sat with you at dinner to keep you quiet because you were drunk. Now shut up and leave me in peace."

When he spoke again there was a nasty edge in his voice. "I was good enough for you once . . . plenty good. What's turned you so nasty nice?"

I did not know whether to disappear or to intervene and if necessary sock the fellow on the jaw. For the time being I was paralyzed by indecision, and before I could move I heard him say, "Good God! You've taken on anything—even jockeys—and now you stick at me. You've slept with half the men at this party . . ."

He did not finish the sentence, but I heard the sound of a violent slap and cursing and I called out, "Mary! Mary!" and came round the corner.

The man was standing still staring at her, and at the sound of my voice Mary said, very quietly, "Get me out of here, Wolcott. Don't hit him. It'll only make things much worse." And she took my arm and fairly dragged me out of the darkness into the light. Then the man began to laugh. It was a horrid mocking sound and it followed us along the whole of the veranda.

Mary said quickly, "Go out and find the car. I'll meet you at the door."

Still bewildered, I obeyed her and in two minutes she was at the door. We drove off in silence and Mary said suddenly, "Did you hear what he said to me?"

"Some of it. I should have knocked him down."

"No," said Mary. "You're wrong there. He was drunk and it would have made an awful scandal. I've been trying to get rid of him since six o'clock."

I said, "Why didn't you call me earlier? I'd have got rid of him."

"It wouldn't have done any good. He was drunk when he came in. I stalled him off until it didn't work any longer." Then very quietly she said, "He was in love with me once. I haven't seen him for four years. He was drunk tonight and he's a cad anyway even when he's sober."

I said weakly, "The whole thing makes me feel like a sap."

"You needn't feel that way. You behaved exactly as a gentleman should. If you had hit him it would have been much worse."

Then suddenly she seemed to collapse. She began to cry and crumpled against my shoulder. I slowed down the car, put one arm about her and kissed her, and at that the sobbing only increased.

Presently she said, "Don't pay any attention to me. I'll be over it in a minute. I'm just tired . . . that's all . . . so bloody, goddamn tired. Just hang on to me, darling, till I come out of it."

I said nothing but kissed her and let her cry. But the sudden collapse startled me. She had always seemed so confident and sure of herself. She always seemed to have everything in life under control, and now she was collapsed, crumpled and sobbing, and the anguish of her cry, "I'm so tired . . . so bloody, goddamn tired!" rang in my ears. It was a cry of real and terrible anguish.

That night at the hotel a new element entered our relationship, for it seemed that she had come to depend on me. She became for that night and from then on softer and in a way more feminine. It was also as if she had become suddenly younger, at times almost like a child. Of all the countless times we made love I think that night was the best of all, for we came that night nearer to what the relationship between a man and a woman in love should be.

It was, of course, a forewarning, a sort of first sounding of the theme of doom in a symphony. In the next few meetings we were both, I think, really happy, happier in the truest sense of the word than we had ever been. I began to think of the whole thing seriously for the first time as a permanent relationship either with or without marriage, and I believe the thought occurred as well to Mary, although we never discussed it. She knew that there was small chance that any such thing could happen, but she knew the reasons why this was so and I did not.

Four weeks later we met in Virginia at a country hotel. She had been staying in the countryside with friends and Nicole was in New York. Mary indeed had scarcely seen her since the ugly incident at the party in Lexington. She met me in Washington at the airfield and we drove impatiently to the village hotel, only stopping on the way at the village post office because Mary said she was expecting a special delivery letter from New York. She hurried into the post office and after a little time came out looking irritated and nervous.

"Damn Nicole!" she said. "She was to have written me two days ago about something important."

She seemed in a bad temper which I managed to break down by making love to her as soon as we reached the hotel and hurried up to our rooms. Afterward she seemed calmer again, but at six o'clock she insisted on driving down to the post office to ask a second time for the letter, again with no success.

That evening we had dinner with some hunting people, and immediately after dinner Mary said, "Do you mind taking me home, darling? I feel like the devil."

She looked very pale and I noticed small beads of perspiration on her forehead.

Back at the hotel she said, "I'll take some aspirin and feel better in the morning."

She went to sleep in my arms, but twice during the night I

was wakened by the faint light from the bathroom and found her there. The second time she was wet with perspiration and shaking violently.

She said, "I think you'd better send for the doctor. I don't know what's the matter with me. It's Doctor Wyndham. You'll find his telephone number on a card in the inside flap of my handbag. . . . No, bring it to me. I'll find it."

I put her back to bed, covered her, and gave her the handbag. Her hands shook so violently that she could scarcely open it, but, fumbling, she found the card at last and gave it to me. She said, "Tell him I'm having one of my attacks . . . that it's serious . . . he'll understand . . . for God's sake to come at once."

It was a country hotel with no telephone in the room and I was forced to go below stairs to the office. It was four in the morning and there was no one on duty, and it took me what seemed an endless time, first to discover how the country telephone worked, and then to rouse the operator at the exchange. Then after a long wait a sleepy voice answered me at the other end of the wire. It was Doctor Wyndham himself.

I tried to explain myself and give him Mary's urgent message, but he seemed to understand at once and to find nothing extraordinary in the situation. He seemed to know what was meant by "one of my attacks."

"Tell her," he said, "that I'll be over at once . . . as soon as I can."

By now I was terrified, and the fear increased when as I approached the door of our room I could hear the sound of Mary's groaning. As I entered the door she fell silent and turned toward me, and as she did so I saw that the pillow was covered with lipstick and what I suspected were teeth marks. I sat down beside her and began stroking her damp hair saying, "What is it, darling? Isn't there something I can do?"

With what appeared to be a great effort she said, "There isn't anything until the doctor comes. Just hold my hand . . . like that. It makes it easier."

"What is it?" I asked, gently enough.

Again with a great effort she said, "It's something that goes wrong with my insides. You wouldn't understand. The doctor knows about it."

Then she began to cry, shaking violently like a small child and burying her head in the crook of my arm. As before on that night at Lexington we came very near to each other. Outside the sky began to turn gray and then pink, and I had that strange feeling, which some people have in time of crisis, of clairvoyance and utter disaster. Somehow I knew that this was the end of something . . . not death . . . but of some part of my life and of hers. It was almost a physical thing, as if I saw not with my eyes alone or with my mind but with the whole of me. And I was afraid suddenly with a fear that was only the same emotion I had experienced that night in Lexington but greatly heightened and touched by a sense of dread, of something which I was about to discover, which lay just a little way ahead of me.

There was something horrible and almost obscene in the sight of her suffering, as if there were a quality of the unnatural about it. At moments she seemed unable any longer to control herself and cried out, and once when I laid my hand on her thigh, she thrust it away fiercely as if it had burned her, saying, "Please! . . . Please, don't touch me! It's agony!" I had had little experience with physical suffering in others and certainly I had never witnessed anything like this. At moments it seemed impossible for anyone to suffer as acutely and still survive.

And after what seemed an eternity, while Mary cried and thrust her body, arched and convulsive with suffering, away from me, I heard the sound of a car on the silent village street. It pulled up to the hotel and stopped, and bending down to kiss her forehead, I said, "It's the doctor, darling. I'll go and bring him up."

As I stood up she reached out and, seizing my hand, kissed it. This was the last action in the world I would have expected of her, and I freed my hand and kissed her again and she whispered, "I want to be alone with the doctor."

"Yes, darling."

I met the doctor in the downstairs hall, still in my pajamas and dressing gown. He was a tall thin man of about sixty with a gentle distinguished pleasant face and wore very clear rimless glasses. I introduced myself and we shook hands and I said, "She's suffering a great deal. I'm frightened about her." But he seemed strangely quiet about it. He said, "I think I know what is the matter. She'll be all right again in a little while. I'll go right up to her."

He left me and hurried up the stairs, and for a while I stood looking out of the window into the street. There was nothing to see but an old brick house and a filling station and some trees, yet today I know exactly how it looks even to the streaks of rust that ran down from the roof across the white face of the filling station. The sense of something coming to an end was still with me and I thought, for no apparent reason at all, "What do I do now? Where do I go?" It was not death, either Mary's or my own, which concerned me, for as I have grown older death has come to mean less and less.

I found myself thinking, "Why am I here in this little Virginia town amongst strangers? How did I come here? What has happened to me?" and for a moment the whole of the affair with Mary seemed completely unreal as if it were something I had dreamed, and I saw myself as if I had been slightly insane for many weeks and had recovered my sanity. All the weeks and months when nothing had existed for me but Mary and the emotions and sensuality which centered in her seemed distant and strange. The memory of it was like something emerging, vague and distorted, in a fog. And then I heard someone at the hotel desk behind me and saw the old man who had been there the afternoon before.

I said, "My wife was taken ill. Doctor Wyndham is with her now."

He looked at me with a rather gentle smile as if he thought, "Another one of those things among the people who come down here!" as if I were a complete foreigner.

"I'm sorry to hear that," he said. "I'm sure it will turn out all right." Then he added, "The cook is here. Perhaps you'd like a cup of coffee."

I thanked him and he led me into the plain empty dining room and pulled out a chair at a table and went into the kitchen, returning in a moment with a cup and a small enameled coffee pot.

"It's fresh made," he said. "Would you like some eggs or something with it?"

I thanked him and said I wasn't hungry. "When the doctor comes down, tell him I'm in here."

"I'll tell him," said the old man, and I had a feeling that, for all his kindness, he wished to wash his hands of me, of Mary, of all people like us.

I had finished the coffee when I saw the doctor, followed by the old man, coming in the door of the dining room. The old man went to fetch another cup, and the doctor, still carrying his little medicine case, came over and said to me, "She'll be all right now in a little while . . . as right as ever."

"What about some coffee?" I asked.

"Yes," said the doctor and sat down.

"What is it with her?" I asked.

The doctor took out a cigarette. He seemed to be neither perturbed nor in a hurry. "I'm coming to that," he said. "In one sense it's nothing to worry about. In another it's terrible." He lighted the cigarette and lifted his coffee cup. I liked him. He seemed calm and gentle with his clear blue eyes, and very reassuring.

He said, "You see, I like horses. That's why I'm down here. I don't really practice any longer . . . just now and then for friends like Mary. It's a good life . . . farming, horses, just enough doctoring to keep my hand in."

I wanted him to get to the point, but I was aware that trying to hurry so calm a man would lead nowhere.

He said, "I meet all kinds of people . . . any doctor does . . . but I get more than the average share of people with a lot of money who somehow get lost along the way. Maybe it's because they never really know where they're going or don't care much whether they go one way or another. . . . This coffee is very good. The Inn's not a bad place really."

Hoping to lead him to the point I said, "It was very good of you to come out at such an ungodly hour."

"That's all right," he said. "I'm fond of Mary. She's one of the ones who got lost along the road. By the way, she wanted me to tell you something. Maybe you know it already. It's hard to believe that you don't, but she is sure you don't." He put down his coffee cup and said, "You know, she's a drug addict. There wasn't anything wrong with her but that she ran out of drugs. She was expecting it by post three or four days ago and it didn't arrive. You see, that woman Nicole didn't send the stuff and she ran out of it."

So that was why the letter at the post office was so important. For a moment I just sat there trying to pull myself together in order to make some coherent or sensible remark. Somehow the sense of doom I had felt was now all connected.

All I could think to say was, "How did she ever get started on that?"

He went on calmly talking as if what he had told me was no more startling than the news that Mary was suffering from indigestion.

"She never talks much about it. I think it began in Italy so far as I can make out, a long time ago. You see, this happened once before, so when you called I knew what was the matter. I've taken care of her for the moment. She'll be all right very quickly." He looked at me sharply. "It's a frightening thing, isn't it? . . . I mean the suffering. I don't suppose anyone can quite describe it. When they're in that condition it's as if the whole of the body is a mass of exposed nerves. The inquisition, the Nazis never thought up any torture quite like it."

I still could find nothing to say and he continued, "I'm surprised you didn't know it already, but Mary said she was sure you had no suspicion. I suppose someone would have to know the signs very well—the little scars, the way she would seem very tired one moment and then disappear for a little while and return gay and full of vitality, the look in the eyes. And of course she never drinks anything stronger than sherry."

It all fitted . . . too well. I had noticed these things without noticing them, perhaps because I did not understand their significance, because I was just too damned dumb and inexperienced.

The doctor went on calmly drinking his coffee and presently in a voice which did not sound to me like my own, I asked, "Can't anything be done about it?"

"It might be possible to cure her—perhaps for good, perhaps not. I don't think she wants to be cured. That is what is difficult in such cases. It all begins in the first place through despair, and usually they're afraid to go back and face that despair. Nearly always they break down again. You see, Mary is very unstable psychologically. It's all very complex and I don't pretend to know the reasons."

Outside it was now quite light and the morning sun was coming in at the windows. I saw people begin to appear in the little village street. The man at the filling station opposite unlocked the door and came out to fill a car with gasoline. But despite the sunlight everything was gray for me, as if the whole scene was enveloped by a fog which penetrated even the bare little dining room.

The doctor said, "All this, of course, is none of my business and there's no bloody reason why I should give anybody advice except that none of us can help it. I don't know who you are or anything about what goes on between you and Mary, but if I were you I'd break it up. Nothing good can come of it. It can only get worse and it might end in tragedy."

"What does Mary think?"

"I don't know. I didn't ask her. It's not only the drugs, you know. It's other things. It may be that you've gotten into something you don't understand at all." He stood up suddenly. "And now I'm going to shut up . . . tight. I'm going to take Mary back to New York this afternoon. I'll drive her to Washington and go from there on the train. She ought to be in a hospital of some kind for a time . . . you know, a private sort of place."

"I could take her," I said quickly.

"No. You wouldn't know the right persons to see or the right place to take her. You see, there's a whole secret inside world that exists for people like Mary. You have to have the key. Besides, she doesn't want you to go with her. She didn't even want to see you, but I didn't see how that could be avoided. If I were you I'd just pack up and clear out . . . at least for the moment. Mary knows I'll take care of her. I've known her well for twenty years. If you stay around under the circumstances it will only agitate her and make things worse. I'll be coming back in an hour . . . as soon as I've packed up. You'd better go separately. Just hire a car and disappear." Then he picked up his little bag and put one hand on my shoulder and said, "Sorry, old man."

He turned away to go and I felt tears coming into my eyes in spite of everything . . . or because of everything. And suddenly he said, "Perhaps you've gotten in too deep . . . where you don't belong. If you go quickly it will be better for Mary and everyone."

I managed to say, "Thank you, Doctor," and suddenly he was gone.

The hardest thing was to get up the stairs and into the room again. I think it was because I was going up the stairs to find a different person from the one I had left a little while before and because somehow the shame of the whole thing had touched me as well. I was ashamed to see Mary. And yet I loved her still, as much as before. But something curious had happened to that love. The elements of it had become precipitated and separate. The sensuality which I know now was the core of that love had become a separate thing, something to be practiced coldly and with calculation. I saw it clearly now. I was not properly a lover but a voluptuary, which I suppose is what happens to men of my age who lose their heads. Mary had given me something I had never known before and possibly would never know again, but I never again would be free from the thought and the memory of it. Perhaps the tragedy was that the knowledge and the experience had come too late.

When I came into the room Mary was lying quite still and calm. She said, "Dick Wyndham told you?"

I came and sat on the edge of the bed and took her hand, but in an odd way it was a different hand from the one I had held a little while before as we waited for the doctor to arrive. I felt no emotion of any kind but only a curious shocked coldness.

"Yes," I said.

She looked away from me rather like a shamed child. "I'm sorry."

"It's all right," I said.

"He told you he's taking me back to New York?"

"Yes."

"I don't want you to come. When I'm straightened out a bit we can get together again."

"Yes."

"You want it, don't you?"

"Of course, my dear."

"It'll be different . . . your knowing. It won't be the same ever again."

"Yes." And then I lied, "It doesn't change anything really."

"Not really, I suppose." She drew her hand away and raised herself on her elbows. "Now get yourself packed up. I'm to be ready to go in an hour or two. You'd better be gone when the doctor comes back."

I dressed and packed quickly without a shower, without even shaving, partly I know now, because I did not want to look myself in the eyes again in the mirror. I had had too much of that.

When I came back into the room she was up wearing a dressing gown and packing her own things. She said, "Of course, you know, this is all Nicole's fault."

"Yes."

"She did it once before out of jealousy."

When I had finished packing and closed my bag she came across the room and put her arms about me, laying her head against my chest, and at the contact of her body the old fierce desire returned and more acutely than before I understood the fashion in which the elements of the whole affair had been precipitated. This was my *body* over which neither my mind nor its reason had any control. I was ready to begin all over again, at once.

"No," she said softly. "Not now. It will be all the better when we see each other again." A faint sigh escaped from her, and with her face still buried on my chest she said in a low voice, "I've done a dirty thing to you. Have you forgiven me?"

"There's nothing to forgive."

"Good-by then for now. I'll write you at once. Kiss me."

I kissed her and it was exactly as before and I knew then that I could never give her up, that I would come back again and again, for I had been corrupted. And I understood everything about Nicole and the peculiar relationship between her and Mary. It was Nicole who got her the stuff. That was why Nicole could never be sent away for good.

The sense of doom, of unreality, of a gray fog which seemed to envelop everything, remained with me during the whole of the trip home. I had no other thoughts but those which concerned Mary and myself, and once or twice it occurred to me that it might have been better if everything had ended cleanly in death without my ever having known. What had happened was a kind of death without any of the finality to which one must become reconciled or perish. What was to happen now? What would it be like when I returned to her? There began to arise in my mind every sort of suspicion as to what Mary's life had been in the past, and I kept hearing the voice of the man called Basil—"Why have you become so nasty nice after taking on everybody, even jockeys?" I saw myself as a fool and a naïve fool, so that I found myself actually blushing. Perhaps the whole thing had been on my side merely an illusion. Perhaps I had been merely used as a convenience—the nearest man at hand.

What troubled me most was the consideration of what it

would be like when I returned to her. Very likely it would become no more than a sensual adventure now that the curious precipitation into elements had occurred in my mind. I could not forget what the kindly doctor had said, "I do not think that she wants to be cured."

Mechanically I had headed for home, why I do not know, except that it seemed the only place to go. I was returning then, exactly as Enid had planned it, exactly as the sob sisters had advised her I would do in their columns. Maybe, after all, they *were* right about most men and what was I but Mr. Smith, having his fling as middle age approached, believing that this had never happened before to any other man? Perhaps I was just another of the myriad Mr. Smiths who should have had all this experience and knowledge in my twenties when it was proper and natural for a man to have it, and was trying now to make up for lost time when it was too late.

I could of course throw everything out of the window and clear out for good to join Mary, but I knew that this was not what Mary wanted and I saw clearly enough even through the gray fog where such an action would lead. We would wander about here and there and it could never be the same again, and whatever there was of stability in me would presently deteriorate and at last disappear. I took too easily to drink. Why should not that point arise at which I too began to take drugs? But despite seeing all this clearly, through the fog, I could not help thinking, "Why not? Maybe that's the best solution." The prospect of going back to Oakdale to disappear once more into the curious kind of conforming anonymity which existed there seemed intolerable.

I took a taxi from the airfield. I had not troubled to send Enid a wire that I would be home earlier than I expected. I had not thought of it at all. And now I would arrive home about five in the evening as a surprise. The thought occurred to me that this was frequently the fashion in which men discovered the infidelity of their wives, but the idea that I might find Enid with a man seemed only ludicrous. Certainly that was not what she wanted.

And of course I found no man. I found Enid playing bridge on the veranda with three women. As she saw me emerge from the taxi she put down her cards and came to meet me on the terrace in full sight of the women crying, "Darling, what a surprise!" and before I knew what was happening she had kissed me violently on the lips and mechanically I had put my arm about her—something which had not happened in months.

I said, again mechanically, "I got through things sooner than I expected," and heard the sentence echoing in my brain as if it were an ironic comment on the whole of the situation. Then the women called out greetings to me and I knew what they were thinking. They were thinking, "He's come back. Enid was right! They all come back in the end!" And they were speculating desperately as to what had happened and about what went on between Mary and me and they would be itching to get home and telephone all their friends. Enid's gesture had covered everything.

I stopped by the bridge table for a moment, acting and talking as if nothing whatever had happened, and then went up to my room followed by the red setter who could not get enough of me, and when I sat on the bed he came over, jumped up, and licked my face. I rubbed his ears and lay down, and presently without being aware of it I fell asleep. I had not slept in thirty-six hours.

It was dark when I wakened and hazily everything came back to me and the pain seemed worse, and now, rested, I wanted to leave at once and go back to Mary. Nothing else mattered. But I did not know where to find her in "that private secret world made for such people." All the unsatisfied desire returned to me and I saw again, with that new understanding, how much of the attraction had been pure sensuality. Again it was my body which wanted to return again and again. It was not really me. My body, my nerves, my sensuality had taken over, then dominated me as the drugs dominated Mary. Even now, here on this island, my body, dominating, cries out in anguish to return. But there is no means of return. I must satisfy it as best I can, to be rid of it.

I went downstairs at last, meaning to take out the car and drive off. I had no objective. I would just drive anywhere at all. And just as I was escaping I heard Enid's voice saying, "Darling, I've kept your supper hot. It's in the oven."

I said, "Thanks. I don't want anything."

She was quite near me now and she said, "If there's anything I can do to help, let me know. I want to help."

I was astonished by the speech but more astonished by the obvious air of sincerity. It was one of the few times in all our life together that she had, I felt, meant what she said. I really think that she meant it all. If things had been different she might have won out for good then and there. I might have gone back and begun all over again and finished out my life in the pattern of Oakdale. But there was too much in the past and I was too wary. I had been betrayed too many times and was unwilling to be trapped and betrayed again into that falsity, that spurious intensity which long ago had become unendurable. Too many memories rushed through my brain.

I was sorry for her, genuinely so, but I said, "Thanks, Enid. I'm just going out to get some air. I'll probably be home early."

She knew that something had happened although she could not in the wildest stretch of her imagination have divined what it was. She hoped, of course, that it was all over between Mary and me, but I think also that she understood in that moment that even if I returned physically to spend the rest of my life in the house with her and the children she had lost me forever.

The next day I went to the office and went through the motions of picking up the loose ends of my business. I was more efficient than usual and demanded perfection from my secretary and the file clerks. And at four I left and stopped by the hotel bar to have a drink, and by the looks on the faces of my friends I knew that the three bridge-playing women had done their work well and the news had spread that I had come back for good, although how they suspected or knew that something serious had happened I cannot even today understand. I think there was sympathy in the faces of some of my friends. They had looked on me as a wild devil and envied me, and now it was over and I was back in the fold again.

It was after six when I arrived home and I found the letter from Mary. She had never written me at home before. The most had been a telegram judiciously worded and sent to my office. Enid, I doubt, could possibly have known her handwriting, but she had left the letter lying on the bed in my room, as if she had wanted to give it an added and urgent importance. My hands shook as I tore it open, and all the desire to be with Mary came rushing back in a great and submerging wave. The emotion was a purely sensual one.

This is what I read:

My Darling:

This is a line to say good-by. I'm going away tonight and I'm not coming back for a long time. Very likely I shall never go back again to the old house that was the only place which ever seemed like home. I shan't see you again.

It hurts me to write this, but there are so many reasons—so many that you know nothing about, even beyond what you discovered in Virginia. It was all wrong from the beginning, you understand, and I knew that it was all wrong. That's what made it the worse and the more wicked on my part, for I could have stopped it at one point or I could never have begun it all. There has been something wrong about me since the very beginning, something which was evil and corrupt, and I can't begin to tell you when it began or why it ever existed. It began when I was quite young and the world in which I was brought up didn't help it much, and when I married it was . . . like touching off an explosion. It is something which I cannot control and long ago I gave up trying to control it.

It is like tearing my heart out to write you this because I really loved you and still love you, darling. You might once have been the means of my salvation, but it's too late for that. Too much had happened long before we ever met that day on the road. It's as if I were two people, one of whom is my enemy whom I cannot trust, who betrays me, who kidnaps me, and does with me as he pleases and then goes away leaving me spent and wretched and shamed and with no peace. I know by now that my enemy will always come back when I am not on my guard and claim me and it will begin all over again. You were not the first man in my life nor the second or the third. There have been many . . . so many that when I am tired I sometimes cannot remember them all. What the man shouted at me on the veranda in Kentucky was true. There have been all kinds of men, yes, even a jockey whom he knew about.

I used to come back home to the big old house for a rest, because for a little time I could escape and because such things were very difficult there. But it happened even there, swiftly and fiercely, never for long, but it happened as if I were nothing but an instrument for my own destruction. It happened with men that you perhaps know. Naming them would do no good. It would only make things worse. It happened there first many years ago with the golf instructor at the club. I cannot even remember his name. So I am a monster and that is how I want you to think of me, always.

It was an evil chance that you picked me up on the day that I had the accident on the road. The thing was coming on again and what happened might have happened with any man who came along at that moment, but with you the worst of all things happened. I saw suddenly that you looked very like my father and after that I no longer had any control. I had to do what I did. You understand that I came back willingly every year from Europe. I kept the house exactly as it was because of *him*. And now I am free of the place. I need never come back again. Something has happened to me and I think you are the one who has set me free because you gave me what no other was ever able to give and now I needn't ever see the house again. They can tear it down. They can burn it. It can rot away. I am free. And it was you who set me free although you knew nothing of what you were doing.

But I loved you for yourself as well, perhaps more than I have ever loved anyone. Why? Because you seemed decent and clean and you were such an innocent when you came to me. You were all the things I had not known for so long, all the things indeed which I have never known and never experienced with any man. You needn't be ashamed of your innocence. You were the most wonderful lover I have ever known and I do not speak without experience. Giving you up forever is the hardest thing I have ever done, but it must be done. If it went on it could only progress into corruption because I am at heart corrupt and long since beyond salvation or redemption. I only hope that I have not already corrupted you beyond saving.

Oh, darling, I am so confused, so wretched, so frightened. When I cried out that night that I was tired, it was a cry from the heart, from beyond the grave. I am tired of struggling, tired of forever failing myself and everyone else. For a time you lifted me above all of that, but it could not last because I am what I am.

You will not see me again, even if you tried to follow me. I would not see you even if I had to destroy myself to prevent it . . . and that would be much easier than you think. I go to sleep every night not caring in the least whether I waken in the morning. I am only afraid of physical suffering. You must have seen what a coward I was that night in Virginia. Perhaps if that had not happened it might have gone on a little longer . . . but after that night I knew that it would never be the same again—that something was changed and that from then on everything would only become progressively more evil and more corrupt. Why do I know this? Because that same knowledge all happened to me once before in Italy when I was much younger. Only then it was myself who was the innocent and the corrupted. That is how I came to begin the whole business of taking drugs. That time I was not the corrupter but the corrupted.

Somewhere in a book I once read a quotation which I memorized and have never forgotten. It was written in French and runs thus: *"Dans la damnation le feu est la moindre chose; le supplice propre au damné est le progrès infini dans le vice et le crime, l'âme s'endurcissant, se dépravant toujours, s'enfonçant nécessairement dans le mal de la minute en progression géométrique pendant l'éternité."*

It is a pity that you do not understand French, for it is very terrible and very beautiful in French. I will try to translate it for you, badly. It runs something like this, "In the course of damnation the fire is the least thing; the real punishment of the damned is the infinitely slow progression into vice and crime, in which the spirit grows constantly more brutish, more hardened, constantly more depraved, losing itself through necessity again and again in the transient evil of the moment, in a geometric progression throughout eternity."

Do you understand what that means? No one who is not damned can really understand it, but perhaps after what has happened between us you are enough damned to fathom a little its meaning.

When we were together I tried not to tell you anything, to let you see anything, even the smallest thing, and that was all right so long as we loved each other in a world in which no one else existed or came near us. Perhaps if we had gone on as we began, in that old house, I might have managed it . . . I mean loving you without corrupting you too much. I don't know why I have written what I have just written because it could never have gone on like that and because what I have written is not true. It is only that while we were together I tried perpetually to deceive myself as well as you, and out of that deception no good could ever come.

The terrible thing is that I cannot see the end or indeed any end. I am alone and each year I grow a little older and a little more desperate. What happened between us was a blessed respite which I knew always in my heart could not last.

I could not have written you thus if I were not at heart an honest woman and a fairly intelligent one. I could not have written you as I am doing if I had not loved you—and, God help me, did not still love you. I am writing you this because I want you to understand, if only a little, that I am both better and worse than I must have seemed to you.

So I am going away. Do not try to find me. Remember or forget me—whatever is easiest for you and best. I ask you only to remember one thing—that you were not like all the others. The beginning perhaps was the same and then something happened. It was not like anything that ever happened before. I *loved* you. That is what made it different. And I shall be forever grateful to you because for a little time I came alive. For a little time everything came together into a pattern that might once have saved me. And then I discovered that it was too late for salvation.

I shall go on, distracting myself. I shall perhaps at times find life possible and I shall even know the fierce, evil, physical pleasure of the act that has been my damnation . . . the act alone! Do you know how terrible that can be, how vicious and degrading and calloused? And for a woman it is so much worse.

I could not debase myself more than I have done in this letter, and somehow the lacerating confession has made me for a little time at least feel cleaner, as if I had atoned and been absolved. But perhaps I am only a fool and fancy that what you gave me was more than the others gave and that I only *think* you are different and that what you gave me was different. When I kissed your hand that night I was trying to say in a futile meaningless gesture what I have written here . . . all of it. You know that I am a proud woman and a fiercely independent one and that such a gesture could only have come from the depths of my heart out of the most profound gratitude and emotion.

And so good-by. I shall be all right. I hope you will be. I think everything has changed for you. I know it, for I watched it happen without your ever knowing. I was aware of what was happening. You see, darling, there are so many things I know that you never knew and may never know. I think I must have been born knowing them. It made me a lonely young girl and later a lonely woman. Good-by again . . . and God bless you.

Mary

XIV The Jungle

I AM COMING NEAR THE END OF THE RECORD WITH A FEELing that there must be some real and definitive end, like the period at the end of a sentence, both to the record and the substance out of which it has come. Setting all this down has been at times an agony. At other times the narrative seems to have run along easily, telling itself like a newborn brook flowing from a spring. But out of it has come a kind of satisfaction, even perhaps, in the sense of eternity, a kind of purification and the realization of a purpose, without which my life would have remained incomplete and even confused and meaningless. I have begun to feel a sort of peace, the kind of peace which a great writer or sculptor or painter or architect or engineer must feel when a given objective of creation is realized and achieved. There is blended with it a feeling of self-respect such as I have never known before, of having had a purpose and carried it through. Whatever happens now I have at least done something.

I have purged myself, awkwardly, by a great effort, with all the discomfort and miseries of a difficult gestation, for, not being skilled and experienced as a writer and in the whole business of putting into words that are understandable the thought and emotions and intuitions of this thing called my body, I have been called upon to exercise vast powers of will and determination. Yet in the exercise of those powers, in the very discipline involved I have achieved satisfaction and even peace. Despite the frustrations, the birth pangs, the desperate effort to see things clearly and honestly, I shall be sorry when there is no more to write. I am even a little afraid of that moment. It is, I think, a terror of becoming lost all over again.

When it is finished what shall I do then with my time, with my interests, with my thoughts? I am beginning to understand that I shall never turn back, that I shall never see Oakdale again or Enid or the old life since it would be impossible for me ever again to be a part of all those dead things. I have tried earnestly to set down in honesty what I am and why I am what I am. Perhaps it is a task too complicated, too complex, too difficult for any man. Alone here in the jungle I have put upon paper things I have never told any man, things which it would be quite impossible to tell, no matter how earnestly I might wish to do so. At moments, alone in the jungle, I have felt myself blushing. And so I have done a "Self-portrait of the Artist."

There is little left to tell except the end and, of course, I shall not be here to set that down, to write the postscript of what may seem a trivial and tormented existence.

After the break-up with Mary I lived for a time in what might be described best perhaps as a state of suspended animation in which I had neither will nor purpose, in which nothing that happened had any interest or value. Twice I tried to break through to her. Once a letter was returned marked "address unknown." The other letter was never answered. Once I planned again in detail the perfect means of destroying Enid. All three impulses, I know, were dictated by a single force—that of sensuality, of wanting passionately to experience again and indeed forever merely the sensual satisfaction which was forever linked to Mary. How often is that pure sensuality confused with love, yet it is nevertheless an integral and indispensable part of any complete and satisfactory love. In that sensuality my own body was regenerated and made younger. It became for a time something apart from me, a kind of instrument which I myself admired and even glorified, so that the sight of it, seen naked accidentally in a mirror, roused in me an emotion of gratitude and admiration. Perhaps that is the way all of us should feel toward our bodies if we were honest and truly decent. For a time, even though it may have been an illusion (and that I shall never know), I did experience what might be called by the French designation *amour*, complete and liberating and satisfactory. In that, even though it may have been an illusion, I was more fortunate than most men who rarely even approach such an experience.

In that period of suspended animation I seemed to have acquired a curious gentleness, and save for the two letters to Mary and the morbid planning of Enid's destruction, things went better in my relationship with Enid. At least I was not consciously cruel to her. I accepted her nonsense, her complacency, her power of pretending, her devastating emptiness and superficiality, or perhaps I ignored it because it no longer had the power to touch me. I think this was one of the happiest periods of her life because the pattern which she had set up for herself became for a little time to have some semblance of reality. I was docile because I did not really care about anything and so was no longer annoyed by her lack of honesty and her make-believe. I did not strike back. I no longer even felt any revulsion.

I found that I slept a great deal, partly because it provided the escape of a "little death" and partly because there was no reason for waking, having a shower, and starting a new day.

And then came the unexpected and unplanned opportunity provided by a war of which, until then, I had taken little notice. They needed "businessmen." They needed "administrators" and "executives," and so they took me, and almost at once they forgot the whole purpose of taking me by sending me out here to sit on this evil and lovely and uncomfortable island where Enid writes to me as if our life together had always been a satisfactory and even a happy one, as if nothing at all had ever happened. The erring husband had come home, exactly as the advisors to the lovelorn had predicted.

Even the final, savage, heroic quarrel which occurred the day before I left, in which I said cruel and vicious things I never said before and, whatever happens, will never say again because they hurt me far more than they hurt Enid, has made no difference. She "forgave" me at once even though I had told her that she was a humbug and worse than a liar because she lived a lie and was utterly detestable to any decent man. Afterward I went outside into the darkness and was sick in the rose garden. But it was all for nothing. She did not even know what I was talking about. What happens to her or to me is of little importance. The tragedy is that there are so many like her. That I am nowhere near her, that she goes through day after day, week after week, without ever seeing me, is of no importance. In the eyes of the world and in so far as she is concerned I have been recaptured and everything is all right again. The letters she writes me, like the one about cutting down the hedge and her difficulties with Ronnie, my boy, are dull and small-minded but illuminated by a sense of triumph. I do not think it would matter at all to her if I died or were killed. For a time it would bring her a sense of importance in the community. Materially she is well-off. She would be a "war widow" whose husband had died, one way or another, for his country. She can, barring utter economic collapse of a whole great nation, keep her automobile, her refrigerator, her neo-Georgian house, her plumbing. She can send the children off to college, possibly to waste four years of their lives, to return as empty and as uneducated as Enid and I returned a generation earlier. She might conceivably marry again an older man less eccentric and peculiar and more comfortable than I have ever been, a man who fitted the pattern of her world and culture, a man *who had never dared to look at himself, his wife, or the world in which he lives.*

There is a double and complicated irony in the sense of triumph I find in Enid's letters. She has never understood that in the very moment I came back to her she had really lost me forever. It did not matter whether I was living in the same house or separated by half the earth, as we actually are. She had lost me. I was simply not there at all whether my body was in Oakdale or in the South Pacific. I suppose I am not alone in such an escape. There must be others. Only I have written it all down.

Last night the Sergeant came in again for some gin rummy. He seemed a little more calm than he had been in the past. It may be that he is becoming worn down by monotony and despair. I had to tell him that there was still no news regarding the possibility of leave and he took it not too badly.

I think I shall miss him, or rather perhaps the complete extrovert stability which he represents. He has a kind of animal warmth and vitality which somehow rubs off on you when he has been around for a little time. Most of all, I think, it is because we are friends. I think of him as a friend, even when I attempt to analyze why this is so . . . more a friend perhaps than any man I have ever known. Why? Perhaps because we do not question each other or our motives or thoughts, because each gives the other what it is he wants and needs.

A friend is a very difficult thing to analyze. "Friend" is a word which is used carelessly and often enough without meaning. When I sit down and try to list my *friends*, the number emerges surprisingly small. Mere community of interests is not enough. There is a certain give-and-take, a certain mutual compensation which is not easy to define, since more often than not it arises from impulse and intuition beyond the realm of the conscious. I suppose you get what you give, and my own life has been perhaps crippled and limited because I did not give enough and so got back little. Sometimes I think that in this hurried mechanical world in which we live there is too little time not only to live decently and richly but even to maintain and cultivate the thing known as a friend.

I think the Sergeant and I would each go to any length to do a service for the other. Sometimes I think that perhaps we could have a very satisfactory existence for the rest of our lives, merely beachcombing together until at last one of us dies. We have never discussed any of this. I could not bring myself to do it and in any case such a discussion would scare him to death. At the root of everything perhaps lies on my side the realization that in him I have met an honest man.

He won all evening at rummy and went away in high spirits. I heard him whistling as he crossed the sand in the moonlight to his own hut, and it occurred to me that not only was he an honest man but a free man and that he would never do a nasty thing. That is the reason he cannot understand a specimen like Homer, the wool-hat. That is the reason why, out of sheer moral indignation and frustration, he gives Homer a "going-over." In him and his kind perhaps lies the salvation of the world, not in science or "liberalism" or do-gooding or sentimentality or respectability or politics or womb-to-tomb philosophies, but in primitive virtues like simplicity and honesty and decency.

The sound of his whistling has died away in the moonlight, and back at my battered typewriter I find that, for me, with all my limitations and all my inhibitions, I have nothing more to write. I am sitting here fumbling with the keys, obsessed by a strange feeling of emptiness. Perhaps it is because there is no more to tell. I am purged and clean but empty.

The quick red fox jumps over the . . . Somebody is shooting again. Probably that noble "underprivileged" specimen Homer . . .

I shall have to go and see what the rumpus is about. I go empty and finished but clean. . . .

NOTE: That is the way the manuscript ended and it is perhaps as good as any other ending. It just may be that there is a kind of symbolism in the fact that middle-class "Mr. Smith," with all his limitations, his weaknesses, his aspirations, was destroyed by Homer, the wool-hat—Homer, one of the swarming ever-increasing "underprivileged."